In Keane We Trust

THE STORY OF A FOOTBALLING CITY'S FAITH IN ONE MAN

*A record of Sunderland's
2007-08 season*

an imprint of the Small World Publishing Group

SMALL WORLD PUBLISHING

ireland ✧ england ✧ switzerland

First published by SPORTS-i, July 2008

Trade enquiries: sales@smallbookwholesalers.com

© Graeme Anderson

ISBN 978-0-9554634-8-8

Typesetting: Seanchai Multimedia | Small World Creative

Cover Design: Paul Taylor

Printed by La Grafica Nuova S.C.R.L., Torino

WWW.SMALLWORLDCOMPANIES.COM

CONTENTS

7-10   Foreword

11-18   Prologue

21-46   Homecomings, Incomings, Outgoings and Shortcomings

47-74   Boom and Bust

75-133   One Step Forward, Two Steps Back

134-159   Tough at the Bottom, Tougher at the Top

160-182   On the Up and A Poison Cup

183-211   The Road to Redemption

212-235   All at Sea and A Dose of the Blues

236-269   Villains and Heroes and Mission Accomplished

270-289   Beginnings at the End

290-300   Games

301   Goalscorers

302   Appearances

303   Bibliography

ACKNOWLEDGEMENTS

AT Small World, thanks are due in huge part to editor Robert Allen for first persuading me to write this book and then helping me see it through. His copy-editing made a huge difference and was an education in itself. As was his patience. Thanks too go to Muriel Lumb for reading through the final edit. Any errors remaining in the text are entirely my own. My gratitude goes to former Sunderland Echo colleague Paul Taylor for producing the book cover under such short notice and to such professional effect. Also to Andrew Barker at Results Network PR for his constant support and good advice; Tim Rich at the Daily Telegraph for his helpful suggestions in the early chapters; my mother and my brothers for their encouragement; Matthew Moore for his forbearance. And, above all, to Marion for her love and patience while I worked on what follows.

I feel this season was one of

the biggest in Sunderland Football

Club's history. I really mean that.

ROY KEANE

FOREWORD

THIS is not a Roy Keane book. It is a Sunderland Football Club book – the story of the 2007-08 season. Yet, so influential a character has Keane become at the club, he inevitably looms larger than anyone else between these pages. That is only right. For rarely in the 129-year history of the club has one figure so quickly come to dominate its landscape. The manager is always the most important person at any football club. In Keane's case at Sunderland he embodied the role.

By a curious confluence of circumstances his prominence has been emphasised by the reluctance of others to seek the spotlight. Board members at other clubs occasionally emerge to sabre-rattle. Not at Sunderland. The Drumaville Consortium preferred to watch from the wings even before Keane's appointment. The seven Irish businessmen, one from Sunderland, who own the club have never called a press conference or contacted a reporter to give their views on the state of play at the Stadium of Light, the club's grand home on the banks of the River Wear.

Their efforts in acquiring Sunderland in the summer of 2006 were not aimed at self-promotion or driven by self-aggrandisement, but at giving the new chairman, former player Niall Quinn, the sporting chance he craved – to revive a club he believed in so passionately. Quinn was possessed of such faith in Sunderland's potential. It was infectious.

His backers invested in that faith, but they wanted none of the publicity that was there for the taking. They were happy for Quinn to take centre stage and, initially, he did just that. Quinn is one of the most articulate and intelligent players ever to lace a football boot and in the early days he used that eloquence to best advantage. He talked up the club, the fans, the players. He tried at every turn to give belief back to people who had lost it on the back of recent anguish-filled seasons. He would pop up, often unannounced, at functions, at civic events, in Sunderland pubs; all the time trying to create a buzz and get across the message of a 'New Sunderland' on the horizon. He delivered that message when his board appointed Roy Keane.

It was one of the great leaps in the dark in recent football history, a real act of faith, and it paid off spectacularly with the club's stunning return to the Premier League in the charismatic young manager's first season. The pact from the start – the agreement, which originally got Keane to the club – was that he would be allowed to run it his way, with no interference from anyone. Quinn took that a step further, scaling back substantially his own media appearances. He restricted himself generally to talking about season ticket prices, general developments and new initiatives. He was not going to be a talking-head chairman treading on the toes of his manager; even though no one talked better than him.

The new image of the club was to be Roy Keane. The dominating image on publicity leaflets urging fans to buy season tickets: Roy Keane. The person wearing a Sunderland Football Club strip on BBC television's Match of the Day credits: Roy Keane. Sunderland was to be Keane's own personal ball game. Keane would be allowed to shape it in the way he saw fit. Quinn would go out on a limb for a remarkable player in the belief he would become a remarkable manager. And, as the board and the chairman took a back seat in the public eye, there were few other challengers to Keane's profile.

At some clubs the assistant manager is almost as well known a figure as the manager, an occasional stand-in for the boss in interviews. Keane's assistant, head coach Tony Loughlan, shunned all publicity.

On the playing side, too, few people drew the spotlight away from the manager. In part, that was down to the reduced accessibility of players in the modern era. For, while it's true we live in a more media-controlled world than ever before, it's also the case that football clubs at the highest level exist in a more 'controlled-media' environment than at any time in the game's history. The days when journalists and players were friends and phone numbers were freely given out, interviews being garnered at the drop of a hat or the lift of a receiver, is increasingly the hallmark of a bygone era.

Even so, the players in the 2007-08 Sunderland squad were hardly the material to titillate the tabloids. Dwight Yorke was comfortably the best known, but his high-profile playboy days were behind him and his interviews few. Newly-recruited striker Michael Chopra made the briefest of forays into OK! Magazine in the early stages of the season. But that was pretty much it. Sunderland's record signing, Craig Gordon, was so self-contained a person that Keane mused, several months into the season, that he'd hardly spoken to him.

Keane had invested in characters rather than personalities, and if anyone typified a Roy Keane player it was his captain Dean Whitehead – a player who turned up on time for training, worked hard, kept his head down and went home.

All of which meant that Keane and Sunderland became synonymous with each other in the public eye far more rapidly than might have been expected. Think Sunderland – think Keane.

With the manager happy to stand or fall by his own idiosyncratic approach to club leadership, the story of Sunderland's season is his, more than anyone's.

There was more, much more, to the campaign than just one man however – there was the consortium, which found funds unheard of in the modern era at Sunderland to invest in a business they freely admitted they were far from experts in; the chairman, whose passion and project the club was all along; the players, some who had been tried and failed in the Premier League previously; many others who were experiencing the Premier League first time around; and, in Yorke's case, a great player on his swan song in the top tier. There was the collective efforts of the club's often unsung backroom staff and the general goodwill of a media that followed them every step of the way.

Above all, the season was about the massed ranks of supporters who had previously made the club great and who would endeavour to do so again with their phenomenal backing, home and away. Before the season was out, they would remind football what a force to be reckoned with they still were. They would help make the club big again. If Keane's pre-eminence was not matched by any individual at the Stadium of Light, even he had to share the attention with the colourful legions that followed in the club's wake and had helped make Sunderland the draw it originally was to him.

This is their story, in their first year back in the Premier

League under the management of Roy Keane. Their story, his story and that of anyone with even a passing interest in Sunderland Football Club.

PROLOGUE

I spent 12 years with Sunderland and I can categorically state that there isn't a club in the land with a better set of supporters. They are as knowledgable as they are passionate. CHARLIE HURLEY

ROY KEANE'S first Premier League season has every chance of being treated unkindly by history.

Almost forgotten, maybe. A footnote, perhaps.

The 'nothing' season.

After all, the 2007-08 campaign brought nothing more than first-round cup exits and a league campaign spent bobbing in or around the bottom third of the table. It lacked the romance of the previous season's surge, when Keane led a team from the foot of the Championship (a team newly relegated with an historic low of 15 points) to promotion as Champions.

Yet, as memorable as Keane's first season was, it was far from unusual in Sunderland's recent history. Almost every season in the previous dozen had been one of high drama, with the club either battling to survive, and often failing, or battling for promotion, and often succeeding.

In comparison the 2007-08 season looked staid. Yet it may come to be seen as the defining campaign in modern times of a football club once fêted as the best in the world; the first club to dominate the Football League – a club that had fallen so far for so long and had now embarked on a journey back towards English football's commanding heights. In that long, upward journey, this season had to serve as a base camp of vital importance.

Successful structures are built on firm foundations and Keane's first task in the top tier was putting those foundations down. It was an extraordinarily significant campaign because relegation could have set the club back a decade, whereas survival might make possible a sustained return to the top half of a table in which so many of the club's formative decades had been spent.

The Championship promotion season had witnessed three public transformations, those of: a badly-bruised giant of a club; an heroic character of the game; and the mood of fans, who had become used to fleeting success only as a means of measuring enduring underachievement. That memorable campaign only highlighted the Sunderland phenomenon of recent years, a sequence of thrilling promotions and catastrophic relegations following on from each other with almost seasonal regularity.

Not just one of England's yo-yo clubs but THE yo-yo club.

It was a boom-bust cycle that Quinn was determined to break. The steepling expectations produced by Keane's instant success saw the fans return to the Premier League on the back of Quinn's 'magic carpet', with hopes high that this was only going to be the start. But after the previous devastating relegations, there existed a natural caution borne from unprecedented pain.

To understand the psyche of the club Quinn and Keane inherited, the mental scars left by the two worst Premier League relegations (up until the 2007-08 season) have to be appreciated. In the 19-point season of 2002-03, Sunderland lost every one of their last fifteen games – a sequence that continued into the following season and eventually stretched to seventeen straight defeats.

Seventeen defeats! To take your support into seventeen games, spread across half a year and see every one of them lost is enough to drain the spirit of any fan. Every week the calamity club seemed to contrive a new way of losing, the most astonishing of which was conceding three own goals in fifteen minutes to guarantee a home defeat to Charlton Athletic.

Since league records began only Lancashire club Darwen produced a worse sequence – an eighteen game losing streak in the 1898-99 season. In the history of football, only the long-dead reporter on the Darwen Bugle could have appreciated how soul-destroying it was writing about a six-month sequence without a win, as I did for the Sunderland Echo. It was the sort of soul-sapping sequence that happens less than once a century.

That would have been bad enough. Two seasons later, after another promotion – this time under Mick McCarthy, Sunderland did even worse with a barely credible three wins in 38 league games. They won only once at home all season and collected just 15 points on their way to another abysmal relegation – a relegation that went a long way to cementing the club's reputation as a byword for failure. Of the five all-time worst campaigns from any team in the history of the English game, Sunderland had claimed two. And not just over the space of 100 years. Only a couple of seasons separated those incredibly depressing campaigns.

It's hard to overestimate the amount of psychological damage those crushing years did to supporter confidence. Sunderland fans pride themselves on a healthy pessimism bred out of generations of dashed hopes, on and off the pitch. But, after the humiliations of their last two relegations, they were looking through a glass not so much half-full as slightly damp. Quinn's purchase of the club, Keane's arrival and their subsequent success had started to change that mind-cast.

No one was allowing themselves to get too excited at the start of the new season, even with Keane and Quinn at the helm. Quinn and the Drumaville board had a long-term plan for Sunderland – mirrored by Keane – to restore the club to the pinnacles of the game. Momentum is critical in football. The maintenance of Premier League status in the 2007-08 season was undoubtedly more important than the largely unexpected bonus of a first-season promotion. If the yo-yo club was to 'yo' just one more time, it would set the club back years, given the litany of disappointments that had preceded it. The benefits of the Keane Factor would have been seriously, maybe even mortally, wounded.

Success has a smell all of its own, but it can be a fragile and fleeting scent. As other heroic footballing figures had found in management – the likes of Bryan Robson, Kevin Keegan, Glenn Hoddle, Stuart Pearce – proud reputations, once tainted by failure, never quite glitter so brightly again. Stay up and the rewards were obvious. This time Sunderland had the financial backing, the facilities and the famous-name manager to re-establish itself as one of the leading names in the game. If they could only bridge the gap in that first season. Then the finances coming into the club, coupled with it being recognised as a Premier League force, might see Sunderland rising to a position of prominence not experienced in more than half a century. It would require a collective unity on behalf of everyone in and around the club, the sort of unity only fleetingly seen since Sunderland's first relegation from the top division. A relegation, we should remind ourselves, that came later to Sunderland than any other English club: 1958.

That was the year the rest of the footballing world remembers for the Munich air disaster, when Manchester United was ripped apart by a tragedy that still strikes the most poignant of chords. Sunderland fanatics remember it as the year that the Wearsiders' proud claim to be the only club in English football never to have played outside the top flight came to an end. Since 1936, and the relegation of Aston Villa and Blackburn Rovers, Sunderland had been the only club in England to play its football solely in the top tier. Ironically it was Keane's former club that delivered the killer blow to that unique record. In the wake of the Munich plane crash, the patched-up remnants of the great Manchester United team managed only one win before the end of the season. It was a win over Sunderland and it was enough to condemn the Wearsiders to an agonising drop. On the last day of the season, and on goal difference, naturally. For the club has always attracted last-minute dramas.

In a way, maybe it was fitting that exactly fifty years on, it should be a man most associated with Manchester United, who was looking to restore the Wearsiders to the big stage from which the last of the Busby Babes had originally ejected them.

Modern-day Sunderland did have a few important factors in its favour as it looked to re-establish itself once again in the top division. There was the universal popularity of Quinn among fans – in direct contrast to his predecessor, long-serving Bob Murray; there was the immense respect felt towards the man Quinn had brought in to boss the club; and, finally, the substantial finance the club now had behind it to make an impact in the transfer market.

However, the man upon which everything hinged was Keane.

In the summer of 2007, in the wake of promotion, it was impossible to overestimate the appreciation and admiration with which the Wearside public regarded him for what he had achieved in just ten short months. And the kudos that a person of his stature brought was a balm to those who had proffered support through thin and thinner. In his debut season in management Keane had given the club back its pride and its Premier League status. That was the completion of a task, which had looked like Mission Impossible mere months before. A 5-0 hammering of Luton gave Sunderland the title on the very last day of the campaign.

That summer, Keane eagerly looked forward to the season ahead. For the first time since the 1950s Sunderland competed with the big boys in the transfer market. More than £35 million was spent during the closed season bringing in the players needed for Sunderland's Premier League challenge. It was something fans had not witnessed in generations. But neither the money nor the manager came with guarantees. It would have to be about trust.

After those embarrassing relegations, Sunderland fans would have to put their faith in one of the most inexperienced chairmen in the game, as well as the man who, that season, was the youngest and most inexperienced manager of all, at the highest level.

Those of us who had followed Sunderland's far-too-many fallow years had a gut-feeling that if Keane could only keep Sunderland up, the club would be genuinely set for take-off in the years that followed. The Wearsiders' exciting potential is still not fully appreciated by so many people outside the north-east but, in some ways, that's the least surprising fact of all. A generational memory is reckoned to last about twenty years. And the past twenty years of Sunderland's history, have been, with few exceptions, nothing special.

For supporters across England under the age of fifty, Sunderland are, most memorably, the underdogs who won the 1973 FA Cup – a plucky David beating the Goliath of Don Revie's mighty Leeds United. Apart from that solitary success though, Sunderland were generally the team doing no more than averagely in England's top tier or quite well in its second division.

Yet it was not always so. When professional football was in its infancy Sunderland were the most successful club of the era. Today the richest and most popular club in the world is Manchester United. Yet the very name Manchester United – the name adopted by Newton Heath – was barely a month old when Sunderland were crowned champions of England for the fourth time in 1902. Liverpool – the club that has gone on to become the most successful English football has produced – had won their first title only a year previously.

And that was thanks largely to the guidance of a former Sunderland manager Tom Watson. By the time Sunderland won their sixth and last English league title, in the 1935-36 season, Liverpool were still two behind them and did not match Sunderland's tally until 1964, the year Sunderland won their first promotion. Before the outbreak of the 1939-45 world war only Aston Villa could match Sunderland's title haul.

It was in the success of the 1890s team, dubbed The 'Team of All The Talents' by league founder William McGregor, that the foundations for Sunderland's huge following were first put down, and the game seeped into the lifeblood of the community. By that time, the town of Sunderland had become one of the engine rooms underpinning the British Empire's industrial and manufacturing dominance. It was a focal point of mining, metal-working and shipbuilding and, at one point, was the biggest shipbuilding port in the world. The legions of men drawn in to support and nourish these industries, those many and varied working class trades, also came together collectively in a love of football which formed the bedrock of the club's support.

If life for so many in the working class was, as it was claimed, 'nasty, brutish and short' towards the end of the 19th century, well, for supporters of Sunderland there was respite, pride and consolation in how outstanding their football team was. In 1895, Sunderland won an unofficial 'Championship of the World' game when, as champions of England, they took on Scotland's champions, Hearts, in an exhibition match and emerged 5-3 victors. Given the two countries were the most prominent footballing nations at the time – Sunderland were now the best team in the world, their supporters could argue with a measure of justification.

The communal passion for football among Sunderland fans, bound up in so much more than a game, was to be passed on from one generation to the next and endured even when the team wasn't winning trophies.

Sunderland became big spenders in the 1950s, earning the title 'the Bank of England club' for the number of times it broke transfer records as it tried to live up to past achievements. It went close too – reaching FA Cup semi-finals and being one win away from a seventh league title. But, after a financial scandal broke in 1957 involving illegal payments to players, the club was severely destabilised, leading to relegation the following year. It was a blow to the community, described by one journalist at the time as being 'like a death in the family'. When the Wearsiders were finally promoted six years later, led by Ireland's great centre half, Charlie Hurley, the Cork-born defender remembered watching, with manly pride, the tears falling down the grimy faces of grown men on the terraces – miners, shipbuilders and steelworkers. That 'present-day' team, represented by Hurley and his teammates, was still embedded in and defined by the proud past of previous teams.

The ships, the mines and the steelworks have all gone now. But the obsession with football remains despite nigh on fifty years spent largely in the wilderness. In the wake of the 1958 relegation, Sunderland embarked on that increasingly yo-yo swing – nine relegations in all – and the only real glory they had to feed on was the famous 1973 FA Cup final victory. When Sunderland won their first FA Cup final in 1937 the football world wondered what had taken the great club so long. Sunderland-born skipper, the glamorous Raich Carter, had mused that league titles over the years had almost paled into insignificance against Sunderland supporters' thirst for that elusive cup glory. They had been beaten three times in the semi-finals and once in the final in previous years, and Raich Carter's glory was Sunderland finally landing the one trophy that had escaped them.

By the time 1973 came along fortunes had turned full circle and Sunderland's victory was regarded as one of the greatest cup upsets of all time – small Sunderland beating large Leeds.

The years of decline from being a major force in the game unravelled against the backdrop of a decaying Roker Park – among the best of 19th-century grounds, but a ground which, in later decades, increasingly became emblematic of Sunderland's slide down football's ladder. It had been famous since it first opened its gates in 1899, for the Roker Roar – the wall of noise, which 1960s Spurs' double-winning captain Danny Blanchflower recalled, was the most awesome sound he had ever heard from any terrace anywhere in the world.

Once it had been one of the grandest grounds in the country with its elegant Archibald Leitch latticework. In its last decade what caught the eye was the crumbling brickwork and the corrugated iron, the barbed wire and the paucity of the facilities. Increasingly it was a crumbling relic. But, even before the ultra-modern Stadium of Light replaced Roker in 1997 and revitalised interest in the club, the passion still endured.

When Denis Smith, manager of the club between 1987 and 1991, was sacked, he said Sunderland was the only place he knew where 'you could go out to buy your local evening paper from the newsstand and not only be recognised by the old woman selling the paper but also be told where you were going wrong both in terms of team tactics and selection'.

It's a special place for football, something Keane seemed to grasp instinctively. And it would be something special in a cynical era, if one of the great clubs, the success story of its age during the birthing years of football, could be reborn again. That was the dream of someone as idealistic as Quinn, but it would not be easy.

To make it work, Keane and Quinn – polar opposites in just about all things other than nationality and a shared love of the game – would have to work together in a campaign that would demand everything from them. They would need fans to stay with them through whatever choppy waters lay ahead. They would need players to raise their game.

In Keane's first season in the Premier League, he was to make a journey reminiscent of his first mentor in English football, rather than his second. Brian Clough's task at Derby County and Nottingham Forest, like Keane's at Sunderland, had been to take lesser lights to greater heights. In contrast, Sir Alex Ferguson's had been to try to take an already massive top-flight club to even more success.

Yet in some ways, the parallels to be made are far more relevant to the United manager than Brian Clough. It has been suggested that Sir Alex Ferguson's most important season of all at Manchester United was the one prior to his team winning its first piece of silverware, when the board held its nerve through the difficult times as calls were made for his head. Before the Champions League games, the FA Cups and the Premier League titles Ferguson had to survive the most trying and tricky of seasons, in which he learned so much about himself and all those around him.

It's an intriguing hypothesis. Forget the glory and the trophies that followed. None of it would have happened if the board hadn't kept faith with Sir Alex Ferguson in what turned out to be his third fallow year at Old Trafford.

A year now largely forgotten.

A 'nothing' season.

CHAPTER ONE

Homecoming, Incomings, Outgoings and Shortcomings

I guessed there was goodwill in the air towards us in Ireland but I had no idea how far and how deep it was. NIALL QUINN

I was off work for weeks but I'm not going to say anything against Roy Keane, especially after what he did for my son. BRIAN LOUGHEED

SUNDERLAND'S 2007-08 campaign first opened its eyes and breathed life into itself on the banks of the River Lee in the city of Cork on a sultry summer evening. The visit to Keane's home place was the highlight of Sunderland's preseason. It was in Cork where the elements, which would have such a profound effect in the months, ahead were reassembled – the passion and pride of the red and white army, the virtually unchallenged adoration of Keane and the absolute willingness of players to dig deep for their manager. For the hundreds of 'Mackems' who made the trip maybe there was a touch of déjà vu, for Cork and Sunderland share some striking similarities. To wander around the Irish city was to understand why the Sunderland manager's job had first appealed to Keane.

He had suggested the previous season that it was his destiny to manage Sunderland, just as it had been his destiny to play for Manchester United and Celtic. Perhaps as a son of Cork, he could relate to Sunderland's great history and the role of underdog it had often been forced to play. Cork and its people had shaped his character and such a place would have made it easy for him to identify with Sunderland. Both are river-based working-class communities with a passion for sport, both have known hard times and sacrifice and both have something of a chip on their shoulders over rival cities that have tended to hog the limelight – Dublin for Cork, Newcastle for Sunderland. Gritty rather than glamorous, Leeside and Wearside also share a common affection for one sporting icon: Keane.

That was as evident on the streets of Cork as it was on the terraces of the city's Turners Cross ground, where goodwill between both sets of supporters was unconfined. In the streets and the pubs, in the days leading up to the game, the cities' local papers on either team of the Irish Sea had printed tales of warmth and welcome shown from Cork people to those of Sunderland and vice versa. In a friendly encounter, played on the last day of a warm and muggy July, that goodwill came together when the two teams met on a pleasant evening, at a ground experiencing the feel of a festival more than a football match. A party atmosphere surrounded the stadium, packed to the rafters with Keane supporters. It was an unusual phenomenon to hear a manager's name being chanted from all corners of a ground but it would actually happen twice more before the season was over, with the two games against Manchester United.

Preseason tours inhabit a surreal world for fans, footballers and sports reporters. It's real football but not really football. No points or prizes are at stake, nothing to win or lose of consequence. But the players need to work hard to build up their reservoir of fitness. For them it's work, for the fans it's play, for sports reporters it's a lot of the first and as much of the second as can be seized.

The tour was important for Sunderland Football Club because it wanted Ireland to buy into the club, emotionally or financially – preferably both. From a journalistic point of view it was fascinating because it gave an insight into Keane's readiness to engage with reporters and fans in a way rarely seen in his first managerial season. It would have been a taxing experience for someone so protective of their privacy, but it was as if he was girding himself for the responsibilities and duties ahead in the forensic spotlight of the Premier League.

There was no doubt it would be a huge test for him.

No one gets to become adept in any job overnight and Keane, at thirty six, was less than twelve months into his first managerial role. He would later acknowledge his mistakes – 'four to five hundred' he'd claim – but he would learn from them too. The first, perhaps, was in trying to cram so much into the Irish tour. Three games in five days, against Bohemians, Cork and Galway, was ambitious by any club's standards. Each game was at different compass points of Ireland – east, south and west. That meant three different hotels, three different training grounds, three different press conferences and, perhaps most demanding, three different communities to glad-hand and court.

The tour had kicked off in Dublin when Sunderland took on

Bohemians in an atmospheric night match at the club's venerable old ground. Before the game hundreds of Sunderland fans had made their mark on Dublin's fair city. The streets were splashed with red and white as throngs of supporters enjoyed the hospitality of the Irish capital's pubs and bars, the main two centres of drinking being those owned by Charlie Chawke, the colourful board member of the Drumaville consortium. These watering holes become Wearside Away for the day as fans revelled and quaffed at the Oval pub in Middle Abbey Street, just off the main O'Connell Street thoroughfare, and at the Bank across the Liffey river at College Green on Dame Street.

The Dublin branch of the Sunderland Supporters' Association held a special open day for fans at the Oval. The Bank was decorated with Sunderland colours draped over its doors and packed with fans within. It was noisy but heart-warmingly relaxed stuff (Sunderland Echo photographer Tom Yeoman and I found time for a beer in each pub). Chawke's son David, behind the bar at the Bank, sounded a little relieved when he eyed the noisy throngs. 'Sunderland's fans have been a credit to their city,' he smiled. 'They've turned up in numbers, enjoyed their few drinks and had a good few laughs.'

It was exactly the sort of image Quinn had hoped to project to the Irish public. The feel-good factor among the travelling faithful continued when the tour got off to a winning start against Bohemians. The Black Cats emerged 1-0 victors thanks to a 78th minute headed goal from Trinidad and Tobago striker Stern John but it was no stroll in Dalymount Park. Sunderland might have just become a high-and-mighty Premier League club, but the Bohs fans and their team weren't overawed by Keane's newly-promoted team. Some fans booed the Sunderland manager as he made his way slowly across the pitch to the dugout, while the rest gave Keane and Quinn a warm reception.

With Sunderland captain Dean Whitehead absent, Player of the Season Nyron Nosworthy led the team out and went on to distinguish himself with an assured display, full of intelligent running, solid tackling and the occasional 'Libero' touch. The athletic centre half was outshone though by new signing Paul McShane. McShane caught the eye of the watching Ireland manager, Steve Staunton, with his fierce tackling and a stunning block midway through the second half, which denied Bohemians a great goal-scoring chance. Though positives were to be taken out of the game, accuracy in front of goal wasn't one of them. Sunderland were sloppy and debutant striker Michael Chopra was guiltier than most. 'The finishing could have been better generally but I'd be more concerned at this stage if we weren't creating chances,' was Keane's verdict.

Talking with a small huddle of reporters on the pitch after the game, he was asked briefly about the hostile reception from a few fans. He shrugged before murmuring, 'every club has a scum element to it.' It was a throwaway remark, but a potentially poisonous one in uncharitable hands. Louise Wanless, Sunderland's head of public relations, sauntered around jovially suggesting reporters leave the remark out. BOHS SCUM RAGES KEANE was the last thing the north-east press lads needed to see in the Irish media as the goodwill tour got underway. No good for the club. No good for us. For, as far as regional press in England are concerned, preseason is the season of goodwill to their clubs, a time when efforts are usually made on both teams to bond. No big headlines emerged in the wake of Keane's comments. These events were an indication of things to come. Reporters would have to be careful with their interpretation of his words throughout the season.

By the time the Sunderland entourage reached Cork, a couple of days later, word had travelled about the mixed reception and Keane was asked about it in the prematch press conference, held in the bowels of Turners Cross.

'You can get booed wherever you go,' he said, looking almost bored by the question. 'It's no big deal, I might get booed here.'

There was a stunned pause in the questioning.

Then, Cork reporter John McHale said, 'Roy, you're not seriously suggesting you might get booed here, are you?'

Keane paused for a beat before a smile played across his face.

'No,' he grinned, as the room dissolved in laughter.

Keane was held in great esteem in Cork. The idea, among the English reporters, that he might not get total backing at Turners Cross was simply unthinkable to them.

Time and time again Cork people provided the English press lads with tales of Keane folklore – of generosity, kindness, loyalty and unsolicited acts of charity over the years from the city's favourite son. His status is such that there is even a Keane 'pilgrimage' taxi drivers offer to fans disembarking at the airport. It involves visits to the house where he grew up, the home his parents have bought with his assistance, the club where he learnt to box, Rockmount FC where he began his schoolboy footballing career and the pub where he used to drink in his early playing days at Nottingham Forest and Manchester United.

The press conferences in Dublin, Cork and Galway proved Keane's willingness to engage. The day before the Bohemians game he had faced a phalanx of photographers alongside a rut of reporters from television, radio, newspapers and magazines. It looked an uneven battle, an entire roomful of journalists, some virtually on top of one another, all focused on one man. It was also a test for Keane who was facing the full weight of the Irish media for the first time as a manager, since taking over on Wearside. The questions weren't just about the game ahead, they were about his personal creed as a manager.

After a year working with Keane as the Sunderland boss, writers in the north-east of England were far from blasé about meeting one of the greatest players and characters the game has produced. He's not a man to trifle with under any circumstances; dangerous to take for granted. Yet, almost unconsciously, a working relationship develops, which naturally goes beyond that of one stranger meeting another. So it was interesting to see the reactions of fellow journalists on the tour, many not used to seeing Keane at close quarters. It felt, for the most part, like a group of twitchy big-game hunters surrounding a lion. Not that Keane looked on edge. He talked and he talked and he talked. Honestly, openly, passionately, humorously about whatever subject was thrown his way. And the time ticked by, ten minutes, twenty minutes, half an hour and well beyond – the longest single press conference anyone could remember him giving since first being unveiled as Sunderland boss. The underlying message seemed to be: 'Ask me anything, I'm publicising Sunderland.' The effect was disarming. Reporters got great copy. Everyone seemed impressed by the way he conducted himself.

Keane was continuing, that summer, the process of his reinvention – from a snarling player, a force of nature, an inspirational captain who wore his heart on his sleeve, to a carefully balanced manager, more thoughtful and reasoned, leading and lifting his players from the touchline. These meetings with the media in his home country helped push that change further across in the public eye. While the Dublin media were ambivalent but engaged by Keane in Cork, he could have said the Pope was a protestant and journalists would have smiled indulgently and reported sympathetically. In Cork, the press conference was laid-back and he was able to enjoy a laugh and a joke before dropping a bombshell – a smart bomb, as it turned out, and a calculated one at that.

He revealed he was planning to speak to Cork City's leading scorer Roy O'Donovan with a view to signing him from under the noses of Fulham. Up until that point the Sunderland manager's style in the transfer market had been that of Manchester United: business done quietly, talks done privately, signing announced after everything's concluded. But this time it was different; and for a reason. Keane knew he had to act immediately if he was to secure a striker scheduled to undergo his medical at Fulham twenty-four hours later. It was a demonstration of a flexibility and a pragmatism on Keane's part that he was to display time and again in the months ahead – a refusal to be bound by hard and fast rules – even his own. In the cramped, windowless confines of a press room in the Turners Cross ground Keane was asked, as he had been continually over the summer, about his transfer targets. He replied that he was hoping to bring in three new players, 'one of them,' he said, 'not too far from here'.

'Do you mean Roy O'Donovan?'

'Yes.'

The effect was electric on the Cork reporters, as you might expect. The twenty-one-year-old O'Donovan was Cork's star player, still raw, but he had already scored twenty-one goals in the eircom League of Ireland and his move to the Londoners was all but a done deal.

Keane's calculated few words created a media frenzy that would help sweep O'Donovan away from Craven Cottage and into the Stadium of Light, but the deciding factor in the successful chase was not the media speculation; it was the identity of Sunderland's manager.

Cork journalist Noel Spillane rang the player to break the news of Sunderland's interest.

'Hi Roy, Noel here, I've just come out of the press conference with Keane, and Sunderland want to sign you,' he said.

'Jesus!'

'Yep, they're looking to speak to you this evening about the move.'

'Roy Keane himself?'

'Yep.'

'Jesus!'

O'Donovan said his heart started thumping. From that point onwards there was only one club he wanted to sign for.

'Roy Keane has always been a hero of mine and he's a god in Cork,' he said after the move. 'The moment I met him and found he had no airs and graces about him, that just confirmed to me that I wanted to join the club.'

Fulham weren't happy, and neither were Cork City who faced the prospect of getting less for the player than they had anticipated. For that reason discussions dragged on but Roy the manager eventually got Roy the player.

The striker's name did not appear on Cork's team sheet for a game that sold out the 7,500 capacity ground. Instead the game would feature a former Sunderland midfielder, Cork-born Colin Healy playing for his hometown club. It was another Sunderland-Ireland connection, just as we had seen at Bohemians, where Mark Rossiter and Chris Kingsberry, former Sunderland youth players, lined up in opposition.

Healy in his early days was compared to a young Keane but his career in England was destroyed in a Sunderland game at Coventry City where he suffered a double fracture to his leg; one of the most gruesome and horrific injuries witnessed on a football pitch. Remarkably, he battled back to fitness but suffered another leg break, and subsequently dropped down the English divisions before ending up back in Ireland.

'I played against Colin a few times and he had the potential to be a top player, but that's the other side of football,' reflected Keane, talking almost to himself. 'People think it's all millionaires and flash cars but injury can ruin a player's career.'

It was another Cork man who had the most important say on the night; former Glasgow Celtic and Manchester United midfielder, Liam Miller, getting Sunderland off the hook with a fortuitous equaliser deep in the second half. That Miller should have needed to equalise at all was a travesty, for Sunderland dominated the match from start to finish. It was a reality check on an evening in which Sunderland were caught up in the carnival atmosphere of the occasion, only to risk Cork having the last laugh. The home fans in the packed ground had amused themselves before the game with playful taunts of 'going down, going down' and 'you're not English anymore'; but it was friendly fire. The mood of the evening was summed up when Keane, photographers buzzing around him like flies, followed the players out to rapturous applause. It was a warm evening and Keane strode out wearing an open–necked white shirt, calm at the centre of a storm. He looked relaxed enough but he was in the zone, staring straight ahead into the middle distance and in no mood to be waving to all corners as the paparazzi zeroed in on his every move. He alone was trying to transmit the message that this was match-day, not fun-day. The sheer excitement was summed up in one image – two photographers circling Keane collided and fell dazed to the floor as he strode through them looking neither left nor right.

Sunderland dominated, but fell to the sucker punch just before the hour when Colin Healy put in a corner and midfielder Denis Behan triumphed in the goalmouth scramble. Cork fans taunted, 'Can we play you every week?' and, to warm laughter, 'Keano, Keano what's the score?' There were only ten minutes remaining when Miller levelled, rolling through a couple of unconvincing challenges, before firing home from the six-yard box. The never-say-die attitude shown that evening was to typify Sunderland's approach to the season ahead, and the knack of getting late goals would be just as much a feature.

Shrugging off his disappointment at the result, Keane reflected on the demanding nature of the tour. 'The players can get sidetracked, as I think the lads have a little bit with all the travelling and the media commitments, which is part and parcel of things, the visits to hospitals and the events with the kids,' he said. He also gave credit to Cork's battling display. 'The League of Ireland is very good these days. I can't remember the last English team that came out here and hammered an Irish team. They are tough to beat.'

Miller was beaming afterwards, thrilled to score in front of his friends and family, still with much to prove and desperate to succeed on the big stage, after seven years at Glasgow Celtic and two relatively unfulfilled years at Old Trafford. Speaking in the ground where he had first watched the game of soccer, the twenty-six-year-old admitted: 'Of all the games on the tour, this was obviously the pick for me and I'm very pleased to have got a goal because this is an important season coming up.'

The Irish games were enjoyable, though always a side issue to the daily grind of transfer speculation, manager Keane, chief executive Peter Walker and chairman Quinn all sharing exasperation at the long-drawn-out nature of some chases. Championship striker David Nugent was one example, Sunderland eventually pulling out of a move after the Preston player kept the club dangling for months. Nugent joined Portsmouth, suggesting he had been snubbed when he was mulling over the Sunderland offer. Keane, he said, was too impatient.

'I waited five weeks for David Nugent,' responded Keane, 'and if he thinks that waiting five weeks is me being impatient, then he doesn't really know me at all. I met him and even made him a nice cup of tea, so he can't say he wasn't treated well. In the end the deal wasn't sitting right so we moved on. Eventually the player needs to make a decision and if he doesn't then you get doubts. I didn't get Nugent but I'm very happy with Michael Chopra.'

Chopra had arrived at the club for £5 million from Cardiff City and, like the capture of Kieran Richardson from Manchester United for half a million pounds more, was one of a string of buys where Sunderland paid top dollar for players they hoped would justify their fees.

One deal exercising the minds of the board was the on-off move for Hearts' young prodigy, Craig Gordon, a goalkeeper everyone seemed to agree was going to be a Premier League star of the future. Arsene Wenger had him watched. Aston Villa were genuinely interested and ready to offer him a move. Sunderland made three successive bids, eventually reaching a club record offer of £9 million, but Hearts refused to budge on their £10 million valuation. Keane had placed a top goalkeeper at the top of his shopping list – remembering Brian Clough's claim that Peter Shilton had been worth a dozen points a season to Nottingham Forest's trophy-winning team of the late 1970s – and had been disappointed when a long pursuit of Bolton keeper Jussi Jaaskelainen ended with the Finn signing a new contract at the Reebok. Hearts' majority shareholder Vladimir Romanov, who had insisted Gordon was going nowhere after Sunderland refused to go to £10 million, softened his stance. 'I think it's for Craig to decide his own destiny,' he said. 'You can't just hold somebody at the club if he doesn't want to stay.'

Gordon had twenty-three Scottish caps, and the twenty-four-year-old was a Scottish Football Writers' Association Player of the Year. If he could be signed Sunderland could hardly send out a clearer signal of its ambition.

The club and its supporters headed off to Galway in time for the races, and with horse-loving Quinn you knew that couldn't be a coincidence. Sunderland set up their wares next to the 'Guinness and Oysters' marquee, and from there they did their best to sell the club during their 48-hour stay. Inside the sweltering tent on a blistering hot afternoon Quinn was elated when we caught up with him.

'It has been marvellous,' he said looking poised and relaxed, oblivious to the humidity in Sunderland's sauna tent. 'I guessed there was goodwill in the air towards us, but I had no idea how far and how deep it went.

'Season tickets are not really going to have an appeal to Irish supporters, but we are trying to do smaller packages for them. There's a horseshoe of airports around Ireland, from the western seaboard down the south and up the coast on the west, and we want to make flights and packages available all around the country. We're not asking them to come twenty times a year, but maybe four or five times.

'Our core support will always come from a semicircle starting up around South Shields, north of Sunderland, travelling round and down below Durham. Our club survives and is what it is because of that belt but it's nice if we can encourage people from wider afield to buy into the club and, because of circumstances, Ireland was always an obvious target. There's so much to attract people; the friendliness of Sunderland people is a big asset. They have a great history out there in the last hundred or two hundred years since football was formed. They have a great pride in the region which isn't really exported outside of it.'

Quinn is a natural charmer, the role of the genial, ebullient Irishman sitting comfortably on his broad shoulders. A tour like this was perfect for his social skills. He had talked earlier about his first Premier Chairman's meeting, facing a roomful of cynics who warned him to expect only grey hairs and ingratitude. Relaxing and working in equal measure at the Galway Races, he couldn't have looked further away from his first white strand.

But it would be wrong to think that he was all style and no substance. He had already suffered disappointment with the realisation that he would not be able, at this stage, to help change the face of football by freeing clubs of the vice-like grip exerted over them by some agents. The Sunderland chairman had been hoping to be in the vanguard of those seeking a sea change in the game, with clubs uniting to insist from now on that it was players who paid their agents, rather than clubs.

'After all,' he had pointed out, quite reasonably, the previous season, 'if an actor gets a part in a film, the film company doesn't pay his agent, the actor does. If the industry wises up with this new found Sky money and makes the necessary changes, then everyone will have a chance and the fan will be better off.'

Those hopes had been dashed in the summer, with more money washing around the game than ever before. Premier League chairman found it impossible to put the moral high ground above their clubs' immediate self-interest. It was a battle that would have to wait for another day. And it was far from Quinn's mind in Ireland as he concentrated on the task of spreading Sunderland's message.

A central thrust of the charm offensive, in Cork especially, had been the ebullient presence of Charlie Hurley, legendary Sunderland centre half of the 1960s, a man voted Player of the Century by fans in the club's centenary year, a big personality who was more than happy to act as an ambassador for the club.

'Charlie is the King and he has been fantastic,' grinned Quinn. 'Everyone here, from the children to the players, can look up to him. He's one of the most respected people in football in Ireland and it's marvellous to see him getting the credit he deserves. He gets it in Sunderland but I'm pleased to see him getting it elsewhere. Actually, I think he's had a ball, meeting people and charming them, and he's been a great asset to us.'

Keane meanwhile was still waxing lyrical in his media conferences and relishing the arrival of a Premier League season which grew closer by the day. At Cork he had reflected, presciently as it turned out, on the importance of home form in the Premier League.

'Any team wanting to do well has to have good home form, and that's what we'll need,' he said. 'Home form alone has saved a lot of teams and we hope crowds of more than 40,000 will be a big help. Some players get intimidated by that, but that's exactly why I've looked to bring in characters, because I know the passion of Sunderland. Playing in front of that sort of crowd should be something to be enjoyed rather than feared. It's very much a roller coaster place, you're either up a height or down in the dumps, so for me it's about getting a well-working team and a well-working club that can handle that.'

By Galway, Keane had tired of the spotlight and the endless autograph signings. The only time I personally saw him looking relaxed and happy was training with his players in Cork, and posing for a photograph in Galway for the Irish Guide Dogs for the Build Association, when he met dog and owner. He was still great value in the press conferences though, being honest and open about how he needed to improve his Championship winning squad.

'The biggest challenge in the Premiership is strength in depth,' he said. 'I think if I put out my first eleven we'd be fine, but we are short of two or three players at the moment.'

He was reminded that the knowledge picked up from working under two great managers would stand him in good stead, but he was at pains to point out he would be his own man. 'I was lucky Timmy Murphy used to be a good manager for me when I was with Rockmount in Cork,' he countered.

Brian Clough and Sir Alex Ferguson had been colossal influences on Keane. Though he would endeavour to take the best bits from both, he also saw flaws and would seek to be a clone of neither.

'It's true that I played under Alex Ferguson and Brian Clough, and I count my blessings for that. Hopefully I can pass on a few of the things I've learned. But, as great managers as they were for me, they made mistakes, and I've got to be my own man. The beauty of being a manager at a big club like Sunderland is that every day something comes up that you couldn't have envisaged. You're always being tested and you have to expect the unexpected. I don't mind that. It was one of the attractions for me. Getting success is a massive, massive challenge for this club. You have to have dreams in football, and I believe Sunderland can be a top, top club, but a lot of managers have tried to do that and come up short. Now we face the Premiership and it's going to be a steep learning curve, but I'm a fast learner and I wouldn't want to be anywhere else.

'We enjoyed the Championship but I don't want to go back there again.'

In the first two games of the tour he had bemoaned Sunderland's lack of goals, saying his strikers were already under pressure; but against Galway (the weakest of the three games) he saw his players hit the back of the net four times. Sunderland had had to fight against Bohemians, they had almost been caught out at Cork, but at Galway they were finally at the races. Forwards Chopra, John and David Connolly gave them a cutting edge. It was a timely boost for the manager, who was gambling that the players who had won the Championship could form the backbone of a successful Premier League team. For Connolly the game produced a moment of vindication, his goal acting as a reminder that the club's top scorer should still be in the mix. He scored one and made another, despite coming into the game midway through the second half.

'It was especially good for me to play and score here because my dad's family is from Galway,' Connolly said, 'and a lot of my family and friends were here. Hopefully in future I will get more time on the pitch.'

John was another striker from the Championship anxious to point out that the old boys might have just as much to contribute as the new. John had been delighted to avoid the close season clear-out and wanted to spend the rest of his career at the club. The likeable forward had almost been offloaded in the summer when Keane was chasing Nugent's signature, with both John and Connolly rumoured as each being offered as a makeweight.

Nugent didn't come, John remained a Sunderland player going into the new season, and he was determined to take advantage. 'I'm really pleased to still be here,' John said at the end of the training session before the Galway game. 'A lot of clubs forget about the players that were good enough to get them to the Premiership and get rid of them too soon, in my opinion. It has happened to me before and, hopefully, it won't happen now at Sunderland because I can do well for the club this season.'

The Irish tour had finished on a good note. 'One or two players did themselves favours in terms of getting into the team,' said Keane. But new arrivals were imminent. 'We are making progress, but it is very slow progress, and if I've learnt one thing lately it is that these things can drag on a little bit.'

It had been a long summer for Keane, who admitted later that he asked too much of himself, trying to fit in studying for his coaching badges along with making dozens of fruitless phone calls looking for new players. He quickly learned that clubs aren't set up to do much business at the end of the season.

The tour had been demanding but Keane was pleased with his players' conduct. 'There has been a lot of interest from Ireland in Sunderland – there's no getting away from it. But that's fantastic and we should welcome it. It's great when I go back to Cork and see Sunderland shirts. The people in Dublin, Cork and Galway could not have been more welcoming, and the players really enjoyed that. We've done our best to wake people up to Sunderland and the reality is that we want the folks at the matches.' A measure of Sunderland's success that summer was that it sold more than a thousand season tickets in Ireland.

Traditionally, preseason tours are the time when footballers, management staff and reporters get to relax together to build the bonds that can sustain them through the slog of a long hard season. There's no average, but local reporters and club managers usually fall out two, three or four times a year, and preseason is a good time to build up relationships that help put things back on track, or keep them on a positive footing – a chance to remind each other that, on almost any given occasion, interests coincide. That happens less and less in the modern era at the highest level, where increasingly there is a distance. The tour itinerary hardly helped on this occasion. In Ireland the players had moved around by private plane. The journalists trailing in their wake had covered the distance by car and, at jam-packed Galway especially, had to room many miles from the city. It was a hectic tour and, given their tight schedules, there was precious little time to spend with the players or conduct interviews with club management. So, typically, it was very much a wing and a prayer style of coverage.

It was photographer Tom Yeoman who suggested that a two-hour window in Galway would be sufficient to get to the race-course to interview Quinn, negotiate a gridlocked Galway to get photos of the fans in the city pubs and then get back to the football ground in time for kick-off. That was why I sweated so profusely while interviewing Quinn at the race ground.

Tom had become an accidental celebrity during the tour. While taking photographs in Dublin, the Sunderland fans had chanted at him 'one Harry Hill, there's only one Harry Hill', drawing attention to a stunning resemblance to the English comedian. In Galway, on our run through the heart of the city along William

Street, Shop Street, Quay Street and down to the Claddagh, snapping pictures of the fans, he'd had the same treatment. His personal highlight, though, had come at the Turners Cross ground, where he was lining up his shot for Keane's entrance when, from a packed stand, the chant went up: 'One Harry Hill, there's only one Harry Hill'. A Middlesbrough native, Yeoman relished both the recognition and the work and, by the end of the tour, Sunderland Football Club had at least one new fan who wasn't from Ireland. In Cork he bumped into Keane's father who was happy to pose with a drink under photographs of his son. Yeoman was thrilled with his scoop. It would have made a nice, unusual off-diary photograph for the Sunderland Echo but on reflection we decided against using it.

I have learned over the years that it's sometimes surprising what innocuous things can upset people in football. And even though Keane was used to being in the public eye, he might have felt invaded by Sunderland's paper featuring pictures of his father, especially if he'd not known they were taken. You never know about these things. And preseason is the time for bridge building.

Although our paths didn't cross very often, tales constantly came back to us of Quinn's hospitality and hard work. Accompanied on one hand by the Championship trophy and on the other by Hurley, he seemed to be on a one-man goodwill mission, ever relaxed, whether he was meeting business leaders in boardrooms or children and youths at the games.

As for Keane, he was great value with his comments. By Galway's prematch conference he had had enough of the circus, perhaps fed up by the sheer weight of interest in him, which had forced him to spend the night after the Cork game holed up in a hotel room to avoid the intrusive public fascination.

'This obsession with autographs, I don't understand it,' he said with grim force. 'I just don't. I don't see the value of a name written on a piece of paper. Why do people want them? You sign something for someone and then they put a second thing or third thing in front of you to sign. Kids come up for your autographs when you know they've got them three or four times before. I can understand kids, but you get grown men coming up to you in a bar at half past one in the morning asking you to sign a wet beer-mat! What's that about?'

It was classic Keane when he had the bit between his teeth and no one quite knew what to say. That particular media conference stuck in the mind, not for the manager's monologue but as a reminder of the debilitating effect he could have on the star-struck. Two young radio reporters interviewing him at the very end of the long session literally got lost for words.

'Roy,' said the more assertive of the two, 'I just wanted to ask you ... er ... er ... what I was going to ... er ... say was ... er ... do you ... I mean ... have you ever ... erm ... er ... sorry, I've forgotten.'

Turning to his colleague, the crimson-faced lad whispered, 'help me out here.'

His gobsmacked mate could only offer, 'Erm ... er ... Roy ... um ... I've got nothing either.'

Silence descended.

Typically, Keane said nothing. This was the model of the complete professional in his mind – be available, be responsive, but do not engage unless you feel it's necessary.

In Cork there had been a similar moment. Simon Crabtree, of the north-east's Century Radio, had gone first in the postmatch interviews. On his way out of the small room he had automatically turned the lights off. Whether it was jet lag, being half asleep or force of habit, you couldn't really tell with 'Crabbers'. He was one of the most unpredictable journalists on the circuit. For a couple of seconds there was complete confusion as the windowless room was plunged into utter darkness. When the lights came on again there were different expressions on every face, from surprise, to confusion, to amusement, but Keane's remained completely impassive, continuing to stare straight ahead. It was like something from the Simpsons, a Homer-like Zen-ness, with the Sunderland manager having changed neither position nor gaze. Not a muscle twitched. This was the sort of detachment we had come to expect of him when he was in 'media-mode'.

Minutes later that impassiveness was tested to the limit when a radio journalist asked for Keane's autograph. 'No fans in the press box' is a mantra in sports journalists' circles that you are expected to abide by, fan or not. You are there to be a professional. That was obviously a view Keane had bought into. His response to the request, a blood-freezing stare that expressed his disbelief, said enough to make clear that he thought this was out of order. Having paused long enough to convey his message, he picked up the pen and without even looking at the item in front of him, he signed it and passed it back behind him. Silently he seemed to seethe with contempt.

Two of the enduring images of the tour involved the training sessions. The first, at a sun-kissed Turners Cross, saw a relaxed Keane join in. 'If there's not enough players in the training session, I'll sometimes join in to make up the numbers,' he explained later without a trace of irony.

There was something amusing about the idea of one of the Premier League's finest ever players 'making up the numbers', as though he was the last one picked at school. Joining in with the shooting practices, agile and animated, he looked every inch a Premier League footballer, rather than a Premier League manager.

The other session was at Galway, where hundreds of school children had been invited but warned to stay behind the perimeter fence. It proved too much of a temptation when Keane and his players emerged. By the time they had reached the centre circle, one child had got on, then another, and another; in seconds it was pandemonium as the Sunderland squad was engulfed. Neither Keane nor his coaching staff were amused when the crowd eventually cleared to reveal most of the footballs had disappeared! But that 'Pied Piper' moment perfectly illustrated the sheer excitement that Keane's personal appearances could generate.

Brian Lougheed, the Irish Examiner photographer who had been injured when Keane walked onto the pitch in Turners Cross, took pains to praise the Sunderland manager. Though the clash with his fellow photographer looked comical, Lougheed had badly torn ligaments from the injury and was off work for weeks. 'I can't say anything against Keane, not after what he did for my son,' he smiled. 'My son Eoghan was struck down by meningitis a few years ago and was in a coma for ten days. At one stage he wasn't expected to live. It was in the papers and word got to Roy that Eoghan was a Manchester United fan. When Eoghan came out of hospital he was still very weak. I had been sent a get well card from Roy and a Man United shirt signed by the whole team. Eoghan was just blown away by the gesture and he never looked back. The shirt still has pride of place in the house and I'll always appreciate how much it meant to Eoghan, and how much he perked up in the days afterwards.'

The following weekend, Sunderland's Stadium of Light hosted its biggest ever preseason game – an echo of the friendly against Ajax back in 1997, which heralded the opening of the glittering new ground rising impressively above the Wear. The stadium had been built by previous chairman Bob Murray, under the brief platform of stability provided by manager Peter Reid, and was the catalyst for change at the club. The ground and the similarly state-of-the-art academy, which followed at nearby Whitburn, were the twin forces which had powered Sunderland into the twenty-first century as a genuinely modern club.

Quinn – who had been a player during Murray's reign and scored the very first goal at the new ground – could find criticisms of his predecessor, like all Sunderland fans, but was among the first to point out that the facilities he had inherited were second to none and had made his chairmanship so much easier.

To mark the stadium's first decade of existence, Juventus had been invited to the ground. The opposition could hardly have been more fitting. Keane had considered joining the Italian giants when he left Old Trafford. Instead, he fulfilled a long-held ambition by joining Celtic.

Even so, the grand old lady of Italian football would always have a special place on his CV. It was against Juventus that Keane had driven Manchester United to victory in the semi-final of the European Champions League in the 1998-99 season. It was indicative of Keane's character because the key to his performance that night was the knowledge that a booking he had picked up in the game would prevent him playing in the final, if his team could get there. It did not alter the intensity of his performance by a fraction as he dragged his teammates to victory through sheer determination and force of will. Sir Alex Ferguson described it as the greatest act of selflessness he had ever seen on a football field. He had done it against one of the great names of European football, and it was Keane's dream that, one day, fixtures like this would be happening for real for Sunderland, rather than just as friendlies.

This was something that those of us at Sunderland sometimes struggled to get our heads around. In the early stages of his time at the club he had been talking about some facet of football when he said, 'it doesn't matter whether you're talking about playing Leicester or Real Madrid, Bolton or Barcelona ...' and it suddenly struck me that the person speaking was not someone just making bland comparisons. He actually had played against all four clubs.

Intriguingly, the last preseason friendly brought together two managers who had made a trademark of rotating their team. Claudio Ranieri had earned criticism and a nickname for that approach. Keane had won plaudits for a system that had kept all his players on their toes en route to winning the Championship title – never naming the same team twice in a row since taking over, almost a year ago.

Ultimately, the battle of the Tinkermen ended even – a 1-1 draw – but Keane's team got far more out of this showpiece game than Claudio Ranieri's. Theoretically a game full of substitutions should have suited them both, but each played their strongest team up until the break and it was Sunderland who went into half-time a goal up. The lead taken was an early one. Liam Miller swept the ball over from the right-hand corner flag, the gangling Dickson Etuhu's header was parried by Juve goalkeeper Gianluigi Buffon and Irish striker Daryl Murphy scored from a couple of yards out. This was a different Sunderland team from the one seen on the Irish tour as Keane put out a team, which could have been his starting eleven, bar injured right-winger Carlos Edwards. Sunderland played with pace, precision and passing not seen since they were thrashing Luton Town on the final day of the Championship season. Five of the seven summer signings were fielded, including former Magpie striker Chopra, who was warmly welcomed by fans, although the game still took only twenty-eight seconds to register the first anti-Newcastle anthem of the season.

The game was balanced up to the break, Sunderland proving the point that, despite an unremarkable preseason, their best players might just have the ability to compete with a team of European quality. In the second half Juventus enjoyed possession but Sunderland should have doubled their lead four minutes from time when Connolly put over a cross that John sliced over the bar. That would have been neat revenge for the 2-0 defeat on Juventus' previous visit in 1957, a time when Sunderland were as big a name as their Italian counterparts. Instead Sunderland let the lead slip, defender Cristian Molinaro striking a fierce half-volley, which spiralled over Championship-winning goalkeeper Darren Ward from left of goal and into his far corner. Sunderland looked outraged and might have snatched a win but Dublin youngster Anthony Stokes' long-range shot beat the goalkeeper only to strike the post. The meaty performance was exactly what Keane was looking for from his players as he underlined the need to have no fear over what lay ahead.

'There's no need for them to be star-struck in the Premiership,' he said. 'Even when we conceded a goal in the last couple of minutes the lads showed great desire to get back in the lead. That's what you need in a football game.'

Sunderland had two injury worries ahead of the new campaign. Edwards, invaluable for his electrifying pace, still had a niggling groin strain which had troubled him all summer, while gritty, young midfielder Grant Leadbitter tore a hamstring in the prematch warm–up.

'Grant will be touch-and-go, but we expect Carlos to be fit for the Spurs game,' said Keane. But it was to be weeks before Leadbitter was to play again and Edwards setback was a precursor to what was to prove an injury-wrecked season.

Meanwhile Sunderland were continuing with efforts to bring in Spurs striker Ahmed Mido Hossam and Hearts goalkeeper Craig Gordon before the start of the new Premier League season.

Confirming, for the first time, his interest in the Tottenham forward, Keane said: 'We made a bid and we're hoping to get him. We are in negotiations right now but if the deal doesn't happen we move on and wish him well, just as we did with David Nugent and Leighton Baines.'

Keane was a little more coy about his interest in Gordon. 'I'm pleased with my two goalkeepers Marton Fulop and Darren Ward. There's speculation another goalkeeper might come in but that's the sort of challenge they have to live with. I'm learning a lot and I'm learning fast about the transfer market, and one of the things that I have learned is that these things tend to take longer than you expect.'

Keane had one message on the eve of the season. 'People mention the word 'survive' but I don't,' he said. 'We are going up there to make our mark on the Premiership.' The performance against the Italians suggested this was not a flight of fancy. Claudio Ranieri stoked up the optimism. 'I think Roy can do well next season,' he said, 'because he is a character, a strong, good personality and also his team try to play good football. I think Sunderland may be the surprise package of the Premiership.'

Keane had no idea himself how the season might pan out. 'There are question marks over me, over my staff, my players but I don't mind that. Only time will tell how things work out – that's the beauty of football – I can't tell you whether it's survival or surprising people. But I can tell you that if we beat Tottenham in the first game of the season, I won't be jumping off the stands celebrating, and if we lose, it's not the end of the world. I'm lucky that I've got the backing I have from people who just leave me to get on with it. We are behind some teams that have been building for years in the Premiership. We know that, but we are working hard to catch up. People say we are not going to win as many games as we did last year – maybe it's just me – but I don't see why we can't. Obviously there are some big, big teams out there – the Manchester Uniteds, the Liverpools, the Arsenals, the Tottenhams, the Chelseas. They are the four or five teams that you look at and think that they've got fantastic squads. But you look at the others and, well, I think, "Game on". You look at the likes of Manchester City, Everton, Bolton, Fulham, West Ham, Derby, Birmingham and so on and I like to think we'll have a go at all of them.

'I'm starting to enjoy management. We all have to raise the bar. Everyone. Maybe we were just lucky last season. Who knows? I know we won't win so many matches this season as we did last season. Things that you get away with in the Championship, you don't get away with it in the Premiership but we will have a go at all of them.'

The Premier League was happy to have the club and its characters back. 'We welcome Sunderland with open arms,' said Premier League chairman Sir Dave Richards, aware not only of the club's history of vast crowds but also its newfound charisma under Quinn and Keane. Quinn himself would go into the new season as excited as a schoolboy. He had promised the fans a magic carpet ride when he first took over the club and the success of getting Keane to the club, and the club to the Premier League, was still inspiring him. So was the knowledge of just how big a club Sunderland could potentially become.

'The magic carpet ride,' he smiled, shaking his head in an interview with me on the eve of the season. 'That is something that is going to haunt me forever if it doesn't work out! But, you know, at the same time I just know what this place is all about. I know what it is like when it is in full steam.'

41

Sunderland would go into the new campaign with a very different squad to the one that had so inspiringly driven the club from the bottom of the Championship to the top. There were few surprises in the players who were allowed to leave in the summer. Kenny Cunningham left because he was out of contract. He was thirty-six years old and he had not featured in the first team since before the turn of the year. Tommy Miller, a locally born player, had been bought by Mick McCarthy for Sunderland's last Premier League adventure, McCarthy hoped he would prove to be a regular goal-scoring midfielder, but he never came close at the highest level. Although he wasn't banished into outer darkness under Keane, he had hardly figured and was out of contract anyway. Quinn had signed five players during his brief tenure as manager and the last of them at the club, Spanish midfielder Arnau Riera, went to Scottish team Falkirk on a season-long loan. The only slight surprise lay in the sale of Irish striker Stephen Elliott, a key figure under Mick McCarthy, who had never really established himself under Keane, and he linked up again with his former manager at Wolves in a £1.3 million deal. Finally, the club's longest-serving player, injury-prone right-back Stephen Wright – the last remaining player bought by Peter Reid – was allowed to join Stoke City on loan.

Far more interest among fans however centred on the new arrivals.

Midfielder Kieran Richardson – £5.5 million, from Manchester United – a player of undoubted, but as yet unrealised, potential.

Striker Michael Chopra – £5 million, from Cardiff City – one of the Championship's most prolific scorers with a point to prove after failing to nail down a place at Newcastle.

Centre half Paul McShane – £1.5 million, from West Bromwich Albion – a tenacious centre half whose strawberry-blonde mop of hair went flying every time he flung himself into a challenge.

Central midfielder Dickson Etuhu – £1.5 million, from Norwich City – tall and lanky; gifted at breaking up play, compared in style to Patrick Vieira. The Nigerian's challenge was to ensure his distribution matched his tackling ability.

Centre half Russell Anderson – £1 million, from Aberdeen – a one-club man and the Scottish Premier League team's captain, Anderson had generously donated part of his signing-on fee to youth development at the Scottish club.

Defender Greg Halford – £2.5 million, from Reading – at six foot, five inches, a giant of a right back and a young defender whose attacking abilities had caught everyone's eyes in the Championship with Colchester United.

Striker Roy O'Donovan – £500,000, from Cork – a genuine and bubbly character blessed with pace in attack, but raw to English Premier League football.

By Sunderland's standards, these signings marked spending unheard of in the club's history but even that outlay was put into perspective in the week before the season when Keane finally landed his key target. Gordon arrived in a deal worth an eyebrow-raising £9 million. It made him the most expensive goalkeeper in Britain and the third most expensive goalkeeper in history, behind two players, ironically with Juventus connections: Gianluigi Buffon, the £32 million goalkeeper, who had been beaten by Daryl Murphy days earlier, and his predecessor Antonio Peruzzi, who left Juve for Internazionale for £10.5 million.

'Fail to prepare; prepare to fail' had been a saying by which Keane had lived so much of his professional playing life and he had slogged for hours over the summer to make sure Sunderland had the players they wanted. The signing of Richardson, a Manchester United squad player, had been a protracted one. Keane had flown out to meet him with England U21s in the European Championships to talk him into the move and had succeeded when others were circling. Some negotiations were surprisingly quick. Etuhu's deal was agreed in a trice. Keane met Nugent and his agent at Keane's house in Cheshire on the back of one of the coaching courses. He met McShane in the south of England, Gordon in the north-east.

Wigan left-back Leighton Baines arrived in Sunderland when the players had gone for warm-weather training in Portugal over the summer. Baines had eventually chosen hometown club Everton over Sunderland but unlike the last time the club had been promoted, the Black Cats didn't lose out to a single player that summer through being beaten over a transfer fee. Baines went to Goodison Park for less than he would have been on at the Stadium of Light.

Despite the huge amount of money spent – something Sunderland supporters had been pleading for for decades – not all of them were persuaded by the stature of the signings. None of the buys had previously excelled at the highest level and there was little in the way of old heads to help them adjust. When Peter Reid had successfully steered Sunderland back into the top tier at the turn of the century, and kept it there in its first season back, key characters were the veterans Stefan Schwarz and Steve Bould. But it was a route that Sunderland had not taken. 'The road Roy has gone down is getting in young, athletic players who are hungry for success. Players always ready to give and receive the ball and players who have a point to prove,' explained Quinn.

Fans continued to be wary. Fears were raised that Sunderland might have overpaid for the players they had brought in. If you had told supporters back in May after Luton were beaten 5–0 that Sunderland would spend thirty five million pounds on players by the eve of the new season, most fans would have hoped for proven Premier League performers, the likes of Alan Smith, Joey Barton and Mark Viduka – all players who had joined their bitter rivals Newcastle United over the summer. Regardless of the impressive amount of money spent, there was a view that Sunderland had actually spent a fortune on bringing in an unproven striker from the eircom League of Ireland, four Championship players, two Scots who had never played in the Premier League before and a Manchester United player who had not fully established himself as a regular in the Red Devils' first team. There was also the long-running question mark over the manager's concentration on Manchester United/Celtic/Irish recruits but Keane shrugged off the dissenting voices over both price and sourcing.

'Gary Pallister cost Manchester United two million pounds many moons ago, and people were outraged, but he turned out to be a bargain,' he pointed out. 'Hopefully the players I've bought will turn out to be bargains. I'm happy with the price I've paid for the players I've got. I think I've paid a fair price. I'm not buying players to get a few extra fans, it's not about trying to bring in players from Ireland to gain extra support there. I didn't sign Dwight Yorke to get extra Trinidad fans!'

Sunderland fans could be forgiven their anxieties. No fans in the history of the game had had to endure the privations they had suffered in recent years, the record-breaking relegations that left wounds still raw, despite the promotions that followed. They were proud supporters, and hopeful, but they would taking nothing for granted. History had taught them that lesson too many times. Fans had fingers crossed, even though there were doubts aplenty on the eve of the campaign.

But, as Keane reminded them, the best chance of success lay in everyone at the club sticking together, in staying united. They might have misgivings but they would have to trust him.

CHAPTER TWO

Boom and Bust

*My thoughts on the Premiership are 'bring it on' – I'd rather be facing
Tottenham Hotspur first game of the season than a Championship side.*
ROY KEANE

THE Stadium of Light press box sits directly behind the
opposition dugout in the main west stand of the ground. It's
seven rows away from ground level. By Premier League
standards it would be a contender for European qualification.
Nowhere near as good as, say, Arsenal's or Manchester City's,
but better by far than Middlesbrough's, which hangs in the gods,
and preferable to that of Chelsea's or Tottenham Hotspurs', both
of which are set pretty much at ground level – Spurs' White Hart
Lane is so low that all you see is a forest of legs when you're
reporting.

When the Stadium of Light first opened, the Sunderland Echo,
as the local paper, was offered the privilege of being the only
news organisation to select its own seat. I chose the one
nearest to the tunnel. It was the perfect vantage point for a
reporter if fighting broke out or there were exchanges as players
and managers were going in. The decision paid off in the very
first few weeks when there was a ruck going into the tunnel, but
it was not a satisfaction that would last. The club took action
and in the very next home game there was an extendable
covering, which was pulled out on wheels to cover the entire
tunnel area from prying reporters' eyes forever. Its sponsors?
The Sunderland Echo.

On the opening day of the 2007-08 season I was in my usual
place, but with my back to the tunnel covering, looking over a
press box packed with sports journalists enjoying the buzz of a
fresh season and an intriguing opening day fixture. Most
familiar to the fans would be the faces of Sunderland
goal-scoring legend Gary Rowell, sitting alongside Century
Radio's Simon Crabtree as expert summariser, and long-serving
former Sunderland captain Gary Bennett doing the same job
with Radio Newcastle's Nick Barnes – enthusiasts as much as
they were experts.

Over in the far distance I caught sight of our photographer Tom

Yeoman cutting, to my mind, a slightly dejected figure near a corner flag: no 'One Harry Hill' chants emanating from the terraces this time. In reality, though, he was buzzing as much as anyone in the 43,000 plus crowd, excited by a fixture and an occasion to whet the appetite. The return of Keane's Sunderland to the top tier was big news and everyone in the ground knew it.

A club and a manager set to freshen up the Premier League one way or another – no one quite knew which way yet – while their opponents, ambitious Tottenham Hotspur, were determined to end the campaign in a Champions League place, having finished fifth in the two previous seasons. To capitalise on the interest, Sky television gave Sunderland the honour of being the first game of the season, the match kicking off at 12:45 p.m. And, as the stadium filled and noise levels rose, the air grew heavy with anticipation.

Each season for a sports reporter, just as it is for a footballer, is a marathon slog from August to May but every season tends to start exactly the same for reporters, footballers and fans alike – with an infectious excitement for the brand new season and the unknowns that lie ahead. It's a fresh, unwritten page in history and the blank canvas stretching ahead can't help but captivate. That was never more true for me than standing in that press box on 11 August, with bright sunlight beaming down on a Stadium of Light that looked fresh and newly scrubbed – a kaleidoscope of colour and sound to quicken the pulse and gladden the heart. Sunderland had won promotions before and welcomed bright new dawns with wearisome regularity but never had they invested so heavily and confidently and never with a manager so high-profile and so certain that this was the stage on which he belonged. As the last minutes of preseason ebbed away you could sense the raw excitement and passion on the terraces – a Premier League stadium, a Premier League fixture and a Premier League crowd. This was what the 2006-07 season's momentous campaign had all been bending towards.

Now all they had to do was not cock it up.

A few seconds later, that enormous, spine-tingling roar began to swell to a crescendo. Goosebumps formed. A fraction, a split-second of silence as the whistle went. And we were off.

There probably wasn't a home fan in the house who wouldn't have taken a draw before kick–off.

Spurs' strikers Dimitar Berbatov, Jermaine Defoe, Darren Bent and Robbie Keane could put virtually any team to the sword on their day, let alone boys fresh up from the Championship. But, as is the way of football, especially on opening days, the game produced the remarkable. Sunderland won. They did it with the sexiest way to win a game – the last minute goal. And not scored by just anyone. Step forward Michael Chopra, the arch-Magpie, instantly laying the ghosts of his footballing past. Chopra had gloried in his Tyneside roots when he scored two goals in Newcastle's 4-1 humiliation of Sunderland at the Stadium of Light in the 15-point season. He had revelled in scoring against the Wearsiders for Cardiff City the following season, and fans have long memories. A number of Sunderland diehards had felt there were only two things wrong with the Geordie when he was first signed. Overpriced and over here. Former transgressions were forgiven the moment Chopra sealed the perfect day for him, and for them, with a winner three minutes into injury time. Having misfired for most of preseason, he was in the right place at the right time to score the very first goal of England's new Premier League campaign.

The game was watched by the country's biggest league crowd of the day. And they were there not only to witness Premier League football return to this part of the north-east, but also to see Keane's return to the top tier. The manager was studiously indifferent to the crush of cameramen who covered every inch of his three-yard walk from tunnel to dugout, having made up his mind to keep his emotions in check throughout. He succeeded too, apart from the moment when Paul Robinson's net was rippled by Chopra's shot, and raw emotion briefly got the better of him.

'It's hard to stay quiet in games,' he said later, 'but I decided at the start of the season I would make a conscious effort not to be ranting and raving on the sidelines. It's important I keep my focus. I don't find it difficult to be detached when I have to. I'm not trying to be someone I'm not.'

Keane included four of the new faces in his opening line-up: British record goalkeeping signing Gordon; centre-half McShane, who was to be voted man of the match; Etuhu and Richardson in midfield.

Spurs boss Martin Jol was one of the few managers to have spent more than Keane over the summer – £40 million. The only new recruit to start was £8 million centre-half Younes Kaboul.

It was a game of very few chances. Jermaine Jenas, booed throughout for his Newcastle links, produced the first shot but failed to find the target. Sunderland's first shot of the season did not arrive until the twentieth minute when Stokes was even more wayward, closer to corner flag than goalpost. But what the opening thirty minutes successfully showed was Sunderland's ability to contain Spurs' much-vaunted attack. Skilful Steed Malbranque proved a handful for dogged Whitehead as stand-in right-back; but the Black Cats' captain held firm while central defenders McShane and Nosworthy showed no respect as they shackled Dimitar Berbatov and Robbie Keane. Berbatov was to give Gordon his only scare of the match when he steered the ball around the keeper, who had raced to the edge of his box, but as he shaped to score Whitehead was there with a wonderfully-timed challenge to dispossess. Martin Jol tried to get the script back on track by bringing on Darren Bent just before the hour, taking the option of playing with three strikers.

Keane made more telling substitutions. Collins' introduction at left back, allowed the lively Ross Wallace to get further upfield and, crucially, Chopra was brought on to give the team more of a cutting edge.

'I just thought, looking at Michael on the bench, that he just couldn't wait to get on,' explained the manager.

Sunderland finished the game strongly and had a great chance to win it in the 88th minute when a Wallace free-kick bounced off the thigh of Etuhu on the edge of the Spurs' six-yard box. Paul Robinson had to fling himself full length to save the misdirected effort.

Spurs' only real chance in the closing stages landed at the feet of Darren Bent. The striker had wrecked Sunderland's last start to the Premier League, scoring two goals for Charlton Athletic in a 3-1 opening day defeat from which Mick McCarthy's men never recovered. This time, though, it was the last player who had scored two goals against Sunderland who was to have the final word.

Wallace did wonderfully well on the right before chipping over a cross, which landed at Chopra's feet near the penalty spot and it was the work of an instant for the twenty-three-year-old to stab the ball into the bottom left–hand corner of the helpless Paul Robinson's goal. The fox-in-the-box Keane had wanted had announced his arrival in the very last minute of the game. The striker's joy was uncontainable as he wheeled away to join with the Sunderland fans he had been so worried about winning over. In that moment any lingering negativity towards him evaporated. Chopra's face was a mask of unadulterated delight, as were those of the thousands of fans who saluted him – as was Keane's, if only for an instant. That memorable picture of the striker celebrating – arms outstretched, eyes bulging, shock and joy written all over his face and captured by so many photographers – was the abiding image of the game, cementing his acceptance on Wearside. Quinn was later to look back on the entire season and select that moment as his personal highlight. Those who interviewed Chopra afterwards in the tunnel were surprised to find just how deeply affected the young forward had been. There were genuine tears in his eyes as he spoke of his joy and relief at getting off the mark and successfully leaping the Tyne-Wear divide. As far as the fans were concerned now, Chopra was a Mackem.

It is hard to describe to those from outside the region how deeply the divisions sometimes run between Sunderland and Newcastle fans, and quite how big a divide the young striker had just bridged, although Keane was understandably dismissive of that afterwards. 'I don't care whether he's from Newcastle or New Zealand, all I'm interested in is how good he is at putting the ball in the back of the net.'

Only ninety minutes into the season and Sunderland were already up and running and Chopra's Geordie past, which had been a quiet concern for the player, was instantly forgotten.

A good start. A great start.

The last time Sunderland had been in the top tier it had taken them seven games to get to this stage. That 'monkey' – getting a first Premier League win – was off the club's back already. Sunderland fans, if they were quick enough – and many were – could call up and capture a table which showed them top of the Premier league for the first time in their history – even if it was only a matter of minutes before other games kicked off!

Watching the celebrations at the final whistle, you knew that Sunderland might have better wins than this one, this season, but they would struggle to notch a win of greater significance. Though managers are fond of saying that one game, no matter how good or bad, is still just one game, some matches can set the tone. For newly-promoted teams that first win, when it comes, can be critical to fragile self-belief. Keane had spent the summer trying to instil that in his players. Ultimately, though, they had to go out and do it themselves, and on that first weekend, against highly-fancied Spurs, they did just that.

'I got the impression that last time we were in this division they were taking their cameras to the grounds they went to,' Keane told reporters. 'But this is a different club from the one it was two years ago,' he said. 'Different chairman, different manager, different players.'

Victory was intoxicating and Keane wanted his players to develop an unswerving belief that this was where they belonged, and not just where they'd managed to get lucky against the Londoners. For Quinn, who had leapt from his seat with his arms in the air when Chopra scored (unlike Keane, he had made no pact with prudence), this was the sort of day he'd dreamed of when first taking over the club, barely a year previously. This, Quinn hoped, would only be the start for his manager.

'Roy Keane's presence could be the factor that allows this club to go to the next level,' Quinn enthused. 'He's turned this club inside out. We have a lot of good things here but when you add Roy's name into the mix, there's no denying it's a big help and the great thing is the fans have responded to that.

'I was down at the Premier League Chairman's conference earlier this summer, and one night people were talking about season tickets and several fellow chairman all but dropped their tea cups when I told them how many season tickets we already had. But that's great because it was a nice feeling for me, for them to realise how big this club is. They have probably forgotten about that on the back of the abysmal two seasons we've had last time we were up. It's good to change that.'

The Spurs result was a belated birthday present for a manager who had only turned thirty-six the previous day. But he revealed, as he breathed in the Saturday morning air before a ball had even been kicked, that he felt elated rather than intimidated. He looked utterly relaxed, before and after the game. But I suppose that was because the Premier League was where he naturally belonged. It had been the Championship that had been alien to him.

'The Premiership's the place, let me tell you', he said afterwards. 'I felt excited in the morning, excited about what lies ahead, and I spoke to the players about it when I got to the stadium. Tottenham at home on a beautiful day with the punters gathering. Driving up, seeing the fans. It's a great life. Now we want to be part of what we hope will be a great future with Sunderland. I thought when I got up, this is what it's all about – a lovely sunny day and Spurs in the Premiership.'

There wasn't a tear in his eye and he didn't quite mention 'jumpers for goalposts' but the inescapable conclusion was that here was a man happy with his lot, in love with his football and excited about the potential of his players and his club. Asked how he would celebrate the club's fantastic opening day result, he pondered for a few moments and then said: 'I'll have a cup of green tea and then, I think, one of those Time Out chocolate biscuits.'

Amid the laughter there were those who took his deadpan reaction to mean he was unmoved by the result, but they were unfamiliar with his style. He was to give reporters plenty of great headlines before the season was out but he wouldn't have himself portrayed as out on the razzle after one win.

'No, I'm excited by the result and it takes a lot to get me excited. Ask the wife.'

More laughter.

'But I said before the season started that if we beat Spurs I wouldn't dance for joy and if we lost I wouldn't despair. There's a long, long way to go. I was delighted with the players' desire to win the game – even at the end when they could have settled for a draw. It's an ambition that might cost us in games but on this occasion it got us all three points. We got a great late goal and some people might say it is down to luck, but it is not luck – we had plenty of late goals last season too. People think it was all wins last season, but it wasn't. We had plenty of setbacks and bad results along the way but the players and the fans always reacted in the right way. The most important thing about the Spurs game was to get off to a decent start and we've done that.'

As good days at the office go, it didn't get much better for Keane but the avuncular Martin Jol bore the strained look of a kindly father whose wayward son had just disappointed him. It's hard not to like the unassuming Dutchman who, in the run-up to the game, couldn't resist salivating at the prospect of what damage his formidable front foursome might do. 'With the addition of Bent we've now got every strike option covered – pace, power, all-round ability and natural goalscoring talent.'

He was typically honest after the game, and what hurt most was that his team hadn't shown the same desire and application as their opponents. 'When I looked at the two team sheets, I felt there was no reason why we should not win, but we didn't show any urgency. Sunderland worked hard and have a few very good players, especially at the back – the centre backs McShane and Nosworthy were very good – but we should remember it's a long, tough season and the time to judge things is at the end of it.'

Those were to be prophetic words for Sunderland, and also for the Dutchman. When the two teams met later in the season, Martin Jol's name would no longer be on the manager's door.

Three games were crammed into the first week of the season. And after Spurs, thoughts ran to what Sunderland might achieve away at Birmingham City's St Andrews ground and Wigan Athletic's JJB Stadium – for the Wearsiders were in a position to build the momentum that might see relegation fears close to being banished in the first seven days of the campaign!

Keane, meanwhile, unintentionally pushed such speculation into the background by coming out with powerful views, clinically expressed, that no one had either anticipated or expected, and which made waves way beyond Wearside: the Curious Case of the WAGS.

The Sunderland manager holds a press conference usually once a week – more if there is a midweek match – and almost always the venue is the press room at the Academy of Light training ground. Over the course of just over an hour the manager does the local evening papers first, along with the club website in a side room. Then he usually does television in an adjacent studio, followed by nationals and morning newspapers in a lecture theatre; finally, the Sunday papers. He seems more relaxed in some interviews than others, but his mind is always on the move. Perhaps, because of that, his lecture room interviews often seem to have an air of theatricality about them. Keane thinks about everything he says before he says it, but he is never more eloquent than when he is on his hobby horse over some issue that rankles. Then the words flow like water.

He had found it hard going in the transfer market over the summer. At times, very hard, having put in a huge amount of hours, so concerned was he to get things right for this all-important season. Some of that workload was down to inexperience.

'I've learned a lot and one of the things I won't be doing is making twenty or thirty phone calls a day in the first few weeks of the close season. I'll be going away for a few weeks because no one's interested in doing business at that stage.'

More frustrating than the demands on his time had been the task of persuading players to move to the north-east when they seemed to think that was an issue in itself.

'People seem to think the north-east is in the middle of nowhere,' he had said in June. 'I wasn't sure initially whether I wanted to come here myself, but it's not Australia you know!'

His annoyance knew no limits when it emerged that, for some players, keeping their partners in close proximity to designer shops counted higher than their own career prospects. Just as he had railed at autograph hunters in Ireland, Keane turned his fire on the priorities of some modern-day footballers.

'Some players are being dictated to by their wives and girlfriends,' he told reporters. 'If a player wants to come here because we are a top club, fantastic, and we will do our very best for their families. But we had a player this summer who didn't even ring us back because his wife wanted to move to London. Shopping was mentioned. It might astonish many people but it is true. There are players going to London, simply because it is London. To me that is wrong. It's a lifestyle move, not a football move and these are the type of people you don't want at your club. That player is weak because his wife runs his life. I could name three or four big players now and clearly their wives and girlfriends are running their lives because they are doing photo-shoots and all that. They say they are not comfortable doing it – well, don't do it. Obviously it is their partners doing it, and they are being dragged along. These so–called big stars are people we are supposed to look up to. Well, they are weak. They are soft. If people want to go somewhere else, fair enough, as long as it is a football reason.

'A couple of years ago I nearly went to Juventus. People spoke to me about Turin and said it is this and that and that "oh Milan would be nicer' but I replied, "I'm not going there for the bloody shops, I am going because it is Juventus". If there is nothing to do, find something, because people who are bored are boring. You don't need to live in London or Manchester to be happy. If someone doesn't want to go to Sunderland because their wife wants to go shopping in London, it is a sad state of affairs. This side of it, with women running the show, worries me. Maybe it shouldn't, because the players are soft.'

It was a devastating critique and it set in motion a debate that lasted for days, locally and nationally, and I'm sure Roy himself was surprised by the reaction his comments generated. There was no doubt that he stood by every word he said. But privately he was perturbed by the way it was conveyed in some national newspapers – the words 'blast', 'rant' and 'raged' headlined over his words, when he had actually delivered his observations in very measured tones.

It was something he accepted on this occasion, but he would act the next time his reasoned words, earnestly expressed, were relayed as some sort of mad-eyed rant.

Everyone had an opinion on Keane's opinion and most saw it as a healthy reality check for the culture of celebrity and wealth infecting football. A few completely misunderstood what he was trying to say. The Sunday Mirror's Geordie columnist Carole Malone branded him a 'neanderthal', which completely missed the point that his criticism was about undriven, unambitious footballers, rather than their wives. The debate rumbled into the weekend but Keane, having made his point, moved on, with Sunderland's next game dominating his thoughts. Birmingham had been swept aside the last time the two teams had met, and Wigan were no Spurs, which left fans openly wondering could nine points be taken out of nine in the very first week? The only thing certain was that Sunderland would look to shuffle their pack to meet with the demands of so many games in a short space of time.

One to benefit was bright-eyed Roy O'Donovan who had made Keane's extended squad of nineteen for the Spurs game and, although he didn't make the final cut, he had already impressed. The day before the game O'Donovan and Keane celebrated their shared birthdays together, O'Donovan having completed his medical and signed a three–year deal.

'We were both presented with cakes on Friday night at the team hotel,' said the striker. 'It was a bit embarrassing for me really. I did not expect anything like that, to be honest, but it shows the friendship and special bond that is at this club. It's been a whirlwind few days but I'm glad it all went smoothly and I was able to leave Cork City on good terms.'

Having watched the Spurs game from the stands alongside

out-of-favour veteran midfielder Graham Kavanagh, O'Donovan was still on a high. 'The fans here love their football and to see so many grown men almost cry when Chopra scored the winning goal was special. It's like Cork. I want to be a part of days like that.'

O'Donovan did make it into the Sunderland team, coming on as a 71st minute sub against Birmingham. But Keane's selection never reached the heights of their last visit, when Edwards had tormented Steve Bruce's team on their way to edging the Midlanders out of the title. The words 'Carlos' and 'torment' were to be mentioned in this game too, although in a very different context. The pacy winger pulled up with a hamstring tear at the end of the game, an injury that was to seriously hamper Sunderland's cause for months to come.

Sunderland were relieved to get a draw after twice falling behind – first to a McShane own goal, then a Garry O'Connor strike – as the two clubs automatically promoted from the Championship fought out a scrappy game. Chopra netted the Black Cats' first leveller with a spectacular strike, although defeat beckoned until former Blues striker John's late point-saver. For once, Sunderland fans had not travelled in great numbers but, given the ticket cost for a midweek game, you could understand why. 'Thirty-five quid, you're having a laugh,' they sang. But they weren't laughing in the 28th minute when Seb Larsson planted a free-kick in the Black Cats' box and full-back Stephen Kelly's downward header was inadvertently helped across his own line by McShane's chest.

Chopra fired Sunderland level with a devastating finish in the 75th minute – a fabulous volley after turning Liam Ridgewell – a goal, which was to feature on Match of the Day's Goal of the Month competition. But the home team regained the lead six minutes later. Substitute O'Connor kept his cool inside the box to beat fellow Scotland international Gordon.

Keane's team responded. Edwards held off markers to set up John. His header came back off the bar. But the striker, making his 250th league appearance and his first in the Premier League for Sunderland, was not to be denied. In the 90th minute Wallace's deflected free-kick was palmed out by Blues' goalkeeper Colin Doyle to Nosworthy who headed the rebound across goal for John to nod home. O'Donovan made his contribution. He was virtually sitting on Colin Doyle when the ball went in. That did not distract from the fact that, for the second time in two games, Sunderland's late persistence had paid off.

Steve Bruce, who noted O'Donovan's obstruction but accepted Sunderland should earlier have had a penalty for a foul on David Connolly, moaned, 'Stern John. It had to be Stern John. He was a great hero at Birmingham and one of my all-time favourites that I've managed at this club. He got us promoted five or six years ago. So when I saw him warming up, I feared he might have an impact.'

Sunderland were satisfied with the point but there was the disappointment of finishing the game with ten men. Edwards had torn his hamstring after setting up the cross that led to the goal and Keane instantly took responsibility.

'He's missed a lot of preseason and it was touch and go whether to use him. I got that call wrong. I've got to use the squad of players – especially with three games in a week – but clearly I got it wrong with leaving Carlos on too long. When you're tired, that's when your hamstrings can go.'

Edwards had been voted by fans in the Sunderland Echo's annual survey as Keane's best buy in his first season in management. He was one of only two Sunderland players – captain Whitehead was the other – to make the Professional Footballer's Association's Championship XI. A natural right-winger, he had tremendous speed, good crossing ability and, vitally, goals. His manager had been relishing the prospect of unleashing him on the Premier League. In his absence, Keane had no natural right-winger and so problematic was it finding someone to fill the role that the players, privately, were to dub it the 'graveyard shift'. It removed from the midfield a natural balance, which the team would struggle to overcome.

At least Keane could be happy with his goalscorers. 'Chopra is an important player for us and we hope he will have a big influence at our club. He's had two chances and scored two goals and if he keeps that up then we'll all be happy. As for Stern, I knew at half-time he would score. There are pictures of him in the corridors at St Andrews scoring for Birmingham City and I knew he would get us a goal if I brought him on.'

To bring a player on, for that reason alone, might seem a quirky judgement call but it was the sort of gut instinct that Keane was to go with time and time again over the season – just as he had done with O'Donovan's signing. The manager had been setting up a scouting network for Ireland when he was in Dublin in preseaso. It was only as he left for Cork, he admitted, that he'd decided to pursue the young striker's signature. Often these spur-of-the-moment decisions would work in his favour. Occasionally, they would not.

The away draw represented a solid start for Sunderland – four points from six – and the next game, a visit to Wigan, offered another opportunity. The Latics were still a club whose name looked slightly out of place in the Premier League. If Sunderland could get a first away-win on the board, seven points in the first week would have everyone sitting up and taking notice.

Alas, the game proved a disaster for them – a 3-0 scoreline fully reflecting the difference between the two teams on the day. Sunderland supporters had travelled in vast numbers and had no inkling such a poor performance loomed.

All but three of the fourteen involved in the Wigan capitulation were Keane's signings. That, however, would not colour his judgement when it came to who might pay the price for a sub-standard display. He had shown his ruthless side in the past, and he would not hesitate to do the same again. He said afterwards he would avoid knee-jerk reactions, but in the week that followed he would offer left back Collins as a makeweight in a move for Stoke's captain and experienced centre half Danny Higginbotham. Collins was not the only one to come under the manager's scrutiny.

The left back had given away a penalty, as had substitute Anderson, and it was absolutely no consolation to Sunderland that the opening goal from Emile Heskey was clearly offside. Too many players had off days. Stokes, though out of position at right wing, offered nothing. The gifted Richardson had yet to convince. Yorke and Etuhu could not stamp their authority on midfield and right back Halford accepted he had plenty to do to justify the three million pounds Sunderland invested in him in the summer.

The bad defeat deflated the fans. Sunderland had taken what was to be their biggest away support of the season to the JJB, almost 5,000 of them taking advantage of Wigan's generous away allocation. Though they were disappointed, there was the knowledge that the club was still in the top half of the table after the first three games. Typical Sunderland, you might say – a week of the season gone and every emotion encountered.

Keane's emotion after Wigan was anger. Some of his players, he now worried, were simply not good enough. 'There's a thin line between loyalty and stupidity and no doubt I have been stupid,' he said. 'It won't happen again.'

In the wake of the defeat Sunderland pursued Higginbotham, who, at twenty-eight, was an experienced player. With more than 100 Premier League appearances, only Yorke in Sunderland's squad offered more nous. Negotiations were continuing to bring in experienced players, veterans Andy Cole and Ian Harte being lined up as Keane surmised that he needed some older and wiser heads in the dressing room.

Sunderland fans and their manager had got used to winning in the Championship. But as August drew to a close, the fourth game of the season was to bring a Premier League reality check when the Black Cats encountered a 'top-four' club for the first time.

The gulf between the Premier League's powerhouse elite and those who bob in their wake was neatly brought home to Sunderland fans by classy Liverpool. It was the Black Cats' first loss at home in 2007 – an achievement which, for a club so used to failure in previous seasons, deserved special mention in itself. But, virtually from kick-off, it was clear the Championship title-holders were going to struggle.

Title-challenging teams, like Liverpool, boast two world-class players for every position and that squad depth made all the difference. Keane had Whitehead and Edwards missing. Shorn of two of his most effective players, the manager pinned his hopes in the prematch build-up on the fighting chance any underdog has in a scrap. But from the very first minute of the game, when Halford's scuffed backpass nearly let in Ukrainian striker Andriy Voronin, there was no doubt it was going to be a long day for the home team. Liverpool were without Steven Gerrard and Peter Crouch but, unlike Sunderland, the absence of two important players did not hamper them. The Sunderland manager had fumed over the woeful performance at Wigan but he made only one change – Miller coming in for Stokes; though within twenty minutes Stokes was on the pitch when Richardson's back gave up on him.

From beginning to end Liverpool looked like they had gears to change up to if needed. Stokes paid for missing a decent chance just before the half-hour when Liverpool took the lead seven minutes later. Voronin was given far too much space and he teed up Momo Sissoko – Gerrard's stand-in – who struck a fierce low shot home for his first ever goal for Liverpool. Fernando Torres showed his blistering pace when he timed his touch perfectly to sprint straight through the shocked Nosworthy and McShane before being denied by yet another Gordon save. But the game was put beyond Sunderland's reach in the 88th minute when Torres swept the ball out to Voronin on the left and he stepped inside Halford to drive a low shot home.

Despite defeat, Sunderland were not demoralised. For a weakened team to fight so gamely, without Edwards and Whitehead and robbed of Richardson, against such superior forces was heartening to see. Those efforts, if repeated at Old Trafford the following week, could be expected to produce a similar result: respectable defeat. For against the powerhouse sides of the division, it was probably the best Sunderland could hope for.

'When you're up against such big, strong squads you've got to take your medicine sometimes and that's what we had to do,' said Keane.

Sunderland's resources were further depleted when it emerged they were facing the long-term loss of Richardson to a back injury he had been playing through since the fag end of his Manchester United days. Extensive scans were to show that, far from being a strain, the England midfielder had been playing with a broken back! He had been getting through games with a stress facture in his spine, something that explained the agony the midfielder had been in during the summer's England U21 championships. It would rule the young star out of a sentimental return to Manchester United in the next league game and sideline him for months to come.

Before the eagerly-awaited visit to Old Trafford, there was the small matter of the League Cup and, although Keane was not taking the opposition lightly, he fancied a cup run. Liverpool were one thing, Luton Town quite another. Cole, whose Premier League goals record was second only to Alan Shearer, was a boost for the club when his arrival was finalised. Though he would not feature against Luton he would be available to play later in the competition if a successful run could be conjured. Luton were seen as a stepping stone to that success, but it proved a stepping stone lying in treacherous waters.

History, we are told, repeats itself, occurring first as tragedy then as comedy. But there was nothing funny for Sunderland fans in the way their team exited the League Cup at the first hurdle again. True, there was an air of comicality about the manner in which the kamikaze Sunderland 'wall' parted like a red and white sea for Luton's opening goal; not to mention the madness that saw the Hatters' second and third so casually dispatched by such an old warhorse – a thirty-eight-year-old glorying in the name of Furlong cantering through the last lap of his career. But hundreds of long-suffering Sunderland supporters who made the long journey south returned home in the early hours of the morning feeling their team had kicked them in the teeth, just like the old days.

A year previously in the same competition, newly-relegated Sunderland had been beaten by Bury – a team lying 92nd out of 92 clubs in the Football League. It was the lowest point of Quinn's brief managerial career. As he gave his post-match press conference on the Gigg Lane turf, he was as despairing as the fans who had slunk so miserably back across the Pennines to the north-east. Quinn had promised a bright new dawn when he took over but I had never seen him so despondent as he was that evening. That was the night he promised 'a world-class manager' would be brought in.

So distraught was he that evening that some of us wondered where he was just talking off the top of his head – speaking in hope rather than with a definite plan. In the wake of his announcement, Wearside was rife with rumour on who this new man might be. The resting Martin O'Neill had turned the job down originally after agonising over his decision for an age. Sam Allardyce had been on the verge of joining before getting cold feet, leaving Quinn to take the club into the season as chairman and manager.

But who would Quinn's replacement be on the touchline? British or foreign? With a club at the moment or not? In the event, the man who was to be appointed was someone whose name hadn't even been thrown into the ring in all the media speculation.

We were days away from the arrival of the inexperienced, untried Keane. And he was to do wonderfully well.

Pretty much everything Keane touched turned to gold in his

twelve months in charge, but he brought up the anniversary with his third defeat in a row. Arguably the worst of his time in charge. He could hardly be blamed for the Luton performance for he had resisted the temptation to field a young and inexperienced team. Substitutes in the Liverpool match, Leadbitter and Stokes started this one, while Anderson made his full debut replacing McShane in central defence and Ward – goalkeeping hero of the Championship campaign – took the gloves from Gordon for the first time in the season.

Unfortunately Sunderland simply didn't produce. 'My keeper had to make only one save all night,' Luton boss Kevin Blackwell pointed out. 'And even that wasn't too difficult for him.'

'Premiership? You're having a laugh,' taunted the Luton fans. It was a stark contrast to the previous meeting between the teams, that 5-0 Sunderland win just a matter of months ago – the prelude to their rise into the Premier League and Luton's drop into League One.

The low point of the game came with the sending off of Halford. He looked woefully short of confidence and could be seen throughout, head bobbing uncertainly beneath the floodlights like a beaten Rocky waiting for the knockout blow. That came just before the hour mark when, ten minutes after being yellow-carded for a shirt pull, he was red-carded for a hand-ball.

The embarrassing loss meant Sunderland had produced two dreadful performances in three games, which prompted the question: what could be read into this defeat? One view was that, precisely one year on, Sunderland now faced an identical crisis in a different division. The mirror images were spooky – three defeats on the spin, no goals scored; out of the cup at the first attempt after being humbled, once more, by opposition two leagues below them. Were alarm bells ringing? The other viewpoint was that despite Sunderland's indifferent start, they were, after all, back in the Premier League now, had four more points than at the same stage last time around and had invested the sort of ambitious funds that would ultimately establish them in the top tier. Nobody really knew at this stage, but what was worrying was the feeling that the composure of former on-loan signings Jonathan 'Jonny' Evans and Danny Simpson in the heart of Sunderland's defence – such a factor in the club's promotion – had yet to be adequately replaced since their return to Old Trafford. Nor could there be great confidence in a team that had now failed to score in 270 minutes of football.

Understandably it was a grim-faced Keane who 'celebrated' his first year in charge of Sunderland, squeezing into the cramped press room afterwards. It had been a remarkable twelve months at the helm. In the club's history only previous manager Denis Smith had won more games than Keane in his first year in charge; but Smith's task had been milder, guiding the club out of the old Third Division in the 1980s, a league it had slipped into for the first and only time in its history. Keane also joined a select bunch of managers who had led the club to promotion in his first season – Denis Smith, Ken Knighton and Peter Reid. None of that counted for anything at Kenilworth Road as Keane contemplated the Luton defeat and Sunderland's poorest ever result against a team two divisions below them. He was the first to admit it was not good enough. 'I'm as disappointed as I've been since I've taken the job,' he said.

In the wake of the setback at Wigan, Keane had lambasted his players but, while he was possibly even more downcast than at Luton, he knew he simply could not tear into his players with every defeat – no matter how abject the display. Closing ranks was the name of the game.

'This is a massive challenge for me, but I knew that even when we won promotion on this ground five months ago. I wasn't thinking that we'd made it then and I'm not thinking it's the end of the world now,' he said. 'Sunderland Football Club have had their disappointments over the years and I've got to change that. But I will say that results like these make me even more determined to succeed. Overall, what I saw out there just reinforced a few things I was already aware of. You don't get anywhere in games if you don't get the basics right, and it was the basics that let us down all over the pitch. We need more physical presence, and we definitely need a number of players in, but we are hopeful of getting them.'

The Luton defeat was bad enough. Then the manager stunned everyone by revealing the extent of the injury to Whitehead. He had suffered a knee injury in a training ground incident, the very last challenge of the session, we were later to hear, which had been diagnosed as cruciate ligament damage – the injury so dreaded by all footballers. It was expected to end the captain's 2007-08 campaign before it had begun. There was a prospect he might be able to play again some time around March but Keane said he wasn't relying on him being back even then.

It meant Sunderland had suffered serious injuries to three key players in the opening ten days of the season – all of them from the middle of the park. The effects of the loss of Whitehead, Edwards and Richardson in the months ahead on Sunderland could not be underestimated. Few teams in the bottom half of the Premier League would be able to cope well with the loss of three of their four first-choice midfielders – two of them the very best of Sunderland's Championship-winning team, according to their fellow professionals. Whitehead, like Edwards, had only played in Sunderland's first two games and the club had taken four points from six.

The cup defeat and Whitehead's injury were put into perspective by the news filtering through that Clive Clarke – a Sunderland player on loan at Leicester City – had collapsed with a heart–attack in the dressing room, forcing the abandonment of the cup tie against Nottingham Forest. Clarke was to spend the next six weeks in recuperation and it later emerged that the on-loan left back had 'died' twice on the Foxes' dressing room floor and was only revived by determined medics using defibrillator equipment. He was lucky to be alive.

The shock defeat at Luton, the stunning loss of Whitehead and the near-tragedy of Clarke took the wind out of Sunderland's sails. The euphoria of the opening-day win over Spurs had dissipated. But fans now had Keane's eagerly awaited return to Old Trafford to look forward to (more eagerly awaited by the fans and the media than by the man himself).

Keane was polite but almost dismissive about the significance of his return in the press conferences leading up to the game. He knew a media circus would surround his arrival at Old Trafford but he had no intention of fuelling it. Shortly before the transfer deadline, Keane announced a triple signing that raised hope and expectation among supporters struggling to retain their optimism. Former Leeds United stalwart Ian Harte arrived on a one-year contract, the thirty-year-old offering new options on the left; Danny Higginbotham cost £2.5 million in a four-year deal; Kenwyne Jones – a player who had barely registered on the media radar until a few days previously – joined from Southampton for four years with a £6 million price tag.

The signing of Higginbotham was a triumph for perseverance, while Collins did not have to go the other way. 'I was a bit disappointed with what went on but if the gaffer wants to bring players in, that's fair enough,' he said. 'I never actually spoke to Stoke, although the gaffer mentioned it to me as part of the deal with Danny. Bottom line was that I didn't want to leave Sunderland and I just dug my heels in and worked as hard as I possibly could to show I deserved a place in the side.'

Yet the arrival of Jones was the deal Sunderland could take most satisfaction from. Derby County had fought tooth and nail to persuade him to join them. Manager Billy Davies had identified him as his key signing, a Didier Drogba in the making he believed. In the end County could not compete, neither in transfer fees nor wages, although the clincher for Jones was that Keane was the manager he wanted to play for.

Keane had made a critical signing. 'He is a big, strong boy and athletic, the kind of player we've been missing,' he said.

Jones' arrival would not have happened had it not been for Quinn's backing and Keane's attraction – all elements at the club pulling together for a successful outcome. This was the sort of signing that Sunderland had missed out on too many times in previous seasons, mainly, it has to be said, through lack of funds.

The transfer deadline passed with Sunderland fans' summer-long hopes dashed that they might get either of Manchester United's young stars – Danny Simpson or Jonny Evans. Quinn and Keane had known for some time that they had no chance of getting either player. Sir Alex Ferguson, going for glory on all fronts, wanted them in his squad and had signalled behind the scenes that he wasn't going to let any of his young players go in the early stages of the campaign.

Of the dozen signings that Keane made up to the end of the August transfer window, the three the club could be most proud of were Richardson, Gordon and Jones, for, in each of their cases, Sunderland had to fight off strong Premier League opposition in order to land their man.

Jones' £6 million move sent Stern John in the opposite direction. Likeable to the last, John had fallen on his sword for the sake of his young Trinidad and Tobago teammate. 'I would have liked to have stayed at Sunderland and I was told I didn't have to go. But I also knew that the deal for Kenwyne would probably not go ahead unless I was involved in going to Southampton, so I agreed to the move. I have had my time in the top flight and loved it but Kenwyne deserved his chance and I did not want to be the one who prevented his move.'

At thirty-one years of age John was not one for the future. Despite his goal against Birmingham City, few Sunderland fans mourned his departure – although he did score five goals in ten starts and six substitute appearances for Sunderland. He was a good character to have around the club and gave his all in games for Sunderland. Hearteningly for him, he was to prove far from a spent force. He was right towards the top end of the Championship's goalscoring charts at the end of the season and his 19 goals – two on the last day of the campaign – were undoubtedly the difference between Southampton staying up or going down.

Keane, meanwhile, was happy to let the new signings have their share of the headlines in the run–up to the game, even though the subject of his return to Manchester, and the emotiveness surrounding it, was inevitably raised.

'Look,' he finally said, 'let's be clear about this. Sir Alex and the United team will be looking to beat me and to beat Sunderland. That's what I know. That's what I expect. I'm not expecting big hugs and kisses.'

Yet he would not have been human had he not felt a twinge of anticipation ahead of his trip to the Theatre of Dreams where he had achieved so much.

Old Trafford nowadays is one of the world's great stadiums. During increases in its capacity, it occasionally looked lopsided, bordering on the ugly. With all the corners filled in to create a vast bowl and so much work being done on the aesthetics, inside and out, the place reeks of the power and money that have made Manchester United one of the richest clubs on the planet. Barely a year since Sunderland were playing at 'Unfashionable Roots Hall', Old Trafford looked awe-inspiring in the hour before kick-off as it gradually filled up. Faced with this cathedral of cash, you could see why Keane felt it important to regularly remind his players not to bring their 'autograph books and cameras'.

His return to Old Trafford lived up to its billing. Nor did his players did let him down with their performance, even though the end result was Sunderland's fourth consecutive defeat.

Sir Alex Ferguson's programme notes, extolling the virtues of the 1-0 win, proved to be the stuff of clairvoyance. He made the point that in games where teams come to defend at Old Trafford, 1-0 is as good as it needs to be for the home team. The United manager hailed Eric Cantona as the master of producing that particular result, though Keane also played his part in many a marginal victory for the Red Devils.

Not that that would have been any consolation to the Sunderland manager as he watched his former club do to him what he and his old teammates did to so many others down the years – patiently plug away and grind lesser opposition down.

It underlined the fact that these were changed times for Keane, the player who was once the master of this particular stage. He left the Theatre of Dreams as the ultimate all-action footballing hero. He returned as the managerial new kid on the block. Not that you would have known he had ever left the building, judging by the waves of affection and adulation that rolled down from the huge terraces as Keane emerged from the tunnel at kick–off. He was applauded all the way along the touchline to the dugout, by those who revelled in the return of one of their most iconic players. He had been the on-field driving force behind the most successful era in the club's history and the vast 75,648 crowd – the largest league attendance ever to see a Sunderland match, incidentally – were anxious to pay tribute. The air crackled with clapping and cheering as Keane accompanied Ferguson out onto the pitch and walked from the corner-flag entrance along the touchline to the dugout. For Sunderland fans watching the inspiring scene it was a reminder of the stature in the game of the manager they now called their own.

For the Old Trafford faithful it was an emotional day as they celebrated two of the club's all-time heroes. Keane's return coincided with Ole Gunnar Solksjaer's departure – the thirty-four-year-old striker finally forced to retire following a debilitating injury – and the Norwegian was given a guard of honour and unstinting applause in recognition of his own contribution to glorious years. The two former teammates were known to have affection and respect for each other, and there was nothing stage-managed about the warmth of their greeting as they shook hands.

The home fans must have wished they could have had both players back on the pitch in their prime as a forgettable first-half unfolded, with United labouring against a solidly set up Sunderland team. Keane made four changes to the team that lost to Liverpool, giving debuts to Jones and Higginbotham. Tough-tackling McShane, who had proven popular with Sunderland fans because of his committed style and fearlessness, was ruled out. He had needed ten stitches in a head wound sustained at Wigan and injured his shoulder at Liverpool; injuries which only increased his kudos with the fans. The other changes saw left back Collins restored and midfielder Leadbitter starting the game. Sunderland adopted a 4-5-1 approach for the first time that season, Jones the lone striker. He immediately caught the eye and the powerfully-built forward's muscularity in the thankless task handed to him was a revelation to Sunderland fans.

United, who gave a debut to £14 million midfielder Oliveira Anderson, adopted the same formation, Owen Hargreaves sitting in front of the back four, with Carlos Tevez up front on his own. The Premier League champions fielded all four of their big name summer signings for the first time in the season and it was Luis Nani who produced his team's first shot in anger, with a low left-foot drive from the left-flank which flashed across Gordon's goal in the 4th minute.

Jones went for the spectacular in the 18th minute from McShane's right-wing cross, but he scissor-kicked his shot high and wide in what was to be Sunderland's last attack of the half. Keane's team were more intent on defence than attack and did their job excellently, with returning star Yorke's composure, Etuhu's awkwardness and youngster Leadbitter's terrier-like energy stifling the home team so much that their first corner did not arrive until the half-hour. It was a fine, personal moment for Sunderland's only home-grown player, Leadbitter, who was facing his hero and the player he was occasionally compared to.

'I enjoyed coming up against Paul Scholes,' he said. 'In my eyes I think he is possibly still the best player in the Premiership. He's been at the top level for ten years or more and won loads of stuff and he's still hungry for more.'

Leadbitter was arguably the player benefiting from the mentorship of the experienced Yorke and looked up to a player who had achieved so much in the game – the youngest and the oldest Sunderland players on the pitch. Yorke had been Manchester United's record-signing when he moved to Manchester for £12.6 million in 1998. Sitting in front of the defence at Old Trafford, the Trinidad and Tobago legend still looked perfectly at home on his old stamping ground.

After half-time Ferguson changed to 4-4-2, Louis Saha coming on for Oliveira Anderson and the effect was instant. Nosworthy made a couple of poor decisions, which United failed to capitalise on, as Keane moved to the touchline to begin remonstrating with his defence. Five minutes into the second half Carlos Tevez forced a fine save out of Gordon, with the keeper diving on a cleverly swept first-time shot from the Argentinean who pounced on a Higginbotham half-clearance. Former United youth player Higginbotham had an excellent debut on his return to Old Trafford and twice repelled dangerous balls as Sunderland continued to hold. Gordon looked great, as good as he had been against Liverpool. He produced a fine block to deny Louis Saha and then in the 69th minute an even better save to frustrate Owen Hargreaves.

Seconds later, Keane made the only decision open to him and withdrew Jones, who had gone down with cramp. He'd had little in the way of first-team football in the preceding weeks and Keane would have been mindful not only of the care Sir Alex Ferguson had shown in not asking too much of Oliveira Anderson on his return from injury but also the hamstring injury that had sidelined Edwards. Sod's Law would dictate, though, that Jones had barely left the field when his marking abilities were missed. United won a corner from the left in the 72nd minute and two Sunderland players at the near post were unable to make contact with the ball as Louis Saha nipped in between them to glance home.

Whether Gordon should have come for the ball earlier was a moot point, but he must have felt entitled to expect at least one of the players around the United striker to have got closer to the ball. The scoreline, though, would have been far worse had Gordon not demonstrated the potential he possessed. Five minutes after the goal he produced another superb save, this time to thwart Hargreaves. United might have added more before the final whistle but 1-0 was probably a fair reflection of the game – of Sunderland's diligent defending and United's technical superiority.

Among the disappointed Sunderland fans was English cricket's one-day captain Paul Collingwood. The dejected Durham County batsman and Sunderland fan had dragged his international teammates along to a game in which Edwin Van

Der Sar had not had one meaningful save to make all afternoon.

There were positives; not least the impressive debuts of the solid Higginbotham and the willing Jones, and Keane could leave his old club knowing his players had given everything on a ground which no team found it easy to visit.

The last time Sunderland had been at Old Trafford was the night that the Wearsiders' inevitable relegation was finally confirmed in the 15 point campaign, two seasons previously.

That night, the team had been led by caretaker manager Kevin Ball – a former Sunderland captain who was in the same mould as Keane when it came to spirit, defiance and tackling. He ensured his team went down fighting. Keane had recognised Ball's worth when he joined the club and the long-serving captain had remained on the club payroll, bringing on the youths – a model professional teaching good habits to the next generation. Though the mathematical certainty of their defeat was confirmed that night, Ball's team still left with heads held high. They had ground out a 0-0 draw which effectively ended United's pursuit of Chelsea at the top of the table. Under Keane, Sunderland had produced a similarly heartening performance, but trepidation was now creeping into the hearts of many Black Cats' fans.

Sunderland had made it hard for United but had still lost, defeat dropping them to 17th in the table. Six games into the season and those first-day photographs of Sunderland topping the table were now beginning to look ever more ironic.

Ferguson did not fool himself about the quality of the win. Sunderland had been stubborn and made his all-star team, deprived of Wayne Rooney, Cristiano Ronaldo and Ryan Giggs, look ordinary for long periods. But as the old master had suggested, 1-0 does nicely enough on any given day.

Defeat put Keane in new territory as Sunderland manager, his fourth in a row being something he had never experienced in over a decade as a Manchester United player. However he wouldn't be up at night worrying about it, as he had been after the horror shows at Wigan and Luton.

'There were a couple of times I was up at four and five in the morning thinking about those games,' he admitted. 'But I won't lose sleep after this one.'

Keane would now demand the same spirit of resolve in the games ahead that his players had shown him at Old Trafford. 'If you are going to lose, there's a way to lose and the way we lost against Manchester United was something like it – going down fighting and losing by a single goal after giving our all.

'The Man United result is not great but I did appreciate the reception. Very, very nice. I didn't really get sucked into the hype about coming back but the welcome was fantastic and I appreciated it. The United fans have always been good to me and the whole thing was probably overshadowed by the fact that Ole had retired. That's fine by me because he's a top man.'

Chopra, meanwhile, who was played wide right for tactical reasons, was showing early signs of being frustrated at not getting more sniffs of goal.

'If you look at the games after I scored the two goals, I haven't really had that many chances,' he shrugged. 'I had one at Tottenham and one at Birmingham and I put them both away, which was good for my confidence, and it was great to be on Match of the Day's Goal of the Month, especially with this being my first Premiership season at the club. But I'm a player who likes to feed off balls into the box and I haven't had that much so far because we've lost key players in the first few weeks – Dean, Carlos and Kieran.

'United have lost Rooney, Ronaldo and Gary Neville and everyone's talking about the big effect that has had on them. It's a different level but we've lost three players who are just as important to us.'

A lack of goals in the campaign would not only be Chopra's concern. It would be that of all the strikers at the club with Sunderland unable to manage a goal a game until well into the New Year.

In the days after the United match, there was controversy when Stokes failed to report for Republic of Ireland U21 duty. The Dubliner had returned to his native city unaware that his country had not been informed of his withdrawal through injury. 'I thought Sunderland were going to speak to the Irish FA,' he insisted.

Republic of Ireland U21 manager Don Givens was fuming and was critical of both player and club. It was a curious incident because, while the colourful Stokes took the brunt of the flak for the breakdown in communication, some were wondering if the fault was Sunderland's failure to properly inform the FAI.

That would have been ironic, given Keane's long-standing

criticism of the FAI's poor organisation. If Keane and Sunderland did get it wrong over Stokes' arrangements, or, even if they didn't, they got it exactly right in the game that followed, both on and off the pitch, as honours were paid to the premature passing of a Sunderland legend: FA Cup hero Ian Porterfield. Porterfield died after a long battle with cancer, just days before Sunderland's next game; a game against Reading, a club he had formerly managed. And, while one Sunderland great was remembered on match night, another Sunderland player showed the first signs that he might go on to carve out his own special place in the club's history.

Kenwyne Jones had arrived at the Stadium of Light.

CHAPTER THREE

One Step Forward, Two Steps Back

There's a fine line between success and failure in this league. ROY KEANE

SUNDERLAND Football Club's finest moment of the modern era came at Wembley in 1973 when its Second Division team beat Leeds United to lift the FA Cup. It was Ian Porterfield's goal that won it. So there was understandable emotion in the air when, for the first time in the Stadium of Light's history, the rest of the 1973 team walked onto the turf together to pay tribute before the Reading game. The old team were piped on, at their own request, to the theme tune of Z Cars, the prematch anthem at Roker Park, and carried with them the trophy, which had been specially brought up to the north-east on the day.

High up in the west stand, Quinn summed up the continuing significance of the ageing men in front of us. 'Ian's team has been largely responsible for maintaining the spirit of this football club down the years.'

There had been fallow decades before and after but Sunderland fans of a certain age could hold on to that moment of glory, when all things good about the club came together. It was recalled by one and all as a time of great togetherness and both the newspapers of the day and the thousands of recollections of those involved have only reinforced that view. It provided rich memories to sustain fans in the years since.

After Sunderland's League Cup defeat at Luton, Clive Clarke's near death experience had put football into perspective and, after the defeat at United, which left the Black Cats one place above the relegation zone, the death of Ian Porterfield did the same.

Slowly but surely, everyone slips into the pages of the past and now it was Porterfield's turn – the man whose shot echoed around the footballing world – dead at the tragically premature age of sixty-one. 'No age at all,' Keane reflected with a slow shake of his head, as the Stadium of Light flags flew at half mast.

Porterfield's death not only dragged that incredible May afternoon back to the forefront of a generation's minds, it also seemed to remind everyone in the city they were trooping to the beat of the same drum. For some reason it took me back to Sunderland's other FA Cup winning team – the team that lifted the trophy for the first time in the club's history back in 1937 – and the sepia-tinted photographs it bequeathed. One image is as iconic as anything from 1973 – the impossibly-dapper FA-Cup-clutching captain, Raich Carter, beaming the broadest of smiles as he is held shoulder-high by teammates lost in personal reverie. The sun shines down in the picture, as it always will do now, shadowing sweated brows, matted hair and muddy knees as Raich Carter is chaired around the Wembley pitch in front of a crowd whose ecstasies know no bounds.

It is the magic of football, up close.

At its very best, football can freeze a moment in time, just like that moment with Carter; just like Jimmy Montgomery's saves or the be-trilbied Bob Stokoe's race across the Wembley turf; or Bobby Kerr's moment of triumph at the top of Wembley's thirty-nine steps; or, most appropriately of all that week, Porterfield's priceless half-volley. Keane himself, his face and hairstyle changing over the years, is captured along with dozens of other United stars in the gilded corridors off Old Trafford's press area and executive boxes. Physiques and footballers fade, but memories do not. Football really is a glory game. A game to take the mundane and make it special.

And those who provide those moments deserve to be remembered.

In 1992 Sunderland fans were dreaming of glory when the team reached the FA Cup final again, only for remorseless Liverpool to cast them aside in one of the most forgettable finals of recent decades. At the time I was a news reporter for the Echo and given the job of interviewing the last three survivors of the 1937 team – Raich Carter, Bobby Gurney and Johnny Mapson. When I arrived at Bobby Gurney's house the club's record goal-scorer took his time to emerge, not because of his eighty-five years, but because of illness. He had caught a chill from going out in the rain.

'There were a couple of tickets on offer for the final in an Echo competition and to enter you had to know the name of the Sunderland player who had scored more cup goals than any other player,' the old striker explained. 'Well, I thought, hang on, that's me! So I wrote the answer 'Bobby Gurney' and where it said 'entrant's name' I wrote 'Bobby Gurney' there as well.

'Didn't win though,' he chuckled, 'and I got this blasted cold going into town to post the letter.'

Bobby Gurney was an absolute gentleman, gifted as some footballers are with phenomenal powers of memory about the games he'd played in. I was as thrilled with the interview as I was angry that the club had not seen fit to offer him and his remaining teammates tickets. I made contact with the club, determined that if tickets weren't forthcoming we would splash the story over the news pages. As it turned out, almost immediately after getting in touch with the club, the three were offered tickets, as they should have been all along. I recall this because one of the failings of Sunderland Football Club down the years is that it did not respect nor treasure heroes like Bobby Gurney in the way it should have done. Goalkeeper Johnny Mapson, at just nineteen, was the youngest player ever to feature in an FA Cup final – a record that stood until the 1960s. He was on Sunderland's books from the 1935-36 season until 1953, yet the club argued that because his eighteen years' service had been interrupted by the war, he didn't qualify for a testimonial. Even prominent members of the 1973 squad once muttered darkly about how quickly they seemed to have been forgotten by the club. Players like Billy Hughes, a no-nonsense personality even in his playing days, had not been back to the club since Roker Park was demolished, so poorly did he feel former players were treated.

Quinn changed all that in a stroke. One of his first actions was to take the decision that every former player should be entitled to a pair of free tickets for Sunderland matches. His work with the Former Players' Association since then has been aimed at ensuring the club made best use of a unique commodity – the players who are part of the tapestry of the club's history. It wasn't gesture politics either.

The 1973 cup-winning goalkeeper Jimmy 'Monty' Montgomery praised the new regime for this stance. 'The chairman started it and Roy is exactly the same because he's come from a club like Manchester United. If you said to them, "forget about the history, let's just look at now" they would say that's ridiculous. That's what one or two people at Sunderland tried to do. Billy Hughes hasn't been to the stadium since it was built and he loved the way he was treated at the Reading game. With what happened before, he didn't want to come back but he's coming again after seeing what Niall and Roy have done. It wasn't the case before – they didn't want to know us.'

The change of tack had been a boost to Sunderland's Former Players' Association, which was now the second largest FPA behind Manchester United's. To show their appreciation, they nominated Keane's Guide Dogs for the Blind charity as their own and handed over a four-figure sum.

Quinn's, and Keane's, enlightened approach to matters like this, was forging a new togetherness, and a shared vision. It was one of the reasons why, despite misgivings about Keane's success or lack of it in the transfer market in the summer, despite concerns about losing four games on the trot, there had been little dissension in the ranks. The fans trusted Quinn, believed in Keane and put their faith in both.

Personally, I was pleased that Ian Porterfield's passing was marked so well. In the days when I had the luxury of being a supporter rather than a reporter, I'd been persuaded by mates to go to Roker Park and pay good money to be part of a minute's silence. Sunderland were in the middle of yet another poor run but I was told I had to. There was to be a minute's silence for the great England World-Cup-winning centre back Bobby Moore and we were playing West Ham United, the club where he'd displayed his talents. Bizarre thing, going to a game for sixty seconds of silence rather than ninety minutes of football, but I'll always be glad I went.

Kenneth Wolstenholme's famous commentary on the last seconds of the 1966 World Cup final, when Geoff Hurst scored to seal a 4-2 England victory over West Germany, was played over the tannoy as a respectful Roker Park hushed. In the seconds that followed, all that could be heard was the sound of seagulls and the metallic click of turnstiles as fans silently made their way into a ghost-silent ground. The ear-bursting applause that followed after the referee blew his whistle also showed that the thousands of Hammers fans, who had made the long journey north to honour a legend, were grateful for the respect shown by Sunderland's fans.

Sunderland Football Club got it right that day. And they got it right for Ian Porterfield too. Before the Reading game, the sound of Brian Moore's commentary on Ian Porterfield's 32nd minute goal was played, followed by a minute's applause. His death was a reminder to all Sunderland fans that their greatest footballing triumph since 1937 was passing from recent history into just history. The occasion would stay in the minds of tens of thousands of Sunderland fans, just like the Moore memorial stayed with me. Ian Porterfield helped give Sunderland the FA Cup trophy. In return, everyone connected with Sunderland – fans, club, media – had given him the send off he deserved. I only spoke to him a handful of times but I think he was the sort of character who would have appreciated the minute's applause, in memory of his death, far more than any aching silence.

His former teammates paid tribute at Bob Stokoe's statue – the manager's arms aloft at the start of that Wembley jig of joy – which stands in the shadow of the Stadium of Light. Wreaths were laid and then, in a never-to-be-forgotten moment for those present, the 1973 team were spontaneously applauded by supporters all the way into the stadium.

The atmospheric evening match, though, was about more than Ian Porterfield's death. There was a game to be played and Keane knew that the best tribute of all would be to send the supporters away with a victory. Going into the Reading match, Sunderland were still without Richardson while Edwards had broken down in training, again – an occurrence that was to happen with depressing regularity throughout the season. Sunderland had now gone four hours without a goal and managed just eight shots on target all season. Their only consolation was that Reading had scored even fewer.

The game was a Sunderland nostalgist's dream – Bobby Kerr, Billy Hughes and Monty on the pitch again, an instinctive shot giving Sunderland a 1-0 lead around the half-hour mark and Ian Porterfield's name on the lips of everyone. The spirit of 1973 was everywhere. On a day dominated by looking back, it was fitting that Sunderland's current team should produce a positive performance. You knew it was a day to be remembered when you saw Keane's team-sheet and realised that for the first time in 49 games he had chosen to field an unchanged team. The starting eleven, though, wholly justified their manager's unique decision.

Reading dominated the opening minutes but Sunderland carved out the early openings. Jones, on his home debut, and Leadbitter both went close with eye-catching strikes. Jones had already shown signs to the home fans that he had more to offer than just physical presence. He was quick, he was hungry and in the 29th minute of the game the striker put his team ahead with a goal of craft and cunning. With his back to goal, he took a short pass from Leadbitter, spun away from defender Ivar Ingimarsson in the blink of an eye and clipped home a bouncing left-foot shot from twenty yards out. Marcus Hahnemann tried to get there, moving to his left, but the quick shot had taken him by surprise and did him for accuracy as it rolled just inside the post.

As the crowd celebrated the birth of a new hero, they were stunned and delighted when he sprinted into tumbling somersaults to celebrate. It was not something they had expected. Tumbling somersaults have not been the forte of Sunderland strikers over the years and Jones had just added a dash of glamour and style to Sunderland's season. Of the goal celebration, Keane said wryly, 'if Ken breaks his ankle doing that, then I'll be quite disappointed – but you have to enjoy scoring. That's what you work all week for and it's the best feeling in the world.'

In the minutes that followed Sunderland continued to threaten, Jones, Ross Wallace and Higginbotham all going close. They should have doubled their lead five minutes from the break when Collins put in a great cross from the left which found Jones unmarked eight yards out. He headed the ball so forcefully into the turf that it bounced over the bar.

Steve Coppell, the Reading manager, believed that, having got his team in at half-time only a goal down, they could get something out of it. It was a false hope. Within 60 seconds of the resumption Jones chased a loose ball down the right-wing, earned possession and shrugged off the attentions of four Reading players. He pulled the ball back across the face of goal and Wallace stabbed home at the far post.

Keane made substitutions, going 4-5-1 in a bid to refresh his midfield and close the game out. Reading gained heart from Sunderland's growing tendency to sit deep, and in the last ten minutes they threatened. Leadbitter gave away a free-kick twenty-five yards from goal. Graeme Murty lifted it goalwards and Dave Kitson guided an 86th minute header inside Gordon's right-hand post. It meant the last few minutes held an anxious moment for the home team, but Sunderland saw it through.

On a day reserved for heroes on Wearside, Sunderland

delivered a victory which ensured fans could be proud of both their past and their present. About a quarter of an hour from time the stadium had risen unbidden to the spontaneous chant of 'Stand up for Ian Porterfield' and near 40,000 people applauded the 1973 hero. It was an amazing knee-jerk of unorchestrated appreciation. A magical moment – a tribute to Sunderland fans themselves, as well as Porterfield – and one which Keane later admitted made an impression on him.

'Someone was telling me the players had never been at the ground before as a group and, if that's true, I find it amazing. Some clubs go overboard the other way and invite teams back too often but, when you look at the lack of success the teams up in the north-east have had over recent years, it's important to remember your achievements.'

Keane was always careful to show due respect to that cup team but, I sensed sometimes, coming from the hugely successful background he did, that he was almost bemused by the fact the game was still so freshly recalled. Keane had won the FA Cup four times during his time at Manchester United and for him, silverware was expected.

'From my own point of view, I'm a great believer in looking forward but you can't get away from the team that wins the FA Cup and teams that do that deserve to be remembered,' he said. 'When you are looking at clubs who win trophies year in, year out, it may be slightly different. But a club like Sunderland who have not won many recently, well, they should remember the teams that did do it for them. You have to.

'But we have to look forward as well. We want to see the players we've got in the team now go on to win things. We want to see their pictures up on the wall in the next few years.'

It was Reading's third defeat in a row. Was it Second Season Syndrome (the theory that the second season up in the Premier League is sometimes more difficult than the first)? Sunderland fans had no sympathy. Second Season Syndrome was something they could only aspire to. Coppell put defeat down to a striker, rather than a syndrome.

'Kenwyne Jones did really well for Sunderland, no getting away from that,' he frowned. 'He was a physical and skilful presence who scored one, made one and was involved in a lot for them. We didn't defend against him very well.'

Keane knew the potential of the player he now had on the

club's book. 'There was competition for Kenwyne and we knew that would be the case because he was never going to stay at Southampton. But from the moment we talked to him, he wanted to come here. It's just a shame he won't have his friend Carlos putting in crosses for a while. That would have been an ideal situation but that was our mistake.'

Jones was frank about his admiration of the manager after he collected his man-of-the-match award. The beaming striker recalled his first meeting with Keane, 'I had a trial at Man United in 2002,' he revealed. 'I don't think the manager knows it but I have a picture of me and him. He was being typical Keane. Composed. Picture. Then move off. There was no conversation because they were off to training.'

'Did he smile?' Jones was asked.

'No,' replied Jones, a broader grin spreading.

The Reading win put Sunderland back into mid-table and lifted spirits considerably.

'I don't think Reading could handle Kenwyne,' Keane said. 'He's a big, strong, physical lad and that will mean sometimes his skill on the ball will be underestimated, but it shouldn't be because he scored a cracking goal for us. We're not the biggest of teams and Kenwyne gives us that presence that we've lacked previously.'

Keane also believed that the mercurial Wallace, at five foot six inches, the joint smallest player in the Premier League along with Chelsea's Shaun Wright-Phillips, could play his way into Scotland's senior team. The young left-winger had followed up an excellent preseason by being involved in every one of the Black Cats' early season games.

'You look at Ross and you have to say that there's no reason why he can't get a squeeze into their squad. He's one of those players that have come up from the Championship with us, who we hope will do well in the Premiership. His preferred position is left-wing but he has done very well for us at left back because he's got a bit of quality on the ball. He gives us options. You look at the Reading game where he scored one and was really unlucky not to score another. It's no coincidence that he's played in every match so far this season.'

The only downside to his performance was another booking for removing his shirt in celebration, a reaction he vowed he wouldn't repeat after two cards during the Championship season for exactly the same exuberant offence. Keane wasn't without sympathy.

'Listen, there's no better feeling in the world than scoring a goal and sometimes it's hard to control your reaction in the heat of the moment. But you just hope the penny drops.'

Wallace, a bubbly character in the team, grinned. 'A few of the lads have been having a go at me. But that's alright. I like a bit of banter. I suppose what's worse is I didn't forget at all – I knew what I was doing. It was my first Premiership goal, the feeling was unbelievable and I just thought, "Sack it, I'm going for it". I got a smile from the manager when I walked past him, but no doubt he'll have a word at some stage. I hope he doesn't fine me, though, because I'm not on much as it is!'

Keane had no such intention. 'I've never really been one for going down the road of imposing fines – although our chief executive Peter Walker wishes I would!'

The manager had other reasons to be cheerful. Whitehead now had hopes of an earlier return to the team. The prognosis had changed. 'First of all,' said Whitehead, 'the news from the specialist was terrible. It took me a while to get my head round it, but the manager had his fair share of injuries and he was brilliant. We had a good few chats when I was first told I'd miss the whole of the season and it really helped to have someone who could say the right words at the right time. He knew exactly how I felt.'

A subsequent return to the specialist had suggested surgery was not required and he could be back playing again by the end of the year.

'It was a massive, massive boost to me,' admitted Whitehead.

To the manager too, who relied on his model professional captain to set the tone off the pitch as well as lead on it. Whitehead was one of those unflashy players who sometimes go unappreciated by supporters, but never by their teammates. A cover-every-blade-of-grass player, Sunderland had to be grateful that the emergence of tigerish, young midfielder Leadbitter helped compensate for the captain's loss.

Keane had made a dozen signings before the August deadline and was now working hard to weld them into a unit, develop a new team spirit. Having his captain sidelined had hardly helped. One of the ways he tried to build that togetherness was a series of team-bonding days, which would become a feature of the season. The first was on an army assault course in north Yorkshire before the Middlesbrough game.

'It was nice to see a lot of the lads laughing on the pictures because we're building something new,' said Keane afterwards. 'It was amazing the way the players gelled last season and it's not easy to get that. But I'm a lot happier over the last few weeks. Some managers will tell you it takes years to get a good dressing room.'

Keane wanted to keep these days 'in-house' so it was a surprise to see shots being broadcast on Sky Sports. If the club was going to let a national sports station in for coverage, why not the local paper? When I raised it with the club, I was told that it had been planned to be in-house but at the very last moment the manager had rung and said he wanted the cameras in.

Gut instinct again.

It seemed a strange decision to me initially, but then the more I thought about it, the more I suspected I knew where he was coming from. I think it was an attempt to send a subtle message out to the rest of football. He was trying to push Sunderland as a more attractive prospect nationally. The pictures, of players laughing in hard-hats, wrestling with ropes and just generally having a good time were transmitting the idea that, far from it being grim up north, Sunderland Football Club was an enjoyable place to be. Maybe his mind was on those designer-clothes-shop players. Or, perhaps, the players the club inquired about over the summer who wouldn't even return phone calls. Maybe it was to counter the negative images of himself as some sort of WAG-berating hard man.

He was also trying his utmost to build up the player unity, which had been a key to success in the club's previous campaign. 'We are trying to get last year's spirit back. We lost two massive players in Jonny Evans and Danny Simpson over the summer, two popular players among the lads. And now we are trying to get a new spirit together in the squad.'

In his playing days, Keane had said the game was full of bluffers. Bluffing was something he'd never done as a manager when it came to his own performance. If he felt he had made a mistake, he tended to be the first to admit it. If a situation did not necessarily paint him in the best light, he refused to duck it. Occasionally that frankness left him potentially wide open to his critics, such as his willingness to concede that despite having spent a massive thirty-five million pounds on transfers, his Championship team was superior in some aspects to the one he had just expensively assembled. 'Sometimes I think we are not as strong a team as we were last season,' he pondered. 'When you look at the injuries we've picked up. We are missing Jonny and Danny in terms of a settled team, and Carlos and Dean too. That's what we're missing this year, a settled team, because that's what makes you consistent. But Jonny, if I thought for one minute there was an opportunity of bringing him to Sunderland with the quality he's got, we would consider it. He did brilliantly for the club and it would be nice if we thought he could come back. But it's a big if. He would have hoped to be involved a bit more at United by now but that's the problem of any young player at a big club, be it United, Arsenal or Liverpool. Yes, well and good being there, but ultimately for a lot of players, especially for the likes of Jonny who is playing for his international team and had a run of games for us last season, you can't beat playing. You just can't.

'Jonny and Danny loved their time here and it must be a nightmare for any player to have played and then be back in the reserves. When I was at Forest, I loved playing every week but if someone had said to me you get a game every two or three months, I wouldn't be happy because I would have felt my game was going backwards. Jonny and Danny came here in a pressure situation and handled it really well. It'll be tough for them at the moment but, believe me, it was a nightmare for us to give them back.'

As he was bedding some players into Sunderland, Keane was trying to shift others out. Kavanagh finally gave up his battle for first-team football at Sunderland, the thirty-three-year-old joining Sheffield Wednesday on loan where he was to prove himself more than capable of playing Championship football as he helped steer the Yorkshire men away from the foot of the table. This was to be a theme for Sunderland's squad. Many of them were not consistent Premier League performers, but still good enough to stand out in the Championship.

For Keane, the work in the transfer market had been exacting, but he felt the working relationship he had established with Quinn and chief executive Walker worked well. 'I have meetings every two or three weeks with Niall and Peter and go to the odd board meeting,' he said, explaining what was very much a separation of powers.

He wanted to be left completely free to dictate the playing team of things and he had been granted that. But the more experienced Keane grew in his role, the more he was prepared to consider different tacks.

'It's very straightforward,' he said. 'I stick to the football side. Six months ago, I would have said a director of football was mad, but the more I'm a manager the more I think you need good people around you to share the load.

'In preseason I was on the phone for hours every day throughout my holiday. I guarantee I won't be doing it next year. I had to go through it to learn it. I'm pretty stubborn like that. I have to go through something myself because that's the best way of learning for me. I know now, though, that that approach was a complete waste of time because everyone's on holiday early on and very little gets done.'

Next for Sunderland was Middlesbrough, Keane's first experience of a local derby. The closest he had got the previous season was the game against Leeds United, which, as any Sunderland fan will tell you, is not a derby at all. Keane was fully aware that the game against the Boro was more important than most for fans – thousands of Wearsiders and Teessiders share the same pubs and workplaces and would have been winding each other up about the fixture all week. But that didn't come into his thinking in terms of preparation.

'I tried to go into every game as a player with exactly the same mentality, and that was just to beat the opposition, no matter who they might be,' he said. 'This game is no different. There's always a bit more interest from the media for derby games and, obviously, the fans take it a lot more seriously than other league games. But as a manager, I've not been much different than I was as a player.'

In the wake of the win over Reading, Keane was delighted with the early signs of the Chopra-Jones partnership. 'Chopra was lively and unlucky not to score against Reading, always sniffing about for any balls that were breaking, and I think to get the best out of him he has to play off a big strong player because, himself, he's not the biggest lad out there.'

The manager was also eager that the contribution of Higginbotham was not overlooked. 'It's only been two games since he arrived but the signs are decent with us having a left-footed centre-half in there because I do think it helps with the balance of the team. Obviously we have had Nyron and Paul playing there, and they've done a good job, but when you have a left-footer there it just gives you that little bit extra balance.'

The Boro game was Keane's 50th in charge of Sunderland. 'It's come up pretty quickly,' he admitted when it was raised in the prematch press conference. 'People say that when you're a player your career is over before you know it, and management might be the same. Fifty games. We were doing the team photograph the other day, and it really does feel like yesterday that we were doing the first one, but there's been so many changes from last season. Lots of changes, lots of progress.

'You look at the photograph from last year and compare it to this one and there's probably more changes at this club than any other. Hopefully, there will never be that amount of changes again in the next few years, but we had to go through that, especially for the Premiership. We couldn't just sit back. There are seven or eight managers who have done over 1,000 matches – so that puts fifty into perspective. I'm sure they would say all you do is focus on the next match. You have to have a toughness about you to be durable in this business. All the top managers have that. But it doesn't meant to say you can't be nice. Look at me!'

The manager felt at this stage that those players traumatised by their previous Premier League adventure were beginning to regain self-belief at the highest level. Only four remained from McCarthy's squad – captain Whitehead, cult-hero Nyron Nosworthy, the dogged Collins and the youngster Leadbitter – and this time around they were not having to endure the same horror show.

'We had better delivery, from Grant in particular, at set-pieces against Reading and you have to remember that, for a lot of these players, it is still new to them, doing OK at this level,' Keane said. 'You look at Grant, for example, Danny, Dean and Nyron, and the last time they were in the Premiership they had some bad memories. The Reading game was Grant's first win in the Premiership so it's new to a lot of these players and we can't forget that.'

Wallace insisted Sunderland would take the derby game atmosphere in their stride. 'I've played in quite a few so it's nothing new,' he shrugged. 'I've come on a few times in the Rangers v Celtic games, one of the biggest derby rivalries in the world, so I'm not going to have a problem with Boro. I am looking forward to the Sunderland v Newcastle game, though, and being part of that, but once you get on the pitch it's just another football game. You just get on with it and at the end of the game just hope that when you look over you see your fans celebrating.'

Sunderland went into the Boro game hopeful of securing their first back-to-back victories of the season. That would have pushed them back towards the top half of the table. But, just as the Spurs victory presaged a false dawn, the triumph over Reading was to signal an even worse run for the Wearsiders.

For the opening and closing couple of minutes of the Boro game, Sunderland were irresistible, Leadbitter's determined opener and Miller's spectacular closer earning the Black Cats a valuable Premier League away point. It was the eighty-six minutes in between that caused concern. Sunderland were inexplicably ragged for long periods and at times hanging on as Boro's classy midfield and solid defence dominated. Only Sunderland's never-say-die spirit and a moment of Miller brilliance avoided a third away defeat in four. 'We got away with it,' was Keane's view of a game brimful of incident and commitment from both teams.

Keane hoped to name an unchanged team for a third game but, with a Nosworthy knee injury persisting, Halford came in at right back and McShane reverted to central defence. Boro included former Sunderland hero Julio Arca in midfield and the Argentinean endured the most extreme of games, being at fault for one goal, scoring another and then being stretchered off with a bad injury, all before the half-hour was up. It was Arca who conceded possession to the bullish Leadbitter with barely a minute gone, and the Sunderland man drove forward into the Boro half before passing to Chopra in front of him on the edge of the area. There was a touch of good fortune about Chopra deflecting the ball into the path of his teammate, who had continued his run, but there was nothing fluky about Leadbitter's finish on the edge of the six-yard box, slotting a cool left-foot shot across and under Mark Schwarzer from left of goal.

Leadbitter celebrated provocatively in front of the Boro fans before posting a clenched-fist salute to the Sunderland supporters at the opposite end of the pitch. Wearside supporters loved it. A local hero had scored in the Tees-Wear derby. Boro came back firing on all cylinders and Sunderland couldn't settle. 'From the moment we scored to the moment they scored, we were never in control,' said Keane. 'We needed someone to put a foot on the ball and string a few passes together but we didn't have the Premiership experience to do that, and they did.'

Julio Arca, given the warmest of receptions by appreciative Sunderland fans before the game, started and finished the move that levelled the game on the quarter-hour, passing the ball out to Gary O'Neil on the right before ghosting in to meet the winger's cross at the far post with a powerful header, which went down and in as Gordon clutched at the ball at the base of his right-hand post. The most skilful player seen in a Sunderland shirt in the 21st century was as good as his prematch word that he would not celebrate if he scored against his former club. It was a move that endeared Arca even more to the Sunderland faithful, with whom he shared a special bond, but it was to be his last meaningful contribution of the afternoon. He was badly injured in a challenge with Yorke and was stretchered off in the 27th minute, joining teammate Tuncay Sanli in the treatment room – the striker having suffered a suspected broken leg in the tenth minute.

Although the Wearsiders created half-chances, Boro's grip on the midfield tightened and what looked like being the defining moment came in the 68th minute when Stuart Downing took a crossfield ball from George Boateng, cut in from the left and smashed a shot from twenty-five yards out which swerved in the air and beat Gordon. The trajectory of the ball could not have been easy to judge but Gordon had had a strangely unconvincing game and Downing's shot did not make him look any better – flying into the goalkeeper's goal just a couple of yards left of centre.

That looked to be end of story for Sunderland before Miller's late, late strike.

The midfielder – introduced before the hour for the injured Etuhu – had been largely anonymous but took centre-stage a minute from full-time when he scored a special goal. Jones and Boro centre-half David Wheater went up for a ball on the edge of the Boro area and it bounced back, twenty yards out, to Miller who chested it forwards, moved on to it and smashed a left-foot shot which spiralled into the very top right-hand corner of Mark Schwarzer's goal. It was a strike worthy of pulling any game out of the fire, and all the more dramatic for arriving so late.

Miller's heroics that day typified the contributions of so many players in Sunderland's season. Miller, Chopra, Murphy, Stokes, Leadbitter, McShane would all make match-winning contributions in games. But as young players and young players especially who were inexperienced at this level, they would struggle for consistency. The manager spoke a lot about bedding players in at this stage, but that unpredictability was to prove a frustration to him throughout the season. And one of the manager's difficulties must have been in calculating which players just weren't up to the challenge and which ones were merely raw, needing only encouragement and experience.

Keane praised his team's fighting qualities and Miller's great finish in the wake of the hard-fought draw. But it wasn't fooling him that his players were anything but fortunate. 'It was a brilliant strike, no getting away from it, but I think that was the only way we were going to get back into the game. It was probably written in the stars that Arca would score against us – just like John did for us against Birmingham City.'

As Gareth Southgate sat down to begin his post match press conference he knocked a glass of water over himself. It was that kind of afternoon for the Boro manager, a second bad start to the day. He was philosophical about the spilt water, and the lost points.

Keane had received the first red card of his career for stamping on Southgate in an FA Cup semi-final but that was long since water under the bridge and the two fledgling managers had developed a friendship in the north-east. Southgate had naturally wanted his team to win, but he hadn't let regional rivalry obscure his sense of perspective and the two young managers were to prove helpful to each other in a difficult season for both.

Gordon was criticised for his performance, but his deputy Ward refused to rock the boat. Sunderland's purchase of the Scottish international goalkeeper was tough luck on the experienced and consistent Ward, a mainstay of the team during promotion. While he struggled to hide his disappointment at not starting games, he made the right noises.

'We've had a tough start but I think we've come through it

reasonably well,' he reflected. 'It was great we came up trumps against Reading because that game showed we could really compete. The manager has strengthened the squad by bringing in a lot of players, but he needed to because we have been tested straight away with injury. A lot of the players who have been playing for us in the Championship have still had an early chance to stake a claim this season, because of injury, and obviously that's good for them, but it looks like I'll have to wait a bit longer. With Craig coming on board and the club spending that amount of cash, you naturally expect he's going to get a run in the side and a chance to stake his claim. All I can do is bide my time.'

Edwards had admitted that he thought Sunderland's next game – the home match against Blackburn Rovers – would come too soon for him but, in the event, quite a few more games were to come too soon for him. The twenty-eight-year-old had pulled up with a pain in the back of his leg during a routine training session. One of the most affable guys in the Sunderland squad, his preseason had been ruined by a series of niggling injuries. This was now his third setback. The injury was such a blow because he offered qualities which simply could not be replaced within the current squad. One player does not make a team, but he was one player who could make a difference. While Edwards' loss was a singular setback, Sunderland found themselves with other problems. £1 million summer signing Anderson joined fellow centre half Stan Varga on the treatment table, the Scottish international being sidelined for three months with ankle trouble. Injuries just kept piling up and were beginning to expose early gaps in the squad in terms of quality and quantity.

Keane had suggested, after the Middlesbrough game, that the Teessiders' superior experience and nous had proved the undoing of his young and evolving team. And that was to prove doubly true in the case of the Wearsiders' next opponents, Blackburn Rovers.

For the limitations of Keane's squad were ruthlessly exposed by one of the Premier League's most underrated but effective teams. Sunderland fielded £25 million worth of recent signings but never really imposed themselves, and Keane's best player on the day cost nothing – Academy graduate Leadbitter. Blackburn came, saw, conquered and only looked under pressure in the final half-hour when they began to sit back and defend a two-goal lead. Virtually all over the pitch, Sunderland were marginally less accomplished than their opponents and eventually it showed. From the whistle, Rovers looked the classier outfit, full of ideas and movement, though at the end of a frantic first half it was Sunderland who had the better chances. Leadbitter looked the player most likely to get something for his team. He had a shot deflected wide on 12 minutes and also produced Sunderland's first shot on target on the half-hour, a well-driven effort from outside the area, which Brad Friedel saved smartly.

Despite Blackburn's possession they created little of note before the break and Sunderland came out strongly in the second-half. When their workrate eased Rovers made them pay with two goals in as many minutes. In the 53rd minute, Roque Santa Cruz – Rovers' big money signing of the summer at a mere £3.5 million – picked up possession 40 yards out in the left-hand channel and, crucially, was allowed to make ground unchallenged until he reached the area and had a shot at goal. The ball struck the hands of Higginbotham. Before anyone could appeal for a penalty it dropped to the feet of David Bentley directly in front of goal. The England man made no mistake.

It was a shock to the system for Sunderland. Then they conceded another. If the first goal was a collective failure to close down Roque Santa Cruz, the second came from an individual error – Higginbotham's. The centre half's backpass to Gordon was under-hit. Brett Emerton raced in to seize possession, crash a shot against the Sunderland goalkeeper and then headed the rebound across to the unmarked Roque Santa Cruz who stabbed the ball home from ten yards. Sunderland raised their game and the rest of the match saw the home team enjoying the upper hand, but Rovers' two goals proved enough. When Leadbitter scored in the final minute it was no more than a consolation, the midfielder settling himself perfectly to drive a right-foot shot around Friedel into the bottom left corner of the goalkeeper's goal from the edge of the area.

It was a salutary lesson for Sunderland, illustrating just how difficult a season they faced when 'middle-tier' teams like Rovers could be so accomplished – the Lancashire club hadn't lost on the road in six months. When he was a Manchester United player, Keane's philosophy for testing away games against modest opposition was always the same – get in, do the job, get out. In this game, Keane's former Old Trafford teammate Mark

Hughes had taken precisely the same approach to Sunderland. 'It's always a difficult place to come, the Stadium of Light,' said Hughes, 'and you have to keep the crowd quiet because they need very little encouragement to get right behind their team. But we had good angles to our passing, got good players in good areas and caused Sunderland problems.'

He had words of consolation for his old teammate.

'Roy has done fantastically well, but it's more difficult in the Premier League,' he said. 'I think he is building something here but it takes time. I'm in my fourth season at Blackburn and I've been lucky enough to have a chance to improve the squad season on season. I'm enjoying the benefit of that continuity and I think it showed a few times against Sunderland.'

Intriguingly, Keane, for once saw a different game to the vast majority of Sunderland fans. The manager thought his players' performances worthy of a point at least, though most supporters did not. 'The first-half was very interesting, two good teams, evenly matched and I didn't have a problem with it,' he said. 'Then came the second-half and when you go two goals behind, it's always going to be hard. When you are 1-0 down – with our record of getting something out of games late on, and especially with us being at home – you think we might still go on to win the game, so the second goal was the killer goal. But even having said that, if we'd had an extra five or ten minutes after getting one back, we might still have got something out of it.'

Keane said he wanted his players to learn from these experiences. 'It's still a new team and it takes time,' he said. 'It's not me making excuses, but you hope you learn faster from defeats. This was an example of an experienced Premiership team coming to our ground and doing a good job. I would never take away the fact that we are very attack-minded and like to go forward but we got one or two lessons about when to play and when not to play – especially after we conceded the first goal. That was an important five or ten minutes to say, "Look, there's plenty of time to get something out of the game, let's calm down, clear our heads and look to build again". Two very bad bits of defending have cost us dearly. We might have got away with it in the Championship. Possibly. But you do tend to get punished straight away for bad defending at the higher level.'

As he considered ways of improving on one win from nine games, Keane was eyeing his reserves for reinforcements,

Connolly, Murphy, Stokes, Halford, Harte, O'Donovan all getting run-outs in the second-string match that followed the Rovers defeat.

Nosworthy, meanwhile, had received more recognition of his progress under Keane with his elevation to the Jamaican international squad. Since converting Nosworthy to a centre half in the previous season, the player had made huge strides and his partnership with on-loan Evans from January to May had been the bedrock of that final promotion charge. Former boss Mick McCarthy, who had originally brought him to the club, had moaned that he had also wanted to deploy Nosworthy at centre half but the player just hadn't fancied it. 'I think Roy Keane's powers of persuasion must be greater than mine,' he'd said with a half-smile.

Nosworthy, himself, said he felt there was no way he could turn Keane down. 'He's someone you have to respect,' the London-born defender said. 'Like your granddad. When he comes into the room you just go quiet and sit and listen.'

Nosworthy's new Reggae Boyz status did not cut across his season, but his manager was aware that challenges might lie ahead with players like Edwards and Jones also vulnerable to Caribbean call-ups. While he was pleased to have an increasing number of internationals in his squad he was not envisaging them becoming regular globetrotters.

'We are delighted Nyron has been recognised,' said Keane. 'He has done extremely well. But we are looking at these things, the same as Dickson Etuhu for Nigeria. Any friendly internationals on the other side of the planet, we have to talk about those.'

Sunderland's next game was against Arsenal, a fixture that brought the presence of Keane in Sunderland to the fore. The London club had been so significant in defining his playing career, and now the ex-Man United captain was returning as a manager. Since taking over as Sunderland boss he had been reluctant to talk about his playing days. But he found himself unable to resist dipping into the memory banks when it came to Arsenal. Some thought he would inherit the same abrasive approach to the Arsenal manager as his old boss Sir Alex Ferguson had on occasions, but nothing could be further from the truth.

'Arsene Wenger is someone you have to respect,' said Keane. 'The job he has done at Arsenal has been absolutely fantastic.

94

To build a great team takes something but to build several great teams is a different thing altogether. People talk about all these great young players that Arsenal keep producing but it's not a coincidence. They're not plucking them out of nowhere. He's developed a great scouting system.'

Given his passion for beating Arsenal as a player, some might have been surprised to hear Keane waxing lyrical about a team and a manager who used to be top of his hit-list to beat. 'Personally,' Keane said, 'I never bought into the grudge side of things. It was just brilliant rivalry, absolutely brilliant rivalry. I think it enthralled a lot of people but let me tell you, it enthralled us, the players. We loved it. If we could have played Arsenal every week we would have done, and I'm sure they would have too. Because that's where you've got to be at your best and that's where top players really come to the fore, when you know you have to be at the ready. I loved playing Arsenal. It was always my favourite game, way ahead of anybody else. People used to speak about Liverpool and Man City but give me Arsenal any day of the week. The hype used to build up during the week of the game, at a time when the teams were very close to each other at the top of the table. You couldn't have got a better mix between the two teams and their desire to beat each other.

'You look at the rivalries around now and it's nowhere near the Arsenal against Manchester United rivalry then. I think it was because they were so finally balanced and there were characters in both teams. It was brilliant. I think you'll live a long, long time before you see rivalry between the players and the managers like you had then,' he enthused, his mind almost drifting. 'Highbury was a brilliant place to go. The fans on top of you, baying for blood. I loved it. The pitch was nice and tight, there were plenty of tackles flying in and there was a great rivalry. It was always the game for me. Give me Arsenal any day of the week.

'That was when I was a player of course!'

It was a testing time for Keane, yet there were moments of levity. In the run-up to the game, one national newspaper had insisted David Beckham was on his way to Sunderland. 'David Mackem' was the memorable headline. These sort of left-field tales happen from time to time. They come out of nowhere, cause a brief feeding frenzy and then tend to disappear as quickly as they arrived. The story was ludicrous, but part of the job of a local newspaper is to address every ludicrous story.

'When is he due to arrive,' I asked Keane. 'Is he already here?' Keane just smiled.

'I take it he's not coming then.'

'No.' The one-word answer was all he needed to say on the subject.

Keane marvelled at some of the claims made in the media about possible targets, reflecting that the club had been linked with dozens and dozens of players over the summer. One which proved half-accurate was Teddy Sheringham.

'Teddy?' whistled the Sunderland boss. 'No for this season. Yes for last season. I was interested then.' Then the smile again. 'Teddy has obviously been talking.'

That was one of the things press men had grown to like about Keane at Sunderland. Straight questions tended to get straight answers. He was never going to be your best mate, but he wasn't going to duck issues or fudge answers. It was an exceptionally newsy period but the story that intrigued me most appeared the Sunday after Sunderland's game against Blackburn. It was the revelation in a Sunday newspaper that the telephones of Quinn's predecessor as Sunderland chairman, Bob Murray, had allegedly been bugged during 1995-96, the implication in the story being that someone in the Newcastle United boardroom was involved. Gathering sensitive information on Sunderland's proposed plans to build the Stadium of Light had been part of the mission, according to the bug planter, who had now come forward over a decade later and claimed that the phones of the chairman of the Tyne and Wear Development Corporation had also been bugged. The chairman of the development corporation had indeed been bugged. He'd gone on the record at the time to confirm it. I contacted Bob Murray's PR at the time of rumour in 1995.

'Would they co-operate with a story,' I'd asked.

They considered it, then quietly declined to get involved. Understandably for them, but disappointingly for me, they did not want to be dragged into the murky business, and it was impossible to progress it from there. But the story reminded me of a time when the Stadium of Light was far from a done deal.

Bob Murray, who was Sunderland chairman from 1986 to 1993 and then 1995 to 2006, will always be associated in some fans' minds with the clip from the TV documentary Premier Passions – a fly-on-the-wall account of Sunderland's 1996-97 relegation season – where he is shown evaluating the quality of the new stadium's taps. Had Sunderland stayed up that season – and manager Peter Reid got them forty points we have to remember – Bob Murray might well have been viewed as the most meticulous of chairman; an assiduous man, scrupulous in his attention to the fine print; a cunning chairman who appreciated that the devil is in the detail. But the club went down that season, to the anguish of all fans who had put their faith in Peter Reid, and, in the hail of recriminations which followed, the tap episode was viewed as a spectacular symbol of a latter-day Nero, fiddling while his Rome burned. It was unfair, as all caricatures are.

Life is far more complex than knee-jerk portrayals, but those are the images that football and the modern media thrives on. It seemed to me that 'taps' would always define Bob Murray – phone or faucet – but I think history will eventually be kinder to him. His passion for Sunderland Football Club was undeniable, although there was little doubt in the minds of many fans that his inability to provide the funds needed for Peter Reid at crucial junctures helped undermine the club's only previous chance of becoming a Premier League force.

That is an argument Bob Murray would disagree with. Either way, there was no doubting that in the closing years of his chairmanship, he presided over a club becoming more and more detached from its fans. It was a rift that had become all but irreparable by the end of his twenty years in charge. It was an estrangement, a hurt, which Quinn had devoted a huge part of his chairmanship to healing.

Quinn, though, was the first to acknowledge the debt owed to Bob Murray for his vision in constructing the Stadium of Light. Quinn, the player, felt the millions of pounds spent on establishing the Academy should, at the time, have gone to strengthening Peter Reid's squad. Quinn, the chairman, now acknowledges that the quality of the Academy itself is a real selling point for quality new signings.

In previous years, vice-chairman John Fickling would order that potential star signings arriving at Newcastle airport should be driven, unawares, beyond Sunderland to Durham City, with its beautiful castle and cathedral, before doubling back to Sunderland's out-dated training ground with its portable out-buildings. The manoeuvre gave the best possible impression of the area. Now there was no need for such creativity. New players went straight to the glittering Stadium of Light and the impressive Academy, and that was enough.

Bob Murray's only concession to his own contribution to the Stadium of Light was to have the metal railings that surround the main entrance named the Murray Gates – far less grandiose than those chairmen who have named entire stands after themselves. Although it was a good day for Sunderland Football Club when its longest-ever serving chairman eventually left and passed the club on to Quinn and his backers to take it forward, it is wrong that he remains regarded by many as a pariah. He is still connected with the club, working with the charitable foundation he set up.

Years after the ground was built, I bumped into retired Sunderland Echo editor Andy Hughes in the stadium car park before a game – my first editor at the paper and an old-style journalist, who prided himself on being frighteningly firm but scrupulously fair – and remembered that he had thrown his weight fully behind Bob Murray's vision of the new stadium, when its fate had hung in the balance. It was a decision Bob Murray never forgot. He regarded the paper's stance and support as critical to the stadium being built. It's just about forgotten now but the council vote to allow the stadium construction to go ahead only went through by a narrow margin. It all hung on that.

Many Sunderland fans favoured staying at Roker Park – myself included at the time, as a young news reporter. That way, the club could maintain its history and tradition. It was an emotional stance. Now, from the vantage point of history, it can be seen that the Roker Park diehards got it wrong. The Stadium of Light – ten years old in Keane's first season in the Premier League – was the engine room which would give the club the chance to kick on towards a new era of success. Bob Murray had seen it through when its construction had been far from a sure thing. It achieved no less than ushering Sunderland Football Club into the modern era.

Bob Murray, like Peter Reid, will remain a controversial character among fans for years to come, although Quinn has been anxious to get Sunderland fans to appreciate the contributions of both his former manager and chairman. Gratitude and appreciation are not words often associated with football but Bob Murray's ultimate contribution to the club was undeniable and those who stand at the Stadium of Light and ask what he ever did for the club, should recall the tribute to Sir Christopher Wren at St Paul's. 'If you would see his monument, look around'.

It spelled the end for Roker Park, of course, and the great ground's passing was mourned. But the Stadium of Light quite literally provided foundations on which Quinn and the consortium could build. Initially its capacity was 42,000 but it was soon increased to 48,000 as Peter Reid took the club forward. It is designed in such a way that extension was relatively easy in construction terms. The next step would be to take it up to 55,000, and it is capable of going much higher. Quinn has already said that he would like Sunderland to gain the success needed to begin that process. But the ways in which unfolding events can be affected by the slightest of things was hinted at by that alleged bug tap. There was a time when the new stadium's fate genuinely hung in the balance, but Bob Murray's determination, and the platform of brief stability provided by Peter Reid, had seen it through.

Times move on. Northumbria Police said that it was uncertain whether it would respond to the bugging allegations. Newcastle said they were linked to a previous board of directors and nothing to do with them now. Amazingly, a story that would have blown north-east football apart at the time was simply allowed to sink back into the mud a decade later, with barely a murmur made.

Eyes instead were focused on the now and the new emerging of Whitehead's progress. The captain, taking his first steps towards a return to football, was good news for Keane. A fully-fit Whitehead covered acres in games and was always at the top end of the ratings provided by ProZone equipment. Though he wasn't an eye-catching player, he was a ruthlessly effective one – something which he had shown in the Championship when he drove the club to promotion. And it said much for his ability that he was one of the very few players that Premier League clubs came looking for when Sunderland went down. Quinn did not look back on his own brief spell in management with much joy, but one of the things he was proud of was that, in the wake of Sunderland's fifteen point demotion, Whitehead had been persuaded to stay when Premier League clubs were circling.

'Dean is due to do a bit of light jogging,' Keane told us. 'Light jogging!' he emphasised when he saw the press reaction. 'Don't be reporting he's ready for anything yet. It's a psychological thing, he's on the training ground and moving again. Great news for Deano because I keep saying he's a very important player to us.'

Keane was delighted with Whitehead's progress but his attention at the time was fully focused on the match against Arsenal.

He knew going into the Gunners game it would be an uneven battle, but he wanted his players to learn from the experience, just as he had in his own playing days. 'I'm looking forward to going to the Emirates because I've never been before,' he said. 'I want my players to look forward to it as well because these are the games you've got to enjoy playing in the Premier League.'

The players stayed positive going into the game against the free-scoring league leaders. Gordon, fresh from helping Scotland beat mighty France, caught the mood when he said, 'No team has a God-given right to win any football match'.

But it was his manager who unintentionally sucked up all the headlines once again with a characteristically honest appraisal of the modern-day game. 'I think the game is changing and it's probably a lot colder,' he reflected in the prematch press conference, comparing past rivalries with current competition.

He had laughed when he talked about 'fantastic, brilliant' clashes with Patrick Vieira. Now he looked sad. 'Football is not the game I knew ten years ago. That goes for every club. It's changing and it's sad to see. It's lost its soul and it is definitely for the worse. Maybe it's up to the managers to change it. Players' characters are different, I know people will say it is rich coming from me but every time they're touched they go down. Football is supposed to be a tough physical game. No one begrudges the top players getting a few bob but when you see average players getting a fortune and driving the big cars, people start to ask questions. I think there are players playing in the game these days who don't love football. You might think that's amazing but it's true. Maybe they've had it too easy.'

Football, he said, had become worryingly predictable, with the same four teams at the top; too much money to average players, and gamesmanship rife. Keane also had words for the Football Association of Ireland, wondering why Miller's international prospects weren't better.

'What's holding back Liam Miller is the fact he's from Cork,' he said. 'People think I'm crazy but that will definitely go against him. People don't know the FAI as well as I do. If he was from further up the country, I'm pretty sure he would be in the team. It happened to me when I was seventeen or eighteen years of age, being in squads but not getting a game while the lads a year younger from Dublin did.'

The Premier League might have become moribund, the players more cynical, the financial excess more obvious but Keane speaking his mind certainly added colour and controversy to it. Right now, though, there was a game to be played and it would serve up a tale of the entirely expected, a predictable away-defeat.

When Highbury was going down, so were Sunderland. For the first season the Black Cats were in the Championship, fans headed into London via Kings Cross, eyeing the fabulous structure of the new ground while they were doomed to head off to Selhurst Park or Unfashionable Roots Hall. Sunderland's travelling support had looked forward to the trip to the new Arsenal ground since the start of the season. Even when Highbury was crumbling and dilapidated, it still had a certain cachet. It possessed, even at that late stage, a sense of its own worth.

The fabled marbled halls I'd heard about didn't particularly impress me. I stumbled across them once while I was looking for players to interview after a match and was surprised by how modestly proportioned they were. I had expected a huge marbled arch, an awe-inspiring chamber. It was more an ante-room, somewhat gloomy. The Stadium of Light's marbled entrance was larger. Arsenal's reputation, though, stemmed from a time when other grounds simply did not aspire to marbled entrances and there was always an undeniable air of gravitas about Highbury, from the uniformed greeters on the doors, to the helpfulness of the staff.

The Emirates was on a completely different plane all together. A space-age stadium for the 21st century in which attention to every detail had been paid. Yet it still retained that Highbury class. It's not very often that you go through the entrance to a stadium and find yourself in an underpass. A road runs through the interior of the stadium, which you have to cross to get into the next sanctum. Crossing the road, I saw Arsenal's team bus –

the deserted roadway allows them an untroubled disembarking – but I regretted the fact that fans would not be able to see them get off the bus. I also felt the dark tinted windows separating the players from the outside world were an unnecessary touch. Football losing its soul? Across the road, into the next section of the stadium and the uniformed member of staff is still there to greet you; ours looked like John Gielgud and spoke in similar tones as he steered us into the press room – a veritable Shangri La.

Carlsberg don't do press rooms but, if they did, this would be it. It was the size of a Heathrow terminal with desk after desk stretching as far as the eye could see. All facilities were ultra-modern. It had its own food hall and bar; even the outside of paper cups were covered in mocked-up newspaper cuttings celebrating Arsenal triumphs. Attention to detail. Wherever he was in the building, I'm sure Keane was impressed.

Outside were soft foam seats, plug points, telephone points, telephone screens and a fabulously impressive red and white bowl of a stadium. Setting their radio equipment for kick-off, Simon Crabtree and Gary Rowell, Nick Barnes and Gary Bennett, were all suitably impressed.

The night Chelsea had parted company with Jose Mouriniho Arsenal had been playing, and the national writers were at the Emirates when the news broke. No problem, said the Arsenal staff. Not only did they keep the press room open to 1 p.m., they supplied refreshments for journalists as they completed their stories. A touch of class on their part. Arsenal were still setting the standards off the pitch and, as Sunderland were to discover, were still setting them on the pitch too. It was a high-noon kick-off and the Gunners came out shooting on sight.

Arsene Wenger's team never looked in danger of losing the match, despite the apparent closeness of the 3-2 scoreline. Their possession, passing and predatory instincts were so superior the only real surprise was that Sunderland weren't on the receiving end of a rout. Arsenal did what they've always done in recent memory against Sunderland, race to an early lead, take their foot off the gas and just when it looked as if they might be caught out, step up a gear and cruise classily over the line.

Yet that summary does not quite do justice to Sunderland's sheer defiance, for the way they withstood an onslaught and came within ten minutes of snatching a point from the league leaders in their own backyard. Keane's team scored twice against the Premier League pacesetters – a feat only Manchester United would emulate at the Emirates that season.

Keane opted for a 4-5-1 formation in a bid to contain the most free-scoring team in the country, although Sunderland's starting eleven remained unchanged from the Blackburn Rovers game. The line-up was designed to give the Black Cats the best possible chance of being hard to break down but they looked as though they would be swept away within minutes of the start.

Although Sunderland kicked off, Emanuel Adebayor whistled a shot over Gordon's bar within sixty seconds, and within seven minutes the visitors were behind. Leadbitter was penalised for barging Cesc Fabregas in the 'D' and Robin van Persie arrowed a rocket in off Gordon's crossbar from the free-kick. Was the shot unstoppable? Should Gordon have done better from a shot which went in off the crossbar just above his head? Probably not, given its speed and power. But what was beyond doubt was the quality of the strike, quality Arsenal were to show time after time over the course of the ninety minutes.

The Gunners doubled their lead fourteen minutes in when Jones failed to clear a corner, and Adebayor's ball into the box was scooped home by Philippe Senderos past an unsighted Gordon. Three weeks previously, Derby County had been walloped 5-0 at the Emirates and this game looked to be going exactly the same way. In the press box, Sunderland press officer Louise Wanless got a text from chief executive Peter Walker.

'If we leave now, we should be able to catch the 12:30.'

It was the sort of gallows humour that nervous Sunderland fans in the far corner of the ground would have appreciated.

Arsenal should have been 3-0 up six minutes later when Alexander Hleb crossed from the right for Vassiriki Diaby to score at the far post, only for the goal to be flagged offside. Had that perfectly good goal been allowed to stand, Sunderland might have been staring down the barrel of a smoking gun. As it was they made the most of the reprieve by pulling a goal back through Wallace five minutes later. A raking forward ball from the impressive Yorke was drilled forty yards on to the chest of Jones on the edge of the Arsenal area, the striker taking it down beautifully. Though his shot was beaten out by Manuel Almunia, the rebound fell to the Scot who adeptly switched the ball from right foot to left before smacking a low shot home from fifteen yards. Incredibly, Sunderland might even have levelled within sixty seconds, Miller seeing a fine shot from an almost identical position saved by Manuel Almunia at the base of his left-hand post. It would be unfair to say Arsenal were rocked by Sunderland's resistance but certainly they lost their momentum before half-time, with Gordon in excellent form. And within a few minutes of the restart Arsenal were stunned to find themselves on level terms. Sunderland equalised with a simple move when Miller and Wallace were allowed to exchange passes on the left flank. Miller swung in a cross. Jones rose, eight yards out, to head down and in. Manuel Almunia got a glove to it but Jones was off celebrating with somersaults in front of ecstatic Sunderland fans.

Cancel that train.

Sunderland almost got a third just before the hour when Leadbitter forced a great save from Manuel Almunia down at his near post.

'We're gonna win 3-2,' chanted the Sunderland fans.

The game turned with the introduction of Theo Walcott just before the hour. His pace and energy made all the difference to an Arsenal team running out of ideas and steam. Sunderland had a let off in the 57th minute when centre half Kolo Toure crashed a thunderous shot off Gordon's right upright from fully thirty-five yards out, but most of Arsenal's good work was done closer in. There were thrilling goalmouth scrambles in the minutes that followed. In the last quarter-of-an-hour Nosworthy – an Arsenal fan as a boy – pulled off a terrific clearance from a Theo Walcott cross. Sunderland lay on the ropes and hung on grimly as Arsenal launched raid after raid. Just when it looked as though Keane's men might hold out for a draw, just as the home fans, Arsene Wenger and his own players were threatening to lose their collective rags, the Gunners grabbed the matchwinner. Theo Walcott's good work on the right found Robin van Persie in the centre and the Dutchman controlled and dispatched the ball in the blink of an eye. Gordon got a glove to it.

Sunderland tried to hit back immediately, Stokes and Miller forcing saves from Manuel Almunia but it was to no avail. At the death, McShane saw straight red for an ill-judged lunge on Alexander Hleb, which left the midfielder writhing in pain. Now it was the Arsenal supporters turn to tease.

'Just like your manager,' they cooed as McShane left the pitch and Arsenal queued up to disassemble the ten men with Cesc Fabregas, Emanuel Adebayor and Theo Walcott all having golden opportunities to extend the lead but passing them up.

Defeat at Arsenal reinforced the lesson handed out to Sunderland in the preceding losses to Liverpool and Manchester United; that the elite teams of the Premier League were in a class of their own.

That wasn't fresh news to Keane who pointed out, 'Arsenal are a top team and if you don't start well it can be a long afternoon. When you go two goals down quickly you fear it could be six, seven or eight.'

The manager was satisfied with the way his players competed, in the middle of the park especially. 'Miller and Leadbitter as individuals were outstanding,' he said. 'I thought Liam was terrific. That's what he's capable of. But to be a top player you have to do it week in week out and that's what we've spoken to him about. If he's doing that against them, he shouldn't just be in the Irish squad, he should be in the team!

'It must have been a great game to watch for the neutral. There were plenty of shots, a sending off, five goals and plenty of saves but I only enjoyed it when I thought we might get something out of it.'

Keane had spoken about football losing its soul and Arsene Wenger took up that theme afterwards, pointing out that this game at least was a great advert for football. 'I know what Roy Keane has said and we have said similar things ourselves in recent times. But this game was a really good game of football and it showed that his team and my team have not lost their souls.'

By now, the Sunderland manager had become fed up with the way he was being portrayed in sections of the national media. He was offering frank, if controversial, opinions. He was doing it calmly and eloquently. But, too often, his words were coming across as though he had been foaming at the mouth when making his points. Keane rarely 'talked' in the tabloids. It was usually 'raged', 'blasted' or 'in his latest rant'.

He had been manager of Sunderland for more than a year and never once had I seen him rant or rage. Truth was, Keane had never lost the plot in any of his press conferences, local or national. But the typical perception of him among many neutrals across the land remained that of the vein-bulging captain, or manager at war with the world, and it was an image that some national papers were happy to pander to. Whatever quotes were sent down south, it was the easiest thing for national sports desks to stick a provocative headline on them and use a photograph of a raging Keane to complete the effect.

'Does it bother you?' I asked, 'The way you are being portrayed?'

His reply was a philosophical shrug. The way of the world. Keane had accepted long ago that it was a waste of valuable time and energy to worry too much about the millions of words written about him, positive or negative. But his entry into management had seen a sea change in his approach to the game, a sea change that had been coming even before he hung up his boots. Now it had come to a head.

He might accept occasional transgressions on their part but he would not tolerate being made a parody of his former self. He was trying to achieve something for himself and for Sunderland Football Club, and he would not allow his misrepresentation to become an issue which could affect both. Prior to the West Ham game, he made his point.

He waited until the usual prematch press conference had run its course, then calmly, and in measured tones, Keane said he would not have the trend continuing. That if this was how he was going to be treated, they would get shorter press conferences and bog-standard answers. One journalist attempted to fight his corner, explaining that it was sports editors rather than beat journalists who were to blame but he was instantly silenced.

This was not to be a discussion. It was a point being made. A shot across the bows.

You wonder sometimes how much these things percolate into the consciousness of the public. The sports media, like football itself, is an iceberg. At any one moment, only a tenth of it can be seen above the surface.

A similar thing had happened earlier in the season when the physio's reports on injured players had disappeared from the club's match-day programme. The manager had been unhappy about how much information was coming out about player injuries when he had not sanctioned their release into the public domain – particularly when stories were circulating about players having pain-killing injections or being out for lengths of time. The physio notes were one of the casualties of that decision to keep more information in-house.

This had been an issue long before Keane's arrival. Peter Reid had been incandescent at one reporter who had made mention of a knee injury which centre half Richard Ord had been playing through. The manager fumed that rival clubs might see that report and choose to target one of his key players. It's amazing sometimes how seemingly innocuous stories can cause most offence.

Fans wondered about the disappearance of those injury updates, scratched their heads for a moment, then moved on without question or complaint. A large raft of information had just gone from their view and it had hardly registered. This is the way that patterns in the media subtly shift.

Keane's intervention had the desired effect.

Almost overnight, those rants, rages and blasts of Keane's disappeared from the national sports pages but, like much that happens in the media, did anyone out there really take that in on a conscious level? Reading between the lines is sometimes the hardest art to master when it comes to the sports pages. The manager had got his message over very effectively. Giving good quotes that led to good stories in the media came naturally to him. He was just speaking his mind and he rarely regretted anything he said, no matter what the rest of the world thought about it. He was happy to stir things up when the moment suited. But don't disrespect him by trying to lampoon him.

While the media might have proved an irritation, infinitely more important to him than the off-field distractions were the on-field issues. Far more frustrating for the manager was the defeat at West Ham in the club's next match, when a point or maybe three should have been taken by the Wearsiders. It was an unseized opportunity to pull clear of the relegation zone. All the more galling because, going into the game, Sunderland's squad was stretched to the limit – only sixteen fit players available – yet they performed so manfully on the night.

The game gave one player a welcome opportunity to return.

Halford, his red-card suspension over, spoke of getting his 'last chance', centre half McShane having been used in four of the five games since Luton in Halford's right-back role. Chopra, surprisingly, was dropped for the game which followed. Whether that had anything to do with his appearance in OK! Magazine, which hit the stands at the time, was doubtful, but interesting nevertheless. Keane had talked, when he first got the Sunderland manager's job, about his loathing of such celebrity articles and the young striker had admitted his heart had sank when the manager made his views clear in print earlier in the season. 'I was worried about what he would think,' said Chopra, 'but the deal was already done before I read what he said. I've not spoken to him about it but the lads have been full of it.'

Just days after Keane insisted Sunderland cut out the sloppy goals, his team conceded arguably the worst of all at Upton Park. Ironically, they were the closest they'd been to a first away win of the season before pushing the self-destruct button. It was a match lost by Sunderland rather than won by West Ham.

The Hammers got off to the perfect start in the 8th minute when striker Carlton Cole clumsily side-headed a cross home from eight yards out with Gordon becalmed on his line and the Black Cats' defence static. The teams were evenly matched up to the break, both looking positive in possession.

But Hammers boss Alan Curbishley admitted, 'going in at half-time, 1-0 up, I felt comfortable we'd risen to the challenge of breaking down Sunderland's 4-5-1 formation and I was looking forward to the second-half.'

Keane shook Curbishley out of that comfort zone by overhauling his team with a double substitution on the game's resumption, Chopra and Stokes replacing Wallace and O'Donovan in a switch to 4-4-2 as the Wearsiders went on the offensive. It paid immediate dividends with Jones producing a prodigious leap to nod home a Leadbitter corner in the 51st minute. From there on in, Sunderland enjoyed a spell of ascendancy that saw Leadbitter involved in the pivotal moment of the game when he was on the end of a fine move. He showed marvellous technique to set himself for a volley on the edge of the area, which looked goal all the way, only for Robert Green to somehow fingertip the rocket onto the crossbar. Had that gone in, it would have been hard to see Sunderland drawing the match, let alone losing it. The Black Cats remained dominant, Halford having his best game for the club so far, whipping in good crosses. One found Jones who was inches wide with a 73rd minute header. Minutes earlier Mark Noble had hacked clear an Etuhu header with Robert Green beaten.

Within seconds of Jones' miss, though, West Ham regained the lead. Sunderland lost possession needlessly high up the field and failed to get it back before it reached Luis Boa Morte on the left of Gordon's goal. Halford was unable to stop the cross, Nosworthy mis-kicked his clearance, Higginbotham and Collins were nowhere near the loose ball and Nolberto Solano drove a shot goalwards. It struck the base of Gordon's left-hand post, bounced back out, struck the goalkeeper's leg and rebounded into goal. With Leadbitter's strike and Gordon's goal, Sunderland had been taught a woodwork lesson of the cruellest kind.

Keane looked on in disbelief, not so much by the fluke nature of the goal, but the slackness that had led to its concession. He had reckoned that four of the last five goals conceded going into the West Ham game were preventable. While each of those goals might have been down to a slip here, or a miscontrol there, the killer goal Sunderland conceded against the Hammers was the result of up to half-a-dozen individual errors between the Black Cats first losing possession and the ball crossing the line.

Sunderland tried to hit back but finished with a whimper rather than a bang and it must have been painful for their fans to see ex-Magpie Craig Bellamy apply the coup de grace in the 92nd minute when he got on the end of a Luis Boa Morte cross. For Etuhu, who had played for Nigeria against Mexico days earlier and returned to the dressing room to find he had been robbed of his personal possessions, it must have felt like being mugged twice in a week.

Reflecting on a scoreline which did not reflect the game, Curbishley said: 'We were under pressure a little bit in the second half but we broke and scored, broke and scored again, and sometimes that's the way it goes. I'll take the three points because we haven't had much luck ourselves in our last three games – games which could have been victories ended as three defeats. Jones scored an equaliser and brought them right back into the game, but Green made a match-winning save and that's why he's in contention for England.'

In contrast to Curbishley's easy demeanour a stone-faced Keane refused to accept the gentle full-toss questions lobbed his way afterwards. He was dismissive of the 'unlucky Roy' or 'can you believe you lost that game, Roy?' approach from the assembled media.

'You have to give credit to their goalkeeper for a great save but the word "annoyed" would be an understatement to describe how I feel,' he said. 'This was probably the best we've played this season away from home, but it's a similar scenario to the Arsenal game when we were praised but lost the match. I'm not interested in the plaudits. It's points we need. I'm paid to win football matches and regardless of how well we play in spells, we are not doing it at the moment.'

The one bright spot for Sunderland was the towering performance of Jones. 'He's getting fitter and stronger,' said his manager, 'and he's going to be a big player for us between now and the end of the season.'

Another was Halford's contribution. His statistics were superior to his opposite number Lucas Neill. 'Neill's a Premiership full back,' Halford said. 'How I measure myself is in how I shape up compared to the other full back, so I'm quite happy with the results.'

Halford had been Keane's first signing of the summer, a move Quinn remarked could prove to be one of his most successful. Halford had been unplayable against the Wearsiders in the Championship when Colchester United came to the Stadium of Light. Along with Southampton's Gareth Bale, their performances were head and shoulders above every young player in that division that season. Keane had apparently lured him to the Stadium of Light with the inducement that he could develop into England's right back, but he had not looked anything like that sort of player all season. When he was good – which was occasionally – he was very good. When he was bad, he was frightening.

'I feel as though I'm getting back to my normal self now and the confidence is growing,' he said after the West Ham game. 'I'm pleased that I'm coming on because I'm desperate to succeed at the club.'

Keane was supportive. 'Maybe we should just relax and give Greg a little more time. Some players settle in straight away at a club and other players take time. People should remember that when he joined the club he was only twenty-two years of age after a very disappointing time at Reading and he's come to be part of a team which hasn't been settled because of all the injuries and suspensions we've had.'

Those injuries continued. Chiefly Edwards, who was out for at least another three weeks with a fresh hamstring strain. With the squad under strain, Quinn announced that the board were determined to strengthen Keane's hand when the transfer window opened in January. 'I will try to do everything I can to make sure he gets the signatures he wants,' said the chairman. 'Player recruitment is everything.'

Going into their last game in October, the match against Fulham, Sunderland had won just one in ten and were lying in 16th place, but Higginbotham, who had been relegated from the top flight twice before with different clubs, insisted the atmosphere around Sunderland was different.

'There was a negative vibe at Derby and Southampton when I was with them,' he said. 'Relegation felt like it was on the cards. I don't get that feeling here.'

A survey carried out by a telephone company and published the day before Sunderland's next game revealed the Wearsiders had the loudest fans in the Premier League. Fulham the quietest. The average volume recorded at the Stadium of Light was 129.2 decibels – about as loud as a jet aircraft. That statistic supported the claims to greatness all Sunderland fans grow up with, stretching back to the early days of the fabled Roker Roar. During this game, though, there were times when a measly 330 Fulham supporters outsang a crowd 100 times that number – Black Cats fans stunned into near silence by their heroes' first-half fumblings. It was a candidate for one of the poorest forty-five minutes from a Sunderland team under Keane. They were lucky to go in at half-time only one down – David Healy missed an open goal – and it could have been curtains in the second-half had an early Diomansy Kamara goal not been somewhat generously ruled out.

Inconsistent Halford was red-carded late in the game. His second sending off in just seven appearances. But, against the odds, Jones grabbed an equaliser five minutes from time and Stokes might have nicked all three points in time added on had he made the most of a wonderful opening.

Experience was in short supply in Keane's team and on this occasion it showed. Only the normally reliable Higginbotham in the starting eleven could boast more than fifty Premier League appearances. Even that proved to be no guarantee of grace under pressure. Fulham finally made the most of the opportunities that were coming their way in the 32nd minute when they earned a free-kick thirty yards out and left of target. Specialist taker Simon Davies went for goal with an effort which flew into Gordon's top right-hand corner. It was a strike of wonderful accuracy but it came from a long way out and had to go down as a goalkeeping error, the goalkeeper flat-footed when the ball came in. It looked as if Gordon assumed Simon Davies would put a cross into the crowded penalty box rather than go directly for goal. It was not the best way for the young Scot to celebrate the 150th league appearance of his career in a season when many home fans remained unconvinced that he would become the world-class goalkeeper everyone hoped for. The soft goal did nothing to either lift the home team's confidence or the supporters' spirits and having expected so much, the fans booed Keane's men off at the break for the first time in the season.

'I was nearly booing myself,' smiled Keane wanly afterwards. 'It's unrealistic to think if you play badly you'll get applauded off the pitch. That'll never change.'

The minds of Sunderland's players were focused by a forcefully critical, but constructive, half-time team talk and they started the second half with the sort of purpose they had needed in the first. Jones signalled his intent with two speculative but positive shots inside the opening couple of minutes and within five minutes of the restart Sunderland fans were back on board, cheering the team to the rafters.

Then Sunderland looked undone by the events of the 67th and 69th minutes. First Halford was sent off for a tug of David Healy's shirt, his second bookable offence of the afternoon. Then Diomansy Kamara scored. Surprisingly, the striker's goal was disallowed, the referee ruling Diomansy Kamara had challenged Nosworthy unfairly. And bizarrely, Sunderland went on to play better with ten men than they had with eleven.

They tore into Fulham and in the 70th minute Leadbitter's sweetly struck volley from a Jones lob was denied only by a brilliant Antti Niemi stop – the second time in consecutive games that a wondersave had thwarted a Leadbitter thunderbolt. It was a sign of things to come. Leadbitter, in the left-hand channel, hoisted a teasing cross goalwards in the 85th minute and Jones rose to power home a header from eight yards out – the striker's fourth goal in six games – becoming the first Sunderland player to score in consecutive top-flight games since yesterday's hero Kevin Phillips in 2002.

On the night, the battling, against-the-odds performance won a point. In the long run it had to be seen as two points dropped. The return of key players couldn't come soon enough for Sunderland. If the fans felt disappointment, Keane didn't share it.

'It was a game of two halves but the players were different class second-half,' he said. 'It was a strange day but I suppose if you are 1-0 down with fifteen minutes to go and you're down to ten men then you've got to see it as a point gained. I was glad to get them in at half-time. I don't know if the players were so happy – but we needed to make points to them. We need to start better. When you start slow in the Premiership, it's not like a light switch, you can't just switch it on, and we suffered because of that.'

Keane would consider how to revive his stuttering team for the games that lay ahead, firstly examining his training schedules because he was beginning to suspect they might be responsible for his team's sluggish starts and some of their injury problems.

'Maybe we have to look at the intensity of our training, the tackling and the pace because we could be doing too much and leaving our best stuff on the training ground. I'm not so much talking about easing down. Maybe we're staying out too long. Other managers have sessions shorter but just as intense. Stuart Pearce was up during the week at our training ground and he was surprised by the intensity of it, and if Stuart Pearce is surprised then maybe we need to look at it again.'

Certainly there was no getting away from the fact that Sunderland's most intensive and longest training sessions of the season were also to coincide with their spell of poorest results and most injuries. Keane had a lot on his mind at this stage, for things just weren't panning out in the way that he had hoped in preseason. Sunderland weren't winning the games they should have won, weren't drawing the games they might have drawn. Every point on the board had been won in wars of attrition. And they were too close to the drop zone for comfort. Injuries had taken their toll, inexperience cost points and the revamped squad was yet to fully gel.

It was a testing time for any newly promoted manager – just one win in twelve – and this would be the point when most managers would be using their contacts in the media to get the right message across, explain developments, spread calm. This had not been Keane's way, although he had never been in this position before. He wasn't going to change though. In an interview given before the Manchester City game on Bonfire Night, he had perfectly encapsulated his stance.

'It's important to take the media with a pinch of salt, whether you're the manager of England, Sunderland, Manchester United or Barcelona,' he said. 'If you're winning, things are great. If you're not, you get criticised. Take it with a pinch of salt. Don't get carried away either way. A lot of managers bring it on themselves, becoming pals with the media. They have their mates here and there and all the top managers seem to have their pals they look after. If things aren't going well, they call on them to do a nice piece with them. They need to be careful.

'Trust no one. Trust none of the media and you'll be okay.'

It was hardly heart-warming stuff, especially for local journalists to whom club relationships are traditionally most important. It might be news to some, but not every reporter is a Prince of Darkness or a soul-sucking Dementor. I've got footballers who are friends I've never let down. Even the occasional manager happily takes a phone call.

Keane's stance should have been depressing for local reporters and yet, in a way, it was not. Everyone knew that Keane was a unique character in the game. He had been a one-off as a player and it looked as though he was going to be a one-off as a manager. Unconsciously, we accepted one rule for him and the one rule we would have preferred for everyone else.

In the run-up to the following press conference, the conversation between local journalists about Keane's approach to the media was light-hearted. It concluded with the universal agreement that if Keane was at the Stadium of Light for five years or ten years, he would never address a journalist by their name and never acknowledge a journalist as an individual. Before that West Ham game he had refused to get into a discussion with an individual reporter and we knew and agreed that that would always be the way.

At which point, Keane walked unannounced into the Academy press room and immediately said to me, 'I didn't like your match report.'

So unexpected was it to be addressed personally that I didn't know what to say. 'Sorry?' I queried.

'Your match report. On the Fulham game. It was harsh. All of it.'

For a moment I knew exactly how those tongue-tied radio reporters had felt in preseason.

'I ... er ... I thought my West Ham report was harsher,' I offered.

'You want to be careful,' he said. 'A lot of people will read what you write.'

'I'll ... er ... I'll take it on board,' I said.

'I don't care what you do,' he replied.

That was it. A curtain had been raised for an instant and then we were back into our usual interview mode.

The Sunderland Echo is usually about as supportive of the club as any local paper could be, and maybe the manager felt he really could have done with its backing right then. Certainly, the Fulham match could have been reported either way. A heroic fight back by ten men. Or a fortunate point seized from the jaws of what should have been a crushing home defeat.

For those of us who had lived through the 19 point and 15 point Premier League seasons, the performance in the first hour against Fulham was the sort of display that had brought on those relegations. The local media were criticised in those seasons by supporters for not doing their duty and ringing the alarm bells sooner or being more outspoken. While the Echo aims to be supportive, it's not there purely as a cheerleader. I felt I was doing my duty in the way I reported the shortcomings, but it taught me an important lesson about Keane the manager – a lesson that the nationals had learned a week earlier. He might not want to lie down with the media but he certainly wasn't ignoring it either.

If the manager was unhappy with my report, he wasn't too impressed with Lawrie Sanchez's comments about the game either. Occasionally, during his time in charge, Keane came in and gave a generous nod to the opposition but then felt other managers weren't gracious enough in their comments in return. The Fulham game was such an occasion.

'There was only one team that should have won the game or ever looked as though it was going to win the game,' fumed Sanchez. 'The result depressed me, really depressed me. Jones's goal was the only one he got on the end of all day, wasn't it?'

Keane, felt those comments too, were harsh. His ten men had

fought back and shown tremendous resolve. He felt it was wrong that that was being overlooked.

Jones, by this stage, was rumoured to be interesting Rafa Benitez at Liverpool and, whether that was true or not, he was certainly making a name for himself with his ability to hang in the air on crosses. That was unsurprising, given he was a former schoolboy high jumper. His teammates too were constantly trying to 'lift him'.

'We're always trying to get Kenwyne up for games,' said Chopra, 'because he's at his best when he's riled. He'll just be walking around the dressing room with his big earphones on listening to his music. But when we get him going, he's unbelievable, he can be the best in the league.'

Higginbotham, who knew the striker when the two were at Southampton, agreed. 'He's always had the talent but he was raw there. He's come on in leaps and bounds and there's no comparison to his performances between Southampton and Sunderland.'

Jones' form was a boost but injury problems continued to hamper Sunderland and once again they had only sixteen fit players going into their next game.

The match against Manchester City, early in the week, was always going to be a difficult one for Keane's team, injuries or not, given the fact that the Blues had won every home game under Sven-Goran Eriksson. But the disappointment for Sunderland was that, like West Ham previously, they should have got something out of it on the night.

Eriksson's men weren't at the races in the first-half. They dug in though and ground out a win thanks to the one moment of genuine attacking class in the match – Darius Vassell's twist and cross followed by Stephen Ireland's sweetly struck volley in the 68th minute.

For long spells the home team were second best to a Sunderland team, which edged possession but lacked a cutting edge, a failing not lost on managers David Moyes and Sam Allardyce watching hawkishly in the stands. With centre half Richard Dunne superbly marshalling Jones, Sunderland couldn't break down the defences of a team that had conceded only twice at home by early November.

The game offered a first start for former Leeds United left back, the thirty-year-old Harte, who had feared his chance of joining

Sunderland had disappeared the previous year when a proposed move from Spanish club Levante had broken down.

'Roy wanted me to come across when he first got the job,' said Harte, 'and I wanted to come as well, but the club in Spain were looking for a hell of a lot of money and Sunderland weren't willing to pay that amount. I had one year left on my contract but I wasn't particularly happy at Levante so we came to an agreement and here I am.'

While thirty was hardly ancient, there weren't too many players at a club who could claim they had been teammates of both the manager and the chairman!

Just after the half-hour Keane approached the touchline to a cacophony of boos from the blue half of Manchester as he sought to inject greater discipline into his team. Murphy would head Martin Petrov's corner off the goal-line four minutes later. The hour approached with Sunderland under more pressure, but a rejuvenated Collins was superb in the heart of defence heading out one cross after another. Twenty months ago to the day, Collins had had a nightmare at the Eastlands Stadium, being at fault for the first goal in a 2-1 defeat, which cost Mick McCarthy his job forty-eight hours later, but he wiped away the memory of that night with his best performance of the season so far.

It did not go unnoticed by Keane.

'Danny Collins has pleased me with his reaction. There were a few games where he trained with the reserves and I spoke to him about one or two options that might be available. But he has worked hard and done very well when he's been given a chance. His attitude and spirit has never been in doubt.'

Sunderland went in at half-time feeling reasonably satisfied with their efforts. It was only the second time that Keane's men had finished a first half goalless on their travels. The previous time was also in Manchester, against United. But just as the introduction of a new striker had been key to the defining moment of the game, when Louis Saha came on at Old Trafford, Darius Vassell was an immediate substitution for City at the start of the second-half, and he went on to set up Ireland. The win gave City their best home start to a season in over a century and left the Wearsiders still searching for an away win while Keane considered a run of eleven games without a clean sheet.

Watching manager Sam Allardyce would have been encouraged

by the way Jones was comparatively neutralised and the fact his teammates were unable to find a goal threat. Both Keane and Allardyce desperately needed a victory at this stage of the campaign, and the Tyne-Wear derby game next up had now taken on a significance beyond its local importance.

Keane meanwhile was struggling to cope with the performances of his team and critical of his own. 'We've lost another game and it's not good enough,' he said. 'It's all the more disappointing because Manchester City weren't as good on the night as they'd been recently and we could have got something out of it. But we've felt that about a few games now and come away with nothing from them as well. The bottom line is that we've had thirteen games this season and won just two of them and it's up to me to do better. I didn't feel there was that much between the two teams – we felt the same against Blackburn Rovers and West Ham United – but we ended up losing those games too. There's a fine line between success and failure in this league.'

Keane felt improvements would come when the senior players returned and with Cole and Edwards having a run out for the reserves, and Whitehead and Richardson making steady progress, ahead of the derby game against Newcastle, he was hopeful. On the quiet, Sunderland's youngsters were having a cracking season and they combined with Edwards and Cole to slaughter local team Wolviston 8-0 in the Durham County Challenge Cup at Eppleton's Colliery Welfare Ground. Cole and Edwards finally hit the comeback trail. When they exited to warm applause after an hour, their team were a magnificent seven goals up. Although Edwards in particular oozed class and Cole showed some nice touches, this was a night when the potential of Sunderland's youth shone. There were eye-catching performances from winger Nathan Luscombe and striker Martyn Waghorn in particular. Afterwards, Edwards, who had spent just a week in full training, suggested he was ready to play in the derby if he got the call from his manager.

'I've had no reaction to the injury and hopefully that's the way it will be from now until the end of the season,' he said.

As far as Sunderland and Newcastle were concerned, it had been largely a season of disappointment so far for both clubs – players and managers – the Wearsiders hovering just above the relegation zone, the Tynesiders having fallen away to mid-table.

Often in the Premier League it had been the first derby game of the campaign that had turned one club's season around and plunged the other's into crisis. 'Big Sam' had finally got the big stage he craved and, swapping Bolton for Newcastle, was now in a position to compete with the elite in the game. The previous summer he'd had the chance of taking over at Quinn's newly acquired Sunderland and was within a whisker of taking up the offer (the Echo was within hours of announcing his arrival, the story written). Instead he got cold feet at the very last moment. He appreciated the size and potential of the club he once played for and the ambition of Quinn's consortium, but felt it was too big a risk dropping down to the foot of the Championship. It was a challenge though that the untried Keane would not sidestep.

At Newcastle United, Sam Allardyce was given an instant opportunity to mix it with the top four. The purse strings were opened and proven players Mark Viduka, Alan Smith and Joey Barton joined him at St James's Park. As with Sunderland, consistency became Newcastle's problem, much to the fury of the Magpies' notoriously demanding support and, having made an early exit in the League Cup to Arsenal's young guns, their fading league form had left Tyneside fans simmering with discontent. Nine miles away on Wearside there was excitement about the prospect of Cole or Edwards playing. But the stage seemed set for Chopra to make his mark on a game everyone was anticipating – he had scored two goals in a 4-1 scoreline at the Stadium of Light in his last derby game – Sunderland fans would love him to repeat the feat in their colours. The north-east derby is special because unlike other top-division clashes in Liverpool, Manchester and London, this is not a battle between two clubs sharing the same city and community. It is a confrontation between two independent, proud cities on each others' doorsteps. Only a short distance separates the two cities but the gulf between their sporting allegiances could not be wider.

Chairman Quinn understood the lure of the rivalry. 'When the fixture list came out, they were the first games I looked for,' he admitted. 'I've played in Manchester and London derbies but the Sunderland v Newcastle derby is something else. There's something a bit magical about this one. The place goes gaga for a few weeks beforehand and, depending on how you've done, if you win, it stays that way, while the place where they've lost goes, well, a little bit depressed for a while. It's just immense. The first time we beat Newcastle over there and Ruud Gullit was the manager, I couldn't believe the aftermath. People were writing songs about it! You just thought, this is so important to the people.

'Fans at a lot of clubs at the start of the season would be looking first for the visits of the Liverpools, Arsenals and Manchester Uniteds. Obviously those games are massive for our fans too but Sunderland supporters look straight away for the home game to Newcastle and then the away game to Newcastle, and I'm sure it's not too different for Newcastle fans either. I'm proud we have Tyne-Wear derbies again this season. Hopefully we'll have them regularly from now on and have them in the top flight because we want these particular fixtures to get bigger and bigger, and for them to really start making an impact nationally as well as locally.'

The scene was set for Chopra, not least after England striker Peter Beardsley, a Tyneside derby hero, described him as the best young player he'd ever coached. He had rightly predicted Chopra would score the Premier League's first goal of the season and Beardsley was expecting a special performance from him in this game. In the event, Chopra was to flash one great chance wide and hit the bar with a header in the dying minutes, with goalkeeper Steve Harper beaten. That would have been the winner, which would have given the youngster a special place in Wearside folklore. He was denied by the width of a post which whipped the ball down into the six-yard box and, somehow, away to safety.

Keane bought into the tribal nature of the fixture. 'It was made clear to the me the moment I arrived at the club what this fixture means,' he said. 'People articulate it in different ways. Sometimes you're told "you just have to beat them" or "make sure you beat that lot". Other times, it's more aggressive than that. And that's just the directors!

'The people in the cities don't like each other and this is a chance for all that to come out. I understand it. I always have done. People mentioned this game to me on the first morning I arrived when the two clubs were a division apart.'

Match day was a decade to the day since the Duke of York had officially opened the Stadium of Light but more than thirty years since silverware came to Tyneside or Wearside. Yet success, or lack of it, seemed to have no bearing on the massive crowds either club could command for this fixture. The stadium was a 48,000 sell-out, just as the return fixture would strain St James's Park to bursting point. The intensity of the crowd experience on Wearside on the day was inspiring. Outrageously, it had been twenty-seven years since Sunderland last beat Newcastle on home soil, and they rarely had a better chance to best their hated rivals than in this match. Keane's Sunderland were on a mission from the start, and for so much of the game Allardyce's team were on the ropes yet somehow emerged with a draw. Newcastle managed only one decent goal attempt all game. They scored from it. To increase the sense of injustice, it was a fluke. James Milner's inswinging cross from the left in the 65th minute deceived McShane in the heart of Sunderland's defence and flashed in off the base of the far post with Gordon a spectator.

Sunderland by contrast carved out a string of chances. Wallace spurned one great early opportunity and Leadbitter and Chopra could have had two each before half-time. In the end they had to settle for just the one goal – a sweetly dispatched Higginbotham header, a dozen minutes before James Milner's leveller. Relieved and pleased, Newcastle fans celebrated at the game's end.

'Worst team in history, you're just the worst team in history,' they chanted, a reference to the 15 point debacle.

They knew they'd got away with it, yet in the cold light of day, it was Sunderland fans who might have been happier.

Keane's team had faced a team full of proven Premier League performers – Michael Owen, Mark Viduka, Alan Smith, Joey Barton, Charles N'Zogbia, Belozoglu Emre, James Milner – and were the better team.

All this from a team with half its players rookies to the Premier League. Keane had brought back Edwards, who could have been no more than eighty percent fit. And Sunderland had to cope with the loss of captain Nosworthy midway through the first half, which sent left back Harte to right back for the remainder of the game. Leadbitter took the captain's armband after Nosworthy's exit and gave a captain's performance in the game he most wanted to win. As a local lad with a fierce love for Sunderland and a dislike of Newcastle, Leadbitter put in a Trojan effort. It was clear before the opening whistle just how fired up he was. When the teams moved down each others' lines before kick-off, shaking hands, he was the only player looking only at United's football boots. Nothing was going to distract from his focus. England U21 manager Stuart Pearce had been up to the Sunderland training ground during the week, and selected him for international recognition.

'I think Grant's deserved it,' Keane said. 'Anything that happens in our team, Grant's probably in the thick of things. When I first arrived I wasn't sure whether to keep him or not but I'm glad we did because he's got something.'

Sunderland had not won the derby, despite one of the very best home performances they would produce all season. They hadn't won one either home or away since 2000. But for the first time in seven years fans could come into work the next week feeling the prouder of the efforts of their team and secure in the knowledge that they had been the better team. Keane entered the press room still shaking his head over United's equaliser, 'a freak goal' Gordon called it.

'I've seen the goal once,' said Keane. 'That's enough. We should have finished better in the first half and Kenwyne Jones had a chance at the end but if you don't hit the target you're never going to win a bloody game.

'Newcastle will be disappointed with their performances because of the quality they've got, but by the law of averages they're going to create something and we are going to have to learn quickly that we have to take our chances when we are on top.

'I'm glad that we didn't lose the game though. I know this game means a lot to people. Over the last couple of days, I've felt that in my bones. I sensed it when I was driving up, taking in the atmosphere. These games mean so much to Sunderland and Newcastle fans and I could see that inside and outside the ground.

'It's my first time as a manager in this derby and you sense the tension and the excitement in the build up to the game. It's actually a lot easier to play in the derby than to manage in one because you can affect the game so much more when you are on the pitch. But it's great to be involved in a game like this in any capacity because it is such a passionate occasion. I've seen a lot of derbies in my time. This one didn't disappoint me, put it that way.'

Keane felt it was rawness and inexperience which was holding

Sunderland back after the loss of key players. He was trying to bring them on by his own example on the training pitch. Midfielder Etuhu enthused about his manager's playing skill.

'He still shows he is great in training,' said the Nigerian. 'He absolutely controls the midfield and shows how well he could do if he was still playing and fit. He still runs it, still appeals for everything. You don't really want to be in his team though because, if you are, he canes you all the time. He never stops ordering you about and shouting and talking and encouraging. If you're playing against him, you're in for a hard time. He just lets the ball go at the perfect time, every time. I haven't seen anyone try to nail him yet – but would you?'

Etuhu's statement touched on the fact that, well over a year after his retirement, Keane still looked no different physically to the player who had so dominated the stage for years as a player in the Premier League. Put a strip on him, put him out on the Stadium of Light turf and it would be the Keane of old. People who meet him face-to-face tend to remark on the fact that, first, he is so lean and, second, he's not six foot four inches – they tend to expect a giant character to be reflected in a giant physique. The only concession to Father Time is when he allows a beard to grow and it comes through flecked with grey. But a clean-shaven Keane is indistinguishable now from the person who strutted his stuff at Old Trafford, and it certainly helped maintain that aura of charisma and authority. He would try to give his players the benefit of those qualities.

In the meantime though, the manager's young squad was learning the hard way that more nous was needed. There was a knack to be mastered in carving out and holding onto Premier League points.

In the wake of a derby Sunderland had dominated, and should have won, Keane was left to reflect on the fact that only a little more composure in front of goal denied his team the three points they deserved. 'The disappointing aspect of our previous game against Manchester City was we didn't create chances,' he said. 'Against Newcastle, we created them but didn't take them. I'm pleased with the way we reacted when we conceded. I was thinking to myself "come on, lads, show me what you've got" and that's exactly what they did, so I think they are learning all the time. But what we really needed was someone to put their foot on the ball and slow things down when it was necessary, like Didi Hamann did for City against us. We play very naively sometimes. I'm sure people inside the game will say that. We need to be a bit nastier and a bit more streetwise.'

Though the game finished in a draw, there was one clear winner – the derby itself. Keane's presence in the Sunderland dugout and the uncomfortable situation surrounding Allardyce across the way ensured the game's high profile among the media. It was standing-room only in the press room before the game, most of the national writers pre-occupied by the plight of Allardyce and what his position might be should United lose their third game in a row, this time at the home of their bitter local rivals. The global media interest was far higher than could have realistically been expected for a game between two mid-table clubs in mid-November. That worked in favour of Sunderland Football Club, because the club got maximum exposure out of the spectacle.

Quinn hoped it was the shape of things to come. 'I think they are going to be magnificent occasions and if we could somehow get rid of some of the bitterness, which seems to latch itself on this great sporting occasion, then all the better. I love rivalry. I'd love to see us win these games. It would make my year – but I don't need to do it as a thug. I think it can become the leading sports event of the region. The Great North Run organisers might not agree with that but I just think we have the opportunity to make this derby bigger to everyone else.'

If there was to be a harmonious future for the derby, it certainly wasn't the case on the day. The depth of passion and bitterness between the two sets of fans was perfectly expressed when coaches carrying Newcastle supporters arrived at the ground, many of the fans having been drinking in Tyneside pubs since 9 a.m. The contorted faces of hate and rage behind the bus windows resembled a scene from the zombie thriller 28 Days Later. Large sections around the Stadium of Light became no-go areas as the authorities sought to avoid potential trouble.

'You can always tell it's an important game when you see police cordons,' smiled Keane.

The sheer force of noise around the stadium – created by both sets of fans – reached a crescendo when the players walked out through a Remembrance guard of honour posted by the 206 Signal Squadron. The sound and the fury made hairs stand up on the backs of necks. When Higginbotham rose to head past

Steve Harper, decibel levels were deafening and home fans had a fantastic memory from the day. Here was the clearest evidence yet, of what had drawn Quinn, Keane and Sunderland fans together – the knowledge of how big and powerful the club could become again if steered in the right direction. The fans had trusted in Quinn's words and Keane's character and this game suggested that that faith would be more than repaid. To have faced the club in whose shadow they had largely lived for more than a decade and shown signs of emerging from it, gave everyone on the terraces enormous heart.

Quinn had appealed to fans beforehand to enjoy the game and savour the occasion, to revel in the sheer sense of theatre and event. He wanted both sets of fans to appreciate that, while each might be big clubs in their own right, their fierce footballing rivalry, played out at the highest level, could only increase the stature and significance of them both.

The Sunderland manager had made one of his boldest selection decisions of the season when he put Edwards in the starting line-up. Edwards had played one hour's competitive football since he had been sidelined in the first week of the season with a hamstring injury – caused partially by Keane's decision to keep him on for the duration of the game against Birmingham City. It was an eyebrow-raising decision and it paid off. Edwards lasted the ninety minutes with no problems.

'There was lots to consider about Carlos when it came to his selection,' said Keane. 'One of the things I took into account was his body language. He was very positive. He wanted to play. It was still a risk though, and if he had damaged his hamstring it would have backfired. But he had been training for a while and he felt he wanted to play, and with it being a derby we decided we would let him start.'

Although Edwards was not fully fit, he made an instant difference to Sunderland's play. 'You can see what Carlos gives us,' said Keane. 'Width and penetration.'

Nicknamed 'Roadrunner' by his teammates for his pace, Edwards added a new dimension to the team with his speed. Whitehead had first given him the cartoon character tag and Edwards grinned when he said that he had got used to teammates and staff making the 'beep-beep' noise at him in the Academy corridors. Keane had hopes that Whitehead himself would also return soon. He featured in a game against Scottish

Premier League team Falkirk in a testimonial for their long-serving defender Andy Lawrie. The game ended 1-1 – O'Donovan cancelling out a luckless Halford own goal – but from Sunderland's point of view, the game was all about Whitehead's return to competitive football. Less than 100 days after it was feared his season was over, Sunderland's Captain Marvel was back on a football pitch and already setting his eyes on a Premier League return.

Whitehead and Kavanagh, back from his loan spell, were withdrawn after an hour and Cole shortly afterwards on a night of good news for Keane, who watched from the freezing cold sidelines.

'The plan was always that Deano was only going to get about an hour,' said Keane. 'The temptation would have been to leave him on but there's no need to take risks.'

For Keane, though, the news on the recovering injured was not all good. Nosworthy's hamstring tear was a bad one and he was expected to be out for a couple of months.

Whitehead had eased through his comeback game and was set for another quick run-out when Sunderland played Chesterfield in a friendly ahead of the next league game, against Everton. The captain was thrilled to put his cruciate ligament test behind him.

'It was great to be back,' he breathed in relief. 'There hasn't been any reaction in the knee but I didn't really expect there to be any. It's fine and it feels good and I just need to work on my fitness now.'

How long it would be before Whitehead was pushing for a first-team place again remained to be seen. Keane had said that the natural fitness of both Edwards and Whitehead meant they didn't necessarily need four or five warm-up games in the reserves to be ready. Whitehead wasn't sure.

'My injury and Carlos' injuries were totally different. He had a hamstring injury, which meant he was able to do a lot of fitness work, while my knee meant I was wearing a brace for six weeks. I'll just see how it goes but I don't want to rush it.'

The real news for Whitehead was that less than three months since he thought his 2007-08 campaign was over he was back on a playing field again. 'This is just the start really, and it might take me a few games yet to be ready.'

On the eve of the Everton game, the news emerged that Ricky Sbragia, the popular former youth team and then reserve coach at Sunderland was poised to return. He had left Sunderland in the wake of Peter Reid's sacking and gone to Manchester United as youth team coach where his and Keane's paths had crossed. Later he had become first team coach at Bolton Wanderers under Sam Allardyce, but had not enjoyed the regime after the manager's departure to Newcastle. A former centre half, Sbragia was expected to take over the first-team coaching duties at Sunderland and concentrate specifically on defence. If he was watching the very next game, the game against Everton, he could be forgiven for thinking he had a mountain of work ahead of him.

Sunderland's worst result of the season – their worst result for a quarter of a century – lay just around the corner. This was the game where Keane's preseason optimism about gate-crashing the Premier League party finally faded. He realised he did not have the quality in his squad to follow his natural instincts and fight fire with fire when he came up against the classier teams. After this game, the target for the season had now become survival.

Some fans were beginning to worry that only Sunderland could be so unlucky as to have the most charismatic manager in the game, its most articulate chairman and £35 million to spend strengthening a Championship-winning team, only to come up short yet again. But that was the fearful mentality that emerges from seasons of shocking failure and national mockery in the nation's top league. Sunderland fans travelled to Goodison Park more in hope than expectation, for the trip to Everton had not been a happy one for the Wearsiders in recent times. No league win there in a decade, and the scene of a 5-0 drubbing seven years previously.

This game, though, was far worse than they could have expected, a scoreline to equal their worst loss to Everton in 117 years competing the fixture. They were unlucky to come up against one of those teams hitting top form at a time when the Black Cats were struggling for either fluency or a settled line-up.

Sunderland had been boosted by Whitehead's return, even if it was a surprise to see the midfielder deployed at right-back. Yorke, too, was welcomed back to the team after a six-week absence as Keane went for a defensive centre – Etuhu, recently returned from international duty, next to Yorke. The attack-minded right-footed midfielder Leadbitter was asked to do a job on the left. They faced an Everton team who welcomed back inspirational captain Phil Neville, just at a time when they had clicked into top gear with the return of goal-scoring midfielder Tim Cahill on a run of five wins and a draw in their last six games.

Everton started well and raced into an 11th minute lead. McShane offered an air-shot to a mighty Tim Howard goalkick. Powerful striker Ayegbeni Yakubu held off Higginbotham long enough to strike a shot, which hit the Sunderland centre half's leg and bounced down into the turf, over the head of Gordon and just under his crossbar; the unlikeliest of goals. Everton doubled the lead five minutes later. Yakubu found Mikel Arteta on the right-wing with a cushioned header. The Spaniard produced a visionary pass for Phil Neville and the Everton captain turned the ball back across the face of goal where it reached Tim Cahill. The Australian swivelled to drive a shot past Gordon despite having three defenders close to him. Two minutes from the break Steven Pienaar sprinted down the left-channel, set up Nuno Valente, and took the ball back just inside the area. There, he sent it spiralling over and across Gordon with a first-time shot.

Sunderland were not without chances. Yorke pulled a goal back just before half-time, the midfielder rifling home from nine yards after Jones had rolled the ball back into his path. It was Yorke's first Premier League goal in three years. 3-1 at half-time.

Keane had sat with a face like thunder throughout the first-half. He made two immediate changes after the break: Yorke and Etuhu were withdrawn; Collins and Wallace came on; Whitehead and Leadbitter paired up in central midfield while Collins went left-back; Harte right-back with Wallace on the left flank. Sunderland now looked much more like their normal selves and began to take the game to Everton.

The quarter-hour's football they produced after the break was their best of the game but the good work was undone in the 61st minute when a long ball forward by Joseph Yobo reached Tim Cahill whose clever first touch took him past the floundering McShane. The Aussie midfielder rounded Gordon as though he wasn't there and passed into the net.

Sunderland were not out of it completely. Whitehead and Leadbitter immediately fashioned a superb opening for Chopra, only for the striker to contrive one of the misses of the season, sidefooting high and wide from the edge of the six-yard box with the goal at his mercy. That was it – the mountain was just too high to climb. Chopra was withdrawn for Cole to make his first appearance of the season. The veteran produced some nice touches but the goal-scoring threat was to come at the other end as Sunderland's misery deepened into embarrassment with three more goals in the last quarter-hour. Sunderland fans, their team 4-1 down, amused themselves with chants of 'Andy Cole, Andy Cole, Andy, Andy Cole. He gets the ball, he scores a goal – ten years ago' – a cruel, if witty, bastardisation of the Magpie refrain from years past. They also shouted for Connolly to be given a chance but Connolly's time in red and white colours was over. The twin chants revealed something, however. Keane's decision-making was being challenged subtly. Even so, no fans turned on the manager.

Mikel Arteta tormented Harte all afternoon and, even when the left-back was switched to the opposite flank, there was to be no escape. Mikel Arteta was immediately shifted over to continue the torture, as the Irishman failed his Spanish inquisition. He was never to start another game for Sunderland.

It was the Spaniard who helped set up Everton's fifth in the 74th minute, playing in Leon Osman. When his shot was blocked by Gordon, Yakubu was there to make no mistake from eight yards. Substitute Andy Johnson grabbed the sixth when he outpaced McShane to a long ball from Phil Neville, dinking the ball over Gordon. The glut was complete in the 85th minute when Leon Osman won the ball just inside the Sunderland half and waltzed forward unchallenged, glided into the box and dismissed the attentions of three red and white shirts, before contemptuously passing a shot home from six yards out. A wonderful solo effort.

Seven goals reflected one hell of a beating and, but for several Gordon saves, some important defensive blocks and some luckless Everton finishing, Keane's team could have been looking at a far heavier defeat.

'It's difficult to put it into words how hard it is to take,' said Whitehead.

'It hurts like hell,' said Keane.

Sunderland were now preparing for a six-game December and Keane had to remain positive. Leadbitter was a genuine threat in midfield, also Whitehead's best position (now closer to match fitness after the ninety minutes at Goodison Park). Edwards was near full fitness. Wallace, Leadbitter, Whitehead and Edwards were an exciting midfield option now available for the first time since the first week of the season. Cole, it was hoped, could provide genuine competition up front, though Sunderland fans were not so sure.

It was the defence that was the worry. No clean sheet since the first day of the season and more goals conceded away from home than any team in the division, including bottom team Derby County. Nosworthy remained sidelined and the back-four was short of consistency and confidence in front of a goalkeeper who had yet to produce the match-winning performances he was believed capable of.

Problems aplenty and a devastating defeat to come back from.

It was an understandably sombre Keane who entered the press room at Goodison Park. Old-style and at the very top of the ground, the press room is accessed via a narrow staircase. The room itself is cramped and journalists claustrophobically surrounded the Sunderland manager as he sat. He had just spent an hour locked in the dressing room with his players going over the game, an inquest only disturbed by the intervention of the law. A policeman had approached a member of Sunderland's staff.

'We're only paid to be here for an hour after the final whistle, so you wouldn't like to tell Roy Keane to finish up, would you?' he said.

'You're right,' was the response. 'I wouldn't!'

If there had been fire and fury in the changing room, journalists were not to hear about it. 'I believe what is said in there should stay in there,' Keane sighed. He made sure he kept a tight rein on his temper as he went through the unavoidable analysis. 'I think that when you come to grounds like Everton, as good as they are, you have to make sure that you perform well too. I would say of the seven we conceded, we gave four or five goals away. We had belief that we could get back into the game when we were 3-1 down or even when we were 4-1 down and Michael Chopra had a chance which would have made it 4-2. But we didn't do that and we end up with a 7-1 scoreline.'

This was about as bad as it gets in football for any team and Keane was the first to acknowledge the scale of the loss.

'It's a major setback and I won't dress it up as anything else. There's no shying away from it. I take full responsibility and I have to learn from it. Football has a habit of kicking you in the teeth. I've seen that happen at other places but in this game it was my turn. I know that if you didn't have lows, you wouldn't appreciate the highs. But this goes down as a real low though. I hope this is as low as it gets.'

Keane later admitted that he had played the wrong team that day. 'Dickson was on the back of two tough internationals and Dwight hadn't played for a month. We could all learn lessons from it but no one learned lessons more than me. I also allowed us to be too cavalier in the second half and those are things I've taken on board. In the last half-hour of the game we were still charging forward, committing half a dozen players into attack at a time and leaving ourselves exposed at the back. We paid a heavy price for that and, while cavalier football can be great for the fans to watch, it wasn't the right way to go. One thing I do appreciate now is that you can't afford to go away to top teams chasing games and going all out for a win. To lose 7-1 is something that stays with you forever. It will be with me to my dying day and I expect occasionally, I'll have flashbacks to the game. The two days afterwards were difficult. I stayed in bed all weekend and didn't leave the house for forty-eight hours. I'm inexperienced as a manager and that inexperience was shown up.'

By a cruel twist of timing, Whitehead and Nosworthy were presented with their joint North-East Player of the Year award the following night for their part in Sunderland's surge to the Championship title. The duo were given the rare accolade of a joint win by the North-East Football Writers' Association because the region's journalists could not separate the value of their contributions in the title-winning campaign. They received the award at a packed Ramside Hall hotel near Durham, watched by club chairman Quinn – himself a former winner of the honour. The award had been won in the past by players of the stature of Quinn, Kevin Phillips, Thomas Sorensen, Shay Given, Kevin Keegan and Alan Shearer, but it brought little cheer to the Sunderland pair. They talked the talk. 'I've looked at the names of the players who have won this in the past,' monotoned Whitehead, 'and it is a privilege to be counted among their number.' The normally outgoing Nosworthy mumbled. 'It's great to be given this award and I accept it in recognition of what was a great team effort.' Each wore tombstone expressions. The

Everton disaster had punched the hearts out of them. At least it brought a smile out of Keane a few days later though. 'It's bad when you have a night like that following a day like Everton,' he sympathised as the bruises began to heal.

No one had been more badly winded by the result than Keane but he expected his badly-beaten players, like himself, to do some serious soul-searching and come out firing on all cylinders against Derby County. In the first training session after the Everton game he gathered his players around him for a further inquest with a meeting designed to ensure everyone put the game mentally to bed and moved on.

Defeat at Goodison Park dropped Sunderland into the relegation zone for the first time in the season and the game against Derby had taken on a 'must-win' dimension. The manager expected his players to stand up and be counted. 'We have a decent dressing room and the players have to show their desire to go out there and compete for Sunderland,' he said. 'Everyone connected with our club will be hurting but we have to come back and everyone has to take responsibility, myself included. It's a learning curve and the hardest place to learn is the Premiership, because teams like Man City and Blackburn Rovers will take quick advantage of your shortcomings. I've had setbacks in my career but you look to turn it around.'

Keane and his staff spent the week before the Derby game putting in long hours, looking at potential targets, their search given extra urgency by the Everton result. The manager watched Liverpool's Champions League victory over Porto and Sunderland Reserves' 2-0 defeat to Manchester United's second string. His assistant Loughlan watched Celtic in their Champions League tie. Elsewhere, the club's scouts were also on duty.

'You're always on the lookout,' Keane said: 'You look at games and watch games, and often it's just to see how prospective opponents play and set up, but you also look for possible signings as well. You're always looking to gather information at games.'

Potential signings were United's two defenders, Danny Simpson and Jonny Evans, who the manager watched keep a clean sheet against Sunderland reservers. Keane joked, 'It was tempting to throw a blanket over the two of them and try to smuggle them back with us on the bus!'

CHAPTER FOUR

Tough at the Bottom. Tougher at the Top

We need to get away from that close but not quite close enough situation in games. ROSS WALLACE

A NERVE-TESTING set of games lay ahead now, beginning with the visit of Derby County, a team making an impressive stab at Sunderland's record low Premier League totals. Just like Spurs on the opening day, just like Reading, Derby was to produce one of the highlights of Sunderland's season. Like those other victories, the light was a false dawn.

Though it wouldn't win prizes on Match of the Day, Stokes' shot, hooked home from a yard out, would be a contender for Sunderland's Goal of the Season when it came to important strikes. The Irish teenager's 93rd minute goal was priceless in the context of the season. It rescued the Black Cats from a draw that would have left them in the relegation zone for the second week in a row, and facing the visit of Chelsea next. Instead, the Wearsiders went up to 15th in the table. Confidence boosted dramatically. Breathing space won.

Sports journalists – drama junkies all – continually look for the pivotal games. Spurs might have been one. Missed opportunities against Newcastle and West Ham could have represented others. Even from a distance, though, any fool could see the importance of the Derby County match. Everyone knew it, no one more than Keane who made the boldest selection decision of his managerial career.

There were five changes to the team hammered 7-1. The chief of them was Gordon, Sunderland's £9 million goalkeeper, dropped in favour of the experienced Ward. Four months into his Sunderland career, Gordon remained an enigma. He had all the attributes of a top goalkeeper, but had yet to really make them count for Sunderland.

In his day, Keane's former boss Brian Clough had also broken the British transfer record for a goalkeeper when he brought Peter Shilton to Nottingham Forest. Clough reckoned Shilts was worth 12 points a season to his team. By the Shilton yardstick it was difficult to see where Sunderland had gained points from the goalkeeper. The Scottish international's finest games, and he'd had some, had all come in defeats – Manchester United, Liverpool, Arsenal – and Keane decided it was time to pull the young goalkeeper out of the firing line.

The decision showed the manager's pragmatism. When you smash the British transfer record for a goalkeeper the tendency must be to stubbornly stick by them, rather than risk accusations that your judgement might have been flawed. But Ward had been a star goalkeeper in the Championship, and Sunderland v Derby had been a Championship fixture just a few short months ago. Keane knew Gordon's time would come again and he did not want to heap extra pressure on the young goalkeeper's shoulders by playing him in this key game.

Elsewhere there were starts for Wallace and Collins on the left, while two more surprises were the restoration of Halford at right back and a full debut for Cole.

Derby's season was becoming failure personified. One win in fourteen; four straight defeats going into the match; five goals scored all season. They had failed to score away from Pride Park all season and had gone more than 600 minutes since their last Premier League goal. But they were re-energised by the arrival of Paul Jewell as manager in place of Billy Davies and attacked the game positively.

Backed by a crowd of more than 42,000, Sunderland started well, but their desire and domination did not translate into a genuine attacking threat. Goal-scoring chances were limited, but three fell Cole's way, only for the striker to fail each time. In front of the south stand, he dragged a twenty-five-yard shot wide, scooped another chance over the bar and then glanced a header across goal from fifteen yards out.

When the game burst into life, five minutes before the break, it was Sunderland in danger. A slip by Higginbotham allowed Kenny Miller to fire off a snap-shot which saw Ward justify his inclusion. The goalkeeper dived full-length to palm the ball onto his right-hand post and prevent a certain goal. A stunning stop. A couple of minutes later, Whitehead cleared a powerful Steve Howard shot off the line.

Sunderland hit back on the stroke of half-time when County goalkeeper Stephen Bywater pushed a Leadbitter shot out to Jones who drove it against the post from four yards out. The giant striker clasped head in hands in disbelief.

The momentum remained with Derby in the five minutes after the break and they tore into Sunderland, putting Ward's goal under tremendous pressure. Then Sunderland went on to dominate the rest of the game but just couldn't get that break in front of goal. The frustration was typified by a vicious Whitehead shot which was goal all the way, until it struck Chopra eight yards out and deflected wide. Chopra was on just after the hour for the tiring Cole. Keane made full use of his substitutes, bringing on Miller and Stokes for Leadbitter and the injured Edwards but the game reached full-time with Sunderland looking at a goalless draw, which would have left their season approaching crisis.

'In my mind, I'd settled for a point,' said Keane but in the 93rd minute, his team found a way through. Miller flighted a diagonal cross in from the right, which Jones glanced goalwards at the near post. Bywater blocked the effort brilliantly and also got a glove on a follow-up header. But there was nothing he could do, as the ball dropped towards the goal line, to prevent Stokes athletically stretching and hooking the ball high into the roof of the net. His first top-flight goal. His first at the Stadium of Light. From struggling draw to salvation in the space of a second. The fans celebrated wildly as the players went ballistic in front of them. Once again that willingness to go all the way to the final whistle and not let their heads drop had paid off.

Defeat kept Derby on six points. At the same stage of the season Sunderland's worst Premier League team, the 15-pointers, had had five. Their relegation was only a matter of time, with December less than a day old.

For Keane it was a first win in eight games. With three points safely secured, Sunderland could look back in relief and celebrate the performances of Halford and Ward. Halford was Sunderland's man-of-the-match – solid defending, fine passing, great attacking play and quality crossing. Ward had taken his opportunity as well as could possibly have been expected. The thirty-three-year-old had produced the save that kept Sunderland in the game and gone on to help his team to its first clean sheet in fourteen matches. It was a personal triumph for him. After a long and proud career, it was his first appearance in the Premier League. It was uplifting that two of the least vaunted members of the squad should combine to make such a telling contribution. The downside to the victory was the emerging news that Edwards had suffered a leg break in a challenge with Jay McEveley. Once again the winger was to be absent for months to come. Once again the graveyard shift beckoned for a string of reluctant players.

The game thrust Stokes into the limelight, but if he thought his goal would see his praises sung, he was mistaken. Keane knocked him off his pedestal before the youngster could even contemplate climbing onto it. No one quite knew what to make of Stokes, the teenage striker signed from Arsenal almost a year previously. Keane addressed that issue.

'We brought Anthony on as a sub because when you bring him on you never know what you're going to get. That can be a good thing or it can be bad, but against Derby it turned out to be good. He can go as far as he wants in the game but, since the day he signed, I think too much has been expected of him. If he had been at a bigger club he would be getting a game every couple of months and not be in the spotlight so much. Sometimes it's difficult for him, especially when I bring him on out wide all the time, when his preferred position is striker. If we were further up the table he might get more of an opportunity there, but the goal will do him good. He does things in training that very few people can, but there's a lot of people out there who do things in training that they don't take out onto the pitch.'

Stokes was one of those players that, some felt, was in danger of settling into his celebrity status before he had earned it. Keane was anxious the striker did not get ahead of himself and was brutally honest when asked about the nineteen-year-old's qualities and his prospects.

'He's a talent,' said Keane. 'He'll go one of two ways, he'll either realise that potential and be a top, top player, or he'll end up in non-league football. You look at Ryan Giggs. He went the one way and has been a world-class player for years. You look at other players, who I won't name, and they had great ability, but wasted it and ended up with nothing.'

Asked what pitfalls the striker had to avoid, Keane responded with an off-the-cuff remark. 'Well, the obvious one is to stay out of the Glass Spider in Sunderland for a start!'

For those of us wondering how plugged in to the area the manager was, it was a revealing quote. Sunderland's centre of drinking, partying and clubbing shifts through the years from one part of town to another. Where to go to be in the in-place can be as unpredictable as Sunderland's league form. But for the last few years the Glass Spider had been the place to hang out. In the days that followed, the Sunderland-supporting owners would enforce a ban on Stokes. For the sake of the club, they said, loyally.

You could feel for the player whose moment of glory had not worked out as smoothly as he would have expected. Keane was right to make the statement though, because too many players have fallen by the wayside (or the Quayside), in the goldfish bowl of north-east football, believing their own publicity too soon. But Stokes felt bruised by the adverse publicity surrounding the scoring of such an important goal, and Keane admitted the following week he regretted that so much had been made over what was intended as a throwaway remark.

'I wasn't suggesting Anthony has a problem with the booze or the high life,' he said. 'I was just pointing out young professionals have to look after themselves and make the right decisions.'

The manager had wanted attention to focus on the win itself. 'The Derby game itself was a big test for everyone and I'm delighted for everyone here because, after Everton, it was a long bloody week.'

He had been his own biggest critic after Everton. After Derby he allowed himself a quiet pat on the back. 'I had to make changes and I know some players won't be happy with that, but I pick the team. I have to make the call. And the most important job I had was making sure I picked the right team. Sometimes you get it wrong, like I did the other week, and sometimes you get it right, like this time around.

'Am I relieved?' he wondered. 'No, that's not it. I don't know what the right word is. Actually, yeah I do. I'm happy, that's it, happy for myself and everyone connected with Sunderland Football Club. It wasn't a classic game and it looked as though it was going to be one of those days. There were some turning points at the end of the first half: Ward's save, Whitehead's clearance, Jones hitting the post. And when that happens you think it's got a goalless draw written all over it. We probably would have accepted that because, no matter what happened against Everton, it's vital we get something out of the games against the teams which are around us. We should have got something out of the Newcastle United game a couple of weeks ago, but we didn't, and you can't keep letting those games slip by. So there's lots of bonuses, a clean sheet, a win, lads coming back into the team, Stokes scoring, Miller setting him up – lads who probably would have been disappointed not to start the game.

'Leaving Craig Gordon out was a call I had to make. I left Dwight Yorke and Dickson Etuhu out too and people might think that's a reflection on the game before, but it certainly wasn't. I was just trying to freshen things up. I think, with our goalkeeping situation, Craig's been under a lot of pressure on and off the pitch since coming to Sunderland and I have to look at that. He's a young man and I said the day he signed that we shouldn't expect miracles from him. I think missing a few games will do him the world of good, mentally rather than physically.

'I wouldn't blame him for any of the goals at Everton. My keeper was facing one-on-ones time after time in that game. I'm delighted with Craig but I have to look at what's best for him long-term and if that means missing a few games, I guarantee long term he'll feel the benefits.'

Keane also saw signs that the team spirit was starting to take-off again. 'After the win I was looking around the dressing room and saw Dickson and Dwight there, who had been left out. And there was Nyron in the middle of it, who was out injured but as happy as anyone. That's where I study people. And I'm happy for them at least hiding their disappointment at not being involved. That was great because we need that bit of bonding.'

While the Derby County victory might have been a point of satisfaction for Keane, for Ward it was much more – a vindication of his ability at the highest level. He had played hundreds of games, but never one in the top flight. There were times before he joined Sunderland, when he was playing second-fiddle to Robert Green, turning out for Norwich City's reserves team in the Championship, that he thought he never would.

Collins revealed how it felt. 'When I was standing in the tunnel Darren was joking, saying his legs felt like jelly. And he's a keeper who has played more than 500 games! I could understand where he was coming from though, because if you're stuck in that bottom three the pressure can really build up on you. It was such an important game.'

In the days afterwards the goalkeeper's mood was

irrepressible. Northern Irishman Trevor Carson, Sunderland's regular reserve team goalkeeper, said he was 'made up for Darren'.

'He's a great bloke and he hasn't stopped smiling since. He's finally played in the Premiership and he said, after the game, that he could look forward to going home and watching himself on Match of the Day – and he did as well!'

Among the backroom staff, there was a significant shift. Former Arsenal and Aston Villa player Kevin Richardson, the reserve team coach, was released in the reshuffle that marked Sbragia's arrival. It must have been hard for the amiable Richardson to take. The reserve team was top of the league at the time. But he went with good grace and dignity, as Keane continued to remould his backroom team.

At the same time, Quinn, Keane and Walker had held a transfer summit to talk about who might come in and who might leave. Keane had spent hours on the road, putting up with cancelled planes and trains as he made final checks on players. His scouting staff continued to supply reports on potential signings, as news emerged that Reading's Stephen Hunt was a top target.

Cole, meanwhile, hoped that the fact he'd started the Derby game would prove a major boost. 'Getting an hour of Premiership football under my belt will have done me a world of good,' he said. 'At my age it takes a little bit longer for injuries to heal and maybe it takes a little bit longer to get back up to full speed.'

Cole rued the missed opportunities he'd had to add to the 188 goals, which made him the second highest scoring Premier League player. 'That last one was the one which got to me,' he sighed. 'I slipped over just as the ball was coming to me and I know that if I hadn't slipped, I would have scored.'

The disappointment would have been compounded by knowing Sunderland's next game would offer far fewer goal-scoring opportunities. The trip to Stamford Bridge represented the toughest away trip in English football. Keane was not to be allowed to go up against Jose Mourinho, something he'd looked forward to in preseason. Chelsea were still bedding in new manager Avram Grant, who was doing much better than he was generally being given credit for at the time. Avram Grant's pedigree as a manager was nowhere near as special as the

Special One. No matter what qualities he had, the lugubrious Israeli did not go down quite so well with Chelsea fans, or players, who felt they were swapping a Bentley for a Banger. The fifty-two-year-old was winning over supporters with a relentless sequence of good results – seven wins in eight games going into this match to quietly revive Chelsea's title challenge.

Sunderland fans travelled in hope, not expectation, knowing London was the unhappiest of hunting grounds for them in the top flight. The inevitable defeat which lay before them was their 13th straight Premier League reverse in the capital, and statistically went down as probably the most predictable loss of Sunderland's entire campaign. A team that had not won away from home all season, and had not taken a point from any team in the top ten, playing away to a team that had not lost in seventy home games and taken sixteen points from their last eighteen.

Sunderland switched to a 4-5-1 formation.

Chelsea were without the injured Didier Drogba, but the absence of the Blues leading scorer was compensated for by the inclusion of £20 million midfielder Shaun Wright-Phillips, while the presence of Andriy Shevchenko up front meant the Londoners were hardly struggling for a quality front-man to turn to.

The enormity of the task ahead of Sunderland was brought home to them in the opening minutes of the game when Ward's goal was put under relentless siege, but somehow survived the battering. Sunderland defended so deeply that fullbacks Ashley Cole and Juliano Belletti were playing virtually as wingers.

It was Halford's 23rd birthday, but the only happy returns he was getting was the ball perpetually reappearing down his flank. It was from his zone that Chelsea's opening goal came. Juliano Belletti, just inside the Sunderland half, pinged a cross-field ball diagonally to the feet of Salomon Kalou on the left of goal. He crossed beyond Halford's outstretched boot to the head of Andriy Shevchenko at the far post, and the unmarked Ukrainian powered a header past the exposed Ward from six yards out. On the touchline Keane looked askance at Halford for failing to stop the cross. It was to be the right back's last game of the season in Sunderland's stripes.

Jones, an isolated figure up front between England captain John Terry and Rodrigo da Costa (Alex), produced his team's first shot on target in the 33rd minute, which Carlo Cudicini dropped left to save. The first half was so one-sided that Sunderland could only improve in the second, even if that merely meant not letting Chelsea have it entirely their own way. There was an air of inevitability about the Blues' second goal, even though it was fortuitous. Frank Lampard hoisted in a free-kick from the left in the 75th minute. Higginbotham yanked back on the shirt of Alex. Referee Peter Walton pointed to the spot and Lampard blasted his penalty to Ward's left as the goalkeeper went right.

Another dispiriting away day for Sunderland fans and, to make it worse, Miller got sent off in the dying minutes. He fouled John Terry. In the resulting melee he retaliated to a kick in the shins from Claudio Pizzaro by raising his hands to the Italian striker. That brought a three-game suspension.

Results elsewhere conspired to send the Black Cats crashing back into the bottom three again as the three teams below them each recorded unlikely but, in the minds of Sunderland supporters, entirely predictable wins.

Avram Grant said what pleased him most was winning without the players who had been voted World Striker of the Year and World Goalkeeper of the Year the previous week – Didier Drogba and Petr Cech. Keane identified three disappointments in the game: both goals and the sending off.

'There's no doubt that when you raise your hands on a pitch you give the referee little option, but I do feel the whole thing should have been avoided in the first place,' he said. 'Maybe you're not allowed to tackle the England captain because Terry made a lot of the incident and so did Pizzaro. They've come up and had a go at Liam and I don't understand that. Obviously it was a foul but there was no nastiness involved. It was the final minute of the game. Now he's going to miss three games. I just wish the referee had stepped in five seconds earlier because the reaction from Terry and Pizzaro disappointed me and if the referee steps in sooner, the situation doesn't arise.'

Keane was stoical in defeat. 'It was vital we didn't concede in the first fifteen to twenty minutes because then the floodgates could have opened. Chelsea was always a tough game for us, but we know defeats at any of the top four clubs won't make or break our season. It's the games against the teams around us which will define where we end up. There are three leagues in the

Premiership: top, middle and bottom. We know which one we're in at the moment.'

Surveying the mini-leagues, Keane's mind was already turning to the January transfer window. 'I plan to strengthen because it needs doing,' he said. 'We missed out on one or two players in the summer and we have injuries to key players and suspensions as well. So there's no doubt we need new players. But identifying players is easier said than done and, once you've identified who you want, it's not necessarily easy to go out and get them.'

How successful the bottom half-dozen teams were in their efforts to strengthen was likely to be key to the outcome of the rest of the season. 'I think the January transfer business will be important. I'm sure there will be lots of teams near the bottom spending. The big teams seem to spend their money during the summer. It is the teams at the bottom who find their squads really tested and stretched and have to act in January. Maybe a lot of us will be after the same type of player.'

Miller's last-minute red card at Chelsea put an unneeded burden on the injury-hit squad, and the manager was irritated at losing the player so cheaply for the games against Aston Villa, Reading and Manchester United.

'Every sending off can have an element of frustration to it, but this one more than most. It was the last minute of the game. It hadn't been a dirty game. And Liam, yes, he'd raised his hands, but it wasn't like he'd taken a swing at the lad or gone two-footed on anyone. It was the same with Paul McShane at Arsenal. It was the last minute of the game and the game is over, but he ends up missing three games. The referee is literally blowing up for full-time and then that happens. Frustration would be an understatement to describe it, to describe how Liam feels and everyone at the club over it.'

The Irish midfielder was fined over the incident, but the bigger punishment was missing out on games. The game against his old club Manchester United would have loomed large on his horizon. 'We keep reminding players about the price they pay for being sent off,' said Keane, 'and that's something that will come home to Liam. We have had Wallace, who has missed games for taking his shirt off; Halford has been sent off twice; Paul McShane; now Liam. And we're not a dirty or nasty team. Yet we've had these cards against us and Dickson has been suspended too. And it does cost you. It does hurt you being without players, especially when you have injuries too.'

The manager reckoned that Sunderland may have paid the price at Chelsea for their defeat at Everton. 'Maybe we were carrying a few scars,' he said. 'We were a bit too defensive, especially in the first-half but I think you can understand that, considering what went before in our last home game.'

Chopra was hoping he and Sunderland could finish 2007 with a flourish. 'I think we've been a little unlucky, especially with the Everton game when we were 3-1 down at half-time, because we could have sat back, but we went for it and on another day we might have got back into it rather than it going the other way. In the previous game against Newcastle, we went for it and were unlucky in a different way. We were as on top against them as Everton had been against us, but it just wouldn't go in the back of the net on the day. That's all water under the bridge and we've got to look ahead. We have Bolton Wanderers at home this month which is a winnable game and we have Reading away, who we've already beaten once. So hopefully we'll beat them away too and pick up another three points.'

Chopra hoped to give Sunderland a happy Christmas, fully aware that his return of two goals in twelve starts was not good enough for a striker who wanted to make his mark on the Premier League. 'I look back on that Tottenham game on the first day of the season, coming off the bench, and that was fantastic, and I've got to hold on to that feeling and try to use it to drive me on. But I do think that the squad as a whole has been unlucky with injuries. We've been missing good players who create more chances for you and I think that, when we get those players back, it will be a different story. I've appreciated the fans being patient with me, but I am trying. And I have a lot of faith in my ability. I believe I will score goals; and I will score goals for Sunderland.'

Wallace meanwhile, revelling in his Premier League progress, was convinced results would pick up. 'We've played well but not killed games off or not scored, that has been our problem,' he said. 'We have been living with teams and at times dominating, but we haven't been getting the goals and that's doubly disappointing because of the defensive situation where we've not been as tight as we should have been. If we get either aspect of the game right, things change in our favour. If we can get them both right, we'll be as much a threat as we were to teams last season. We need to get away from that close but not quite close enough situation.

'Kenwyne will help make a difference, though. As a winger it's good to be playing with him because it means you just need a yard, and if you can get the ball in the general area, you know Kenwyne's going to get on or near it. It means that you don't have to be quite so precise with your crossing and because of that you can get them in quicker. He's strong, physical and good with his feet and he's going to be a massive player for us.

'Last season we never really got going until Christmas time, and there's no doubt we're going to have to step it up in the second half of this season too; but I think we can.'

Wallace was proved right in one respect. Sunderland would improve generally, but just as they were picking up, fate would deal them a cruel blow with a string of Quixotic refereeing decisions that would keep them in the thick of the relegation battle.

We could say, with absolute certainty, after the game against Aston Villa in mid-December that referee Steve Bennett was off Keane's Christmas card list for life. When Collins rose inside the six-yard box to head home Leadbitter's left-wing corner in the 93rd minute it should have been one of the most romantic and inspiring moments of Sunderland's season. As the defender wheeled away to celebrate his first goal of the season and a 2-1 victory that would have hoisted Sunderland to 15th in the table in front of an ecstatic 43,000 plus crowd, Steve Bennett blew for a perceived foul on goalkeeper Scott Carson. Final score: 1-1. Sunderland 17th.

It shouldn't have been that way.

There wasn't a single appeal from any of Villa's outfield players for a foul and though Keane might have been exaggerating when he said, 'The referee was looking to give things against us all afternoon', you had to question a decision that courted controversy so unnecessarily. Television replays showed it was the wrong call. Ironic that in Sunderland's match day programme Steve Bennett had said that the crucial thing for referees was to get the major decisions right.

Steve Bennett left the field to a malevolent chorus of boos and jeers and was immediately confronted by Keane in the tunnel, the manager still raging at the unfairness of the decision. He angrily accused Bennett of cheating Sunderland fans. In the wake of the game, the club was to extend the quarantine area inside the tunnel, a decision that probably owed much to the public airing of Keane's furious words with the referee. Though he might have been sensitive about his outburst, no one could blame Keane for his anger. The confrontation was understandable, if unedifying, and if Steve Bennett did one thing in Sunderland's favour that day it was to exclude the incident from his match report afterwards.

Away from the controversy of the referee's decision-making – and it was hard to get away from it – Keane was pleased with a defensive performance as resilient as Sunderland had produced all season.

It had been a stern examination. The defence had been bombarded by dozens of crosses and tested to the limits by the pace of Ashley Young and Gabriel Agbonlahor, and had only been breached by Shaun Maloney's brilliance from a free-kick.

'We put Dean Whitehead in at right back and as a unit I think they tightened up well,' said Keane. 'I think there were about fifty or sixty balls into the box they had to cope with in the game. The two Danny's did well – Higginbotham and Collins. There's no questioning these lads' honesty and desire to be players.'

'I always felt we would nick it at the end, and we did. We did nick it at the end. We scored a very good goal, an injury-time winner. It would have been a fantastic boost for us. Good for us, good for our supporters. For some reason it was chalked off. I just feel for the fans who have been brilliant, brilliant all season, and they stay behind us in every game. They will be thinking of that last goal tonight. It's them I feel for more than anyone because getting a win in the Premiership is not easy. It's a hard one to take.'

Keane invited disciplinary proceedings with the force of his comments on the referee. 'We should be talking about two good teams after the game,' he told journalists. 'Instead, for the next few days, we're going to be talking about the referee, but I think he'll enjoy that; he'll like to be the centre of attention. I saw him at the hotel the night before the game and I just thought to myself "nah". This is certainly the most angry I've been as a manager after a game. You watch and see it again – he's got his whistle in his mouth ready to blow for the foul as the ball is in the air, and that's what really concerns me.

'Sunderland fans deserve better than that, and the players deserve better than that. I don't want to crucify the referee, although to some officials criticism is water off a duck's back, but everyone should be accountable. I was chatting to Mark Hughes a few weeks ago and I said I found the referees alright. He said "that'll change" and he was spot on. I've not criticised referees since coming into the job, certainly not through the media, maybe through the assessor and I've always tried to be fair, but in this case I've no idea why he's given the foul.

'If it was a fifty-fifty decision then maybe; but no, nothing of the sort. Sometimes a decision goes against you but you can see where the referee is coming from, but I couldn't see it in this game. I'm looking for an angle for the referee, to try to help him, to see where he's coming from, but I just can't see it. Maybe the referee's the only man on the planet who has seen it because it's a header. We score, three yards out. It looks straightforward and the referee disallows it. No one's getting a winner here today. It's a massive call.

'We're on fourteen points at the moment and sixteen is massive.'

In the end, no action was taken against Steve Bennett, but that didn't surprise Keane. 'You speak to the assessors and they say it makes a difference, but I don't know,' he said. 'To be fair though it would be wrong to take him out of the Premiership and put him in the GM Conference because why should we inflict him on their fans and players?'

Higginbotham insisted Sunderland would not let the controversy affect confidence. The centre half had scored a cracking goal but was fully aware the only goal anyone was talking about afterwards was the one that got away. 'We're disappointed it didn't count, but we're not a bunch of players who'd let our heads drop. You'd be out of the door with our manager if you let that happen. I was one of the players who was in there when Grant's corner came in and I certainly didn't touch their keeper,' he said. 'It's very tight at the bottom at the moment, but one win can lift you towards mid-table. Other than the Everton game we've held our own and I don't think we've looked outclassed.'

The centre half's disappointment was compounded by the fact that Sunderland had performed so solidly. 'There's a whole lot of pace in the Premiership and it's how you cope with it that counts. Villa have had a good start to the season and they've got that pace, but I thought we coped well. For us, as a defence, a clean sheet is very important and Ricky Sbragia has come in and done work with us in that direction. Sometimes, though, teams need just one chance. Villa produced a free-kick and we couldn't do much about it.'

Despite Higginbotham's defiant words, there was no doubt that Steve Bennett's decision had floored Sunderland. So who would believe that in their very next game, the match against Reading, questionable officiating would once again be the overwhelming talking point? By a hurtful twist, the player who would score the goal that would crush the Wearsiders in a 2-1 victory would be the one Keane wanted to sign for Sunderland – Stephen Hunt.

It was no surprise that in a game where both teams fought so grittily for gain, they would only be separated at the final whistle by the width of a linesman's flag. It was hard to take for Sunderland that, having been denied two points by Steve Bennett's mistake against Villa, they should fall victim to linesman Steve Rubery's ambitious flagging for a 'goal' which he could not have seen. The fact that Steve Bennett's boob and Steve Rubery's rush of blood happened in the 93rd and 92nd minutes of their respective games only compounded the sense of pain and injustice for Sunderland's suffering supporters.

When Reading winger Stephen Hunt's fierce 92nd minute shot was blocked off the line by the returning and impressive Gordon, the goalkeeper's back was to the official. Steve Rubery, it seemed certain, could not have known whether it had fully crossed or not. Yet still the fatal flag was raised.

Reading were better than Sunderland overall, just like Villa had been the previous week. But football is not a game in which points are awarded for pressure or fine play; only for goals. The reality was that, below par though they were, Sunderland had created a couple of great chances – Cole at the beginning of the game, Jones at the end – to have added to Chopra's penalty conversion and taken all three points. They would have at least gained the single point needed to keep them out of the relegation zone had Steve Rubery not given Stephen Hunt's shot the nod.

With both teams struggling for consistency and form, their managers had opted for different approaches. Steve Coppell made no changes; Keane made four. Ward's three-game spell between the posts came to an end with Gordon returning, while further upfield out went Wallace, Etuhu and Stokes to be replaced by Leadbitter, Chopra and Cole. Cole might have given Sunderland the perfect start, five minutes in, when Yorke lobbed a ball over the top to his ex-Manchester United teammate. The striker sprinted into a one-on-one with Marcus Hahnemann, who got his angles right and made a fine save. It was the last of Sunderland as an attacking force in the first half, and you couldn't help wondering whether the Cole of ten years ago would have been similarly thwarted. Reading got into their stride and began to dominate, their main danger coming from Hunt, who enjoyed a terrific duel with Collins.

Sunderland went behind as a result of linesman Steve Rubery's first mistake, in the eyes of the fans, the official ruling in favour of Hunt being fouled, when it looked as if the winger had in fact fouled Collins. That gave Reading a free-kick on the right where James Harper's delivery was glanced goalwards by Ibrahima Sonko at the near post and, though Gordon managed to block it, the ball ran straight into the shins of Ivar Ingimarsson two yards out and bounced over the line.

With nothing to lose now Sunderland threw everything forward. Their boldness was rewarded when Jones was brought down by Ibrahima Sonko in the 82nd minute for a penalty. It was a pressure moment for Chopra, who hadn't scored since the opening week of the season. Nervelessly, he drove a shot just inside Marcus Hahnemann's left-hand post as the goalkeeper went the wrong way. It was the Tynesider's third goal of the season on the eve of his 24th birthday and he raced towards the Sunderland fans behind the goal to celebrate in now trademark style, arms outstretched.

Chopra, Jones and Stokes all went dangerously close in the dying stages. But just as it looked as if Sunderland would have to settle for a draw, Reading launched a final attack. Lively substitute Shane Long crossed from the right. Stephen Hunt drilled in a shot from the left. Gordon appeared to block it on his line, only for Steve Rubery to make his second and decisive intervention of the afternoon, signalling the ball had crossed the line.

Sunderland had lost three points in two games, purely through a flag and whistle. Instead of 18th in the table, they might have ended the day at 13th. 'If' is the longest word in football though, and the bleak reality was that, as things stood, Sunderland now had fewer points than at the same stage of their 2002-03 19-point relegation season. A statistic to chill the blood of every Sunderland fan. What the Wearsiders really needed now was out-of-form opponents they could beat easily.

Unfortunately, Manchester United were next on the fixture list.

Stephen Hunt's potential transfer to Sunderland was dismissed by Reading manager Steve Coppell, who praised the Irish international. 'I'm not surprised there's been talk about Hunt because he's been terrific this year,' he said. 'He has been a bundle of energy and skill, and his goal capped a terrific performance from him.'

No point crying over spilt milk, was Keane's verdict, but it was delivered through gritted teeth. 'If the referee's assistant gives it,' said Keane, 'he's got very, very good eyesight. I'm told that, in any game, if an official is not sure, they can't give it. We have watched it a few times now and it is still unclear. So if the linesman is sure, all credit to him, because he must have fantastic vision! Gordon feels it was a terrific save and the ball wasn't across the line, but that doesn't matter now. Two big decisions have gone against us in a week, but a lot of other decisions haven't gone our way: the free-kick for Reading's first goal; the throw-in just before the second goal when the ball seemed to go out. It's a combination of a lot of things. The strange thing is that we'd made our minds up to keep calm heads, but for some reason we're getting more and more excuses to lose them. I have seen literally thousands of games in my career – be it watching or playing – where teams haven't played particularly well but they've got a good result, and we nearly got that today. We should have seen the game out, but we didn't, and got punished.

'We know we've got a long way to go, and I've never claimed we're the finished article. That's our challenge. We've got a hell of a lot of work to do. We've been in the Premiership two minutes and we've got a long path ahead of us.'

Defeat left Sunderland in the bottom three again, and struggling. But Keane remained supremely unworried about his future. His attention was on strengthening the club in the transfer window. 'We've been in the bottom three before,' he shrugged. 'Half a dozen managers may have gone in this league but that doesn't concern me. If you get sacked it's not the end of the world. Top managers have been sacked before. Clough was sacked after forty-odd days and he wasn't bad, was he? I know it's tough at the moment but I wouldn't class it as pressure. It's a challenge. I believe we have enough to stay up as it is, but we do need a few more players. Two or three more quality players in the window and there's no reason why we can't get them in. At the moment we are in the bottom three but hopefully people will see the potential at the club, like I did.

'I didn't take over when we were in the Premiership. I took over when we were second bottom in the Championship. And I hope anyone coming in will see just what I saw about this club's potential. Even so, my advice to supporters is – don't be too excited. I think Niall and Peter are making progress with targets but it's the most difficult time to bring players in.'

The season wasn't looking great for Sunderland's fans but former manager Peter Reid, who had experienced successful and unsuccessful relegation battles during his management of the Wearsiders, offered them some hope. 'Sunderland have been big spenders since Roy Keane arrived,' he said. 'The board have backed him in the transfer market and for that reason, and coupled with the amazing backing from the fans on Wearside, they will consolidate at this level. Roy Keane is still a very young manager, but he's had an outstanding start to his career and I think most would agree he has what it takes to be a top manager. Sunderland and Roy are a great match.

'There might have been a few eyebrows raised when he was first appointed, but the job he did in turning things around and getting promotion last season was brilliant. He knew things would step up a notch or two in the Premier League and it hasn't been easy, but he'll be learning all the time.'

It was six years since Peter Reid was sacked, with the club higher in the league than it found itself after the Reading game, but his affection for the Wearsiders hadn't waned. He had come remarkably close to returning to the club when Quinn had first taken it over, only for the move to founder through no fault of either. 'Sunderland are a big club and they should be top ten,' said Peter Reid. 'They have a massive fan base, a wonderful stadium and now financial backing to boot. Jones, Richardson, Chopra and Gordon – they all cost a few quid and put Sunderland in among the top summer spenders, but Jones in particular was an inspired buy. People were wondering why Roy was spending so much on an unproven player but he has shown his potential and it looks like six million pounds well spent. This season, the fans would probably settle for staying up, but then they'll be looking to progress and maybe challenge for Europe.'

Peter Reid knew hopes were sky-high among the fans after the appointment of Keane. Though the Manchester United legend fulfilled all expectations by leading Sunderland to immediate promotion, these were testing times for a young man learning his trade in the most unforgiving of environments. 'When I was there we got promoted, relegated, promoted again and then finished seventh in the Premier League twice on the trot. Finishing so high in the table, the expectation levels just rocketed. It's difficult to manage expectation levels at Sunderland and they have to realise this season was always going to be tough.'

Peter Reid's Sunderland team had been based around the spearhead of targetman Quinn. 'He's the catalyst for everything which goes well for us,' teammate Alex Rae had said at the time. Now Jones was threatening to become equally as influential a player for Keane. After the Reading game, Coppell admitted the key to it had been in taming Jones. 'He had such an impact on the first game that we had to deal effectively with him this time round,' he said. 'And up until that moment when he got the penalty, we'd done just that.'

Coppell reckoned Sunderland were experiencing the same Premier League learning curve as his own Championship team underwent the previous season. 'It's just a hard league, certainly for teams coming up, and on an annual basis, for the foreseeable future it's going to be hard for the three teams promoted. The gap between the top of the Championship and the bulk of the Premiership is bigger than the gap between the top and bottom of the Championship. In the Championship you can be having an afternoon where you're not playing well, but you're still in the game and will maybe only lose by the odd goal if the worst comes to the worst. In the Premier League the elite top-four in particular are playing at a level not seen before and you can find yourselves 4-0 down in a game, having not played particularly badly but having been done by four moments of world-class skill. You are up against world superstars and in the Premiership the depths of skill in the squad are much greater.

'The Championship is a league which doesn't really prepare

you for the Premiership. I think when you start playing in the Premiership there is that "oh, my word" moment where you realise how easily it is to be destroyed without playing particularly badly.'

For Keane, that moment had come at Everton one month previously.

There was no doubt at this stage that Sunderland were in trouble. Many of Keane's transfer signings had not worked out. Sunderland were struggling for goals. Jones was top scorer with four. The club had scored just seventeen goals in eighteen games. Defence was even more of a worry. Sunderland had kept a clean sheet in that opening day game against Spurs but repeated the feat just once more in the nineteen league and cup games that followed. They were scoring goals at a rate of roughly one a game and were to end the year conceding an average of two goals a game.

Though Keane was projecting public calm, he was concerned about league form and, in particular, the problems of his defence. What he was not to know was that Sunderland's fate in that direction had already been profoundly affected in the days leading up to the Reading game. Not by anything happening in Reading or Sunderland. But in Manchester.

On Tuesday 18 December the Manchester United squad held an early Christmas party and the squad's night on the town was to end with Jonny Evans charged with rape of one of the partygoers at Great John Street Hotel. The charges were immediately denied by the player and were to be quietly dropped in March. But at the time they were devastating and enough to sweep Evans out of Old Trafford and up to the Stadium of Light.

For those of us who had met him, the story seemed hard to credit. You could hardly find a player more removed from the cliché of the flash, cocky footballer. Evans had been a model professional in his time on loan at Sunderland, off the pitch as well as on. You would have held the nineteen-year-old up as the ideal template for any youngster to follow. Sometimes it is hard to have faith in the modern-day footballer, but Evans was different. A less likely troublemaker it was hard to imagine.

The central defender was to strenuously and immediately protest his innocence in what was to be the most stressful few weeks of his young life. Manchester United closed ranks around the player, but the immediate consequence of the charges hanging over Evans' head was that Sir Alex Ferguson decided a loan-spell would be the best thing possible for the young footballer's state of mind. Ferguson wanted to keep his young players at the club during this particular season because he wanted the most promising to be available for United when the charge for trophies began on a series of fronts. Evans' problems, with potential criminal charges hanging over him, were obvious. Too much time on his hands was not going to be beneficial mentally. With Ferguson knowing he could offer the youngster very little in the way of first-team action, he took the decision to give him first-team football elsewhere. Many Premier League clubs would have taken him, so impressive had the Northern Ireland international been the previous season on loan at the Stadium of Light.

But the choice was left to Evans. And Evans chose Sunderland.

Months later, Keane was to reflect that, but for Evans' troubles at the time, the young Manchester United player might never have been allowed out of Old Trafford for a second season in succession. There were many on Wearside who'd publicly doubt at the season's end whether Sunderland would have stayed up if Evans hadn't arrived.

His arrival would not happen, though, before the two teams in his life met on 26 December, a festive-day game in which Sunderland's struggles would be cruelly highlighted. Keane however remained bullish going into the game.

'We wanted to bring something to the Premiership and I think we have done,' he insisted. 'Our crowds have been brilliant and I think we have played some very good football at times. But now we have to look at digging in and getting points on the board.'

The game against the giants of Old Trafford was a match as appealing in its glamour as it was daunting in its challenge. To see Sunderland on a match-day such as this was to appreciate the full power of the Stadium of Light. There was something majestic about the steepling banks of people, all focused on the desire to see their team do them proud, even though the likelihood of a victory against the league leaders was slim to none.

In this game, it was Sunderland who were united. United in that kind of Rorke's Drift spirit of defiance. Keane had said at Arsenal he thought his former club had that little bit more than the Gunners when it came to the title race. By this stage of the campaign you could see what he meant. United were performing with the swagger of Arsenal, the remorselessness of Chelsea and a style all of their own. Cristiano Ronaldo and Wayne Rooney were playing fantasy football and Sunderland would go into the match like the blindfolded man awaiting the first shots from the firing squad.

Their fans knew this but would roar their defiance.

On a day like this, the buzz around the ground begins hours beforehand and, by the opening whistle, the tension and excitement is palpable.

It was what Quinn had dreamed of the previous season – Sunderland versus the likes of Manchester United with a full house roaring the team on. It had been quite a journey already for Sunderland fans since Keane arrived at a club bumping along at the bottom of the Championship. A club that had completely lost its way. Perhaps the extent and the speed of that journey under an exciting but completely untried manager only became apparent in the build-up to kick-off – Keane's newly-promoted, freshly assembled team facing the might of the defending Premier League champions in a sell-out arena. The Red Devils' festive visit had been described by Quinn at the start of the season as his and Keane's Christmas present to Sunderland fans. A thank you for your support from Drumaville. A payout on a promise delivered less than eighteen months ago.

'Enjoy the game.'

Unfortunately, Christmas is also a time for giving and Manchester United needed no persuading to accept three points which were so invitingly offered. The match, though, was less about the inevitable result and more about the quality of Sunderland's fans, who showed stirring defiance in the face of overwhelming odds. They sang and they sang and they sang! And it was marvellous for anyone with pride in Sunderland to hear.

Somewhere around the hour-mark, frustrated Sunderland fans – watching their team 3-0 down – embarked on a chorus of 'red and white army' which just kept going and going and going until it filled the ground.

It rolled around the stadium for minute after minute, to which Sunderland's players responded by trying to raise their game, but could offer little in the way of cheer. The fact that United barely let the opposition have a touch of the ball in all that time only offered extra impressiveness to the act of thankless defiance from the terraces. It made you proud. But it also made you slightly sad. They deserved more than this – these relegation-zone fans who produced the biggest crowd in English football on the day – a massed act of faith in the wake of having been completely kicked in the teeth in their last two Premier League seasons.

Taking on Manchester United was never going to be an easy task for a team whose form had been as indifferent beforehand as the Red Devils' had been impressive. But to be swept aside so casually on home turf was hard for any supporter to stomach, especially on a festive day in which entertainment is traditionally the name of the game. This was not so much entertainment, as execution – as big and as comprehensive a home defeat as the Stadium of Light had witnessed in its first decade.

Just as distressing was the realisation that, had United needed to, they could easily have added a few more. Despite Edwin van der Sar being injured and Ryan Giggs rested, United were never remotely close to calling Carlos Tevez off the substitutes bench, such was their ease on the ball, the way they controlled this game. With Wayne Rooney and Cristiano Ronaldo given free roles to attack and destroy, Sunderland were under the cosh virtually from the start.

An unusually large crush of photographers waited for the managers to come out before kick-off, the media still intrigued by the connection between legendary captain and manager – the Master and the Apprentice.

In keeping with the Christmas theme, Keane rang the changes again: Etuhu, Wallace and, the big surprise, youth team player Waghorn starting in place of Leadbitter, Murphy and Cole. Waghorn's inclusion was something of a shock although Keane had dropped occasional hints that the youngster was close. And it was pleasing that the seventeen-year-old left-footed striker was handed a role up front, alongside Jones, rather than being asked to play on the wing, as so many young strikers are when handed a full debut. The teenager rewarded the faith shown in him by producing some nice touches, a robustness and a confidence that did him credit during his ninety minutes. Although he never really got a clear-cut chance on goal, the sponsors voted him their man-of-the-match. A day which would stay with him forever.

It was an afternoon when Sunderland carved out very few chances, but it didn't seem to matter to the fans who were enjoying their break, and the occasion. Former United trainee McShane's first-minute defensive clearance received a mighty roar while fans of both teams chanted Keane's name. When Waghorn won ground up the left a minute later he received a wonderfully warm reception from the crowd as his entranced youth teammates watched from the seats behind the dugout and in front of the press box.

An early scare for Sunderland came ten minutes in, when Higginbotham brought down Cristiano Ronaldo in the Sunderland 'D'. A Ronaldo wondergoal might effectively have ended the game as a contest in its opening stages. As it was, Gordon got his gloves to the swerving ball. Just as it looked as if Sunderland might make a fist of it though, they let in as soft a goal as they'd conceded all season. Wes Brown on the right stabbed the ball forward to Wayne Rooney, who found himself criminally unmarked twenty-five yards from goal. He took the ball in his stride and drove it past Gordon.

United doubled their lead on the half-hour when Collins failed to get a cross in from a Sunderland free-kick, and United counterattacked with devastating effect. Cristiano Ronaldo in the centre-circle swept the ball forward to Wayne Rooney on the left-flank. Wallace tried to contain him. Rooney shrugged off the challenge, and hit the ball across the face of the goal where Louis Saha clipped in a low shot.

The game was up on the stroke of half-time when Etuhu chopped down Darren Fletcher twenty yards out. Cristiano Ronaldo curled the free-kick into the top right-hand corner of Gordon's goal so exactly, and at such speed, that the goal-keeper failed to move a muscle, staring in apparent disbelief. It was a fabulous moment of quality from a player whose strike moved him to the top of the Premier League goal-scoring lists. Sunderland's best effort on goal in the first-half came from a move that saw Wallace force a save out of Thomas Kuszczak in the 40th minute.

They had more of the game in the second-half – United taking their foot off the gas a little, but Sunderland never really threatened to get back into it. The best they could hope for was not to implode completely, as they had in the 7-1 defeat at Everton. Such was the difference in quality between the two teams that when Cristiano Ronaldo was substituted just before the hour, the home fans felt detached enough to applaud the midfielder off the pitch – just as they had done for Arsenal's Thierry Henry on the very last day of their 15-point relegation, when they knew the game was up and wanted to show their appreciation of a genius.

Five minutes from time United got their fourth, Louis Saha scoring from the penalty spot. The defeat left Sunderland second-bottom of the Premier League, 19th, with only Derby below. United's victory also equalled Sunderland's worst ever defeat at the Stadium of Light.

When the stadium scoreboards flashed up results elsewhere, the scoreline Wigan Athletic 1 Newcastle United 0 appeared in neon. The reaction was instinctive – Sunderland fans were unable to stop themselves cheering the Magpies' defeat, even though relegation rivals Wigan had just leapfrogged Sunderland and escaped the bottom three. It felt a little like turkeys cheering for the coming of Christmas.

Keane argued there was little shame in being beaten by the current Premier League champions. 'It's never nice to lose, particularly at home, but at least we've been beaten by a very good team,' he said. 'We started okay, but the goals we gave away were sloppy. Any mistake in the Premiership is likely to be punished but if you give Wayne Rooney space twenty yards out he's going to take it. The fans stayed behind us and we appreciate that because we're in a sticky patch now. We've had a few massive blows but we are still on our feet. We still have a chance. And at the half-way point of the season, I think we're doing okay.'

With no real signs on the pitch that Sunderland were on the verge of turning things around, Keane was reluctant to encourage the idea that the January transfer window would offer the prospect of instant salvation.

'We can't build our hopes up,' he said. 'Let's not kid ourselves that we are going to bring in loads of players. We hope for two or three but that might be it.'

Keane would be right in one respect – how well relegation-threatened teams did in the transfer window would be crucial to their survival hopes. And he was about to play a blinder.

CHAPTER FIVE

On the Up and a Poison Cup

I'm ashamed. People might say that's too strong a word for it, but I don't. I'm ashamed. ROY KEANE

SUNDERLAND turned towards the New Year at their lowest ebb. They badly needed a victory. With the visit of Bolton Wanderers they had a good chance. Sammy Lee had been sacked after steering the club into the buffers. Gary Megson, nicknamed 'the ginger Mourinho' by Bolton fans originally out of mockery and increasingly out of respect, had lifted the club off the foot of the Premier League table into 17th place.

But their revival was fragile and, for the second successive match, Sunderland had the backing of the biggest crowd in the country behind them on the day. That only emphasised the club's depth of support after the 4-0 United defeat, as the Wearsiders' chairman acknowledged.

'There are times I have to remind people just how big this club is,' said Quinn. 'But as time has gone by this season, I think that people are beginning to see where I'm coming from. I believe Sunderland Football Club is the most important identity in the region.'

Keane made three changes to the team that faced United: Miller, Richardson and Cole started in place of Yorke, Waghorn and Wallace. It was Wallace's first absence all season from the squad. Bolton included ex-Sunderland midfielder Gavin McCann in their ranks and former Sunderland target Jussi Jaaskelainen. This gave Sunderland fans a chance to compare Jaaskelainen – the man Keane couldn't get – with Gordon – the man he could. In the end neither could be completely happy with the way their afternoons panned out.

Sunderland drew first blood when Jones and Richardson combined to give the Wearsiders a 13th minute lead. Jones won possession on the right and rode through three challenges on a diagonal goal-bound run. Looking up he saw Richardson gain ground down the left, unmarked by a distracted Bolton defence. The striker found his teammate with a fine pass, and Richardson hit a fierce left-foot shot from six yards out. Jussi Jaaskelainen could only watch as it flashed over him into the net. The same combination doubled the lead just after the half-hour. This time Richardson was the provider. His corner from the right was met by Jones, who rose athletically at the near post six yards out, to head home. Once again the Bolton keeper was close, but not close enough. In between the goals, Wanderers' attacks foundered on the defensive solidity of McShane and Higginbotham, and Sunderland looked to be cruising to half-time two goals to the good.

Then Bolton won a free-kick left of goal twenty-eight yards out. Senegalese midfielder El-Hadji Diouf took it, marking his 100th start for Bolton by scoring the most unlikely of goals. His on-target effort just cleared the head of McShane, who looked as though he had been sneakily shoved in the back. As the ball dropped, Gordon's attention was focused on Kevin Davies who had stolen unmarked into the six-yard box, but the striker failed to make contact and the ball bounced across Gordon and into the corner of goal, a carbon copy of the ugly goal the pairing had conceded to James Milner in the game against Newcastle. 'We should have been looking to see the half out at that stage,' growled Keane.

Wanderers re-emerged in a mood of grim determination and although the best chance before the hour fell to Sunderland – Richardson's long-range shot forcing Jussi Jaaskelainen to tip just over his bar – it was the visitors who had the upper hand. The last twenty minutes must have been as difficult for Sunderland players to play in, as it was for Sunderland fans to watch, as the jitters set in with a string of misplaced passes, poor decision-making and nerviness in possession. Despite the immense pressure Sunderland were under – the crowd screaming at them not to defend so deeply – they managed to hold. And, right at the death, they notched a morale-boosting third. Jones got on the end of a Gordon goal-kick and headed it into the path of Murphy, who surged into the penalty area and fired a low left-foot shot past Jussi Jaaskelainen from left of goal. A clinically confident strike.

The Irishman's goal was greeted with wild joy and relief from the home crowd, a clenched fist and a smile from Keane, who had been as animated on the touchline as anyone had seen him all season. For the first time in the season Sunderland had scored three. They hadn't been too far away from producing a shut-out either. 'We've been working very hard with Ricky Sbragia on keeping a clean sheet,' confirmed a delighted Higginbotham.

The genial Sbragia had been a coach at Sunderland between 1994 and 2002. He only left the club because he was disillusioned by Peter Reid's sacking. He had been a massively positive influence at the club previously and his presence was a major boost to the club's backroom staff. Now his influence was being felt. 'No good at cards,' pointed out Keane. But pretty good at coaching.

Keane was gradually surrounding himself with men he had worked with before. People he felt were like-minded and whose work he rated. His first appointment had been Tony Loughlan, a friend and former youth-team colleague at Nottingham Forest, who had arrived as head coach. Loughlan was a person Keane could trust implicitly and was vital in providing the balance and support the manager needed. Former Manchester United academy coach Neil Bailey had arrived as first-team coach in January 2007. When the scouting network was reviewed, Old Trafford's long-serving chief scout Mick Brown was recruited. Raimond van der Gouw, another Old Trafford old boy, succeeded Tim Carter as first-team goalkeeping coach in July 2007 and Sbragia, who had also worked alongside Keane at Manchester United, continued the process. Even the club's strength and conditioning coach – Mike Clegg – was an ex-United player. Keane quietly but steadily went about building a backroom team he was familiar with and felt could take the team forward. He also wanted people who knew how he wanted to work. They weren't changes for change's sake. Sunderland's youth-team set-up, which involved Kevin Ball, remained. The physiotherapy department headed by Pete Friar was left to get on with its work.

The Bolton win ended a run of three defeats and a draw for Sunderland and changed the mood in the camp completely. Richardson's return suggested Sunderland had a player of real quality and a potential match-winner. His hairline-fracture injury had been more typical of cricketers and field athletes. 'I felt it towards the end of the season at Man United. I thought it might be my bed, but I had fractured my spine,' he said. 'I was in agony in the European Championships. Then I couldn't sleep after the Liverpool game at the start of the season and the scan showed I had a fracture.'

Fans knew there was a long, long way yet to go, but this result sent them into 2008 with a new found sense of resolution. Richardson, who scored one and set up another, added an extra dimension in the first-half before understandably fading in the second and being subbed.

'In an ideal world we wouldn't have started him,' said Keane. 'Ross Wallace damaged his hamstring in training the day before the game so we had to play Kieran. He got seventy minutes when normally we would maybe have given him forty-five, but he did very well for us. This is the situation we're in at the moment. Michael Chopra has been carrying a knock for a few games but has still contributed. As for Kieran, we hope he's over the worst of it now.'

The win was only the second for Sunderland in fourteen games. 'I was relieved when the third went in because, again, we made it hard for ourselves,' Keane said. 'It's a shame Daryl Murphy couldn't have scored half an hour earlier. We needed someone to put their foot on it because experienced lads do suck you in and that's what Bolton had. They are a big, strong experienced team and Premier League experience is what we lack. Grant Leadbitter and Roy O'Donovan, for example, have no Premiership experience to speak of and it tells in certain situations. We are not streetwise and it shows. Five minutes before half-time we should have been looking to shut up shop. In the end we had to win the game twice.'

The pressure Sunderland found themselves under in the second-half, allied to a team selection that was dictated by who was available, only underlined to Keane why he needed to be active in the January transfer window.

'People talk about us being positive in fielding three strikers from the start but that was as much down to the players we had left as it was to clever thinking,' he said. 'Ross was injured and Dwight couldn't have played after playing two in four days, so we were down to the bare bones. We need a few more players to see it through.'

Victory lifted Sunderland out of the bottom three but the manager did not want to place too much emphasis on that. 'I was watching Sheffield United's Championship game against Crystal Palace on the television before our game and that was a reminder that it's all about where you are at the end of the season. You look at Sheffield United and they were out of the bottom three almost all season until the last week, while Wigan were in it virtually all season until the last week and got out of it. So you shouldn't get too bound up by where you are in the table in December.'

As the year turned, Collins drew huge satisfaction from reaching the milestone of 100 appearances for the club in the game against Manchester United. He had played in nineteen of the Black Cats' twenty Premier League games, to go with the thirty-seven starts he'd made in Keane's Championship season. The Welsh international centre half, asked to play left back, had seen off the challenge of specialist full backs Robbie Elliott, Clarke and Harte. Collins, a £140,000 signing from Chester City in October 2004, had had to endure speculation over his future on a regular basis. He had nearly been offloaded to Stoke City in the first few weeks of the season yet had fought his way back into favour. 'I've never thought it should be about how much your transfer fee was,' said Collins, 'it's about how well you train and how you perform in football matches. I'm lucky that the manager sees it the same way. It's not about how much you cost to him, it's how well you do.'

Collins' contributions had been solid rather than spectacular. But he had come to the fore in recent games where he had been a rock of consistency in defence where his courage and combativeness had come to the fore. His century of appearances meant only Whitehead, among those involved in the first-team squad, had made more first-team appearances for Sunderland than him.

Always down to earth, Collins said: 'I have a lot to be grateful for. I enjoyed 2007. The last year has been an eventful one, but then it always seems to be at this club. We started the year mid-table in the Championship but went on to win the league, which was a great achievement, something to be proud of. I played a lot of games last season and have been a regular so I feel it was an important year for me. Now I've just passed the 100 game mark for Sunderland and I'm so proud about that. Not many people play 100 games for a club like Sunderland and it's a big achievement. It means a lot to me.'

Collins was one of those players who was popular with the media, simply because he carried no airs or graces about him and was not one to refuse interviews. Increasingly, footballers see talking to the press as a chore to be avoided. At Premier

League clubs in particular, too many see no connection between media coverage and the growth of the game, which pays their wages.

Football losing its soul.

But at Sunderland, players like Collins, Leadbitter and Whitehead, for example, saw it as something which went with the territory and dealt with media demands professionally. Collins was the latest in a line of Sunderland players who didn't dodge interview requests. He followed on in the tradition of players like Darren Williams, Paul Thirlwell, Martin Smith, Darren Holloway, Michael Bridges, Julio Arca, Kevin Ball, Alex Rae and Chris Makin in previous years, and was respected for that.

Perception is everything. In past seasons the likes of Williams and Thirlwell were sometimes pilloried by fans for talking when the club was struggling. They were criticised for appearing in print. Stirred up by talk-show stations, it was suggested that players shouldn't comment unless their team was winning. The players who featured most regularly on back pages were not attention seekers. They had simply responded politely to a reporter's request. They tended to be very genuine people, players who felt a responsibility to talk to fans, to get a positive message across in tough times. Williams and Thirlwell, and Collins in his time, sometimes took stick for appearing in the newspapers but, often, the only reason they were so heavily relied upon by the press was because other players did not feel any duty or desire to justify themselves or talk to the public. It was ironic that the most down-to-earth and decent footballers felt they owed supporters a duty to give interviews; yet in those tough times, fans were most critical of the only ones brave enough to talk.

Collins was in that mould of the approachable player and had shown that good guys could come first by the way he had handled himself in the most demanding season of his career so far. 'Beating Bolton was important,' he said. 'A massive three points. And we should take heart from that. We have been gung-ho at times, as the manager said, and teams have picked us off as a result. So at the moment we're prioritising strong defence and I think that showed with the recent clean sheet against Derby County.'

The drizzle on Wearside on New Year's Eve wasn't needed to

dampen the spirits of Sunderland fans, who revelled in the new realism that had settled in with the rain. It was an upbeat realism. They were trusting Keane to keep Sunderland in the Premier League. Seeing the club fourth bottom going into 2008 was good enough for most of them, especially after previous experiences.

The new year dawned with news that Stephen Hunt at Reading was the target of a £2.5 million bid from Sunderland. There were also rumours that £1 million had been offered for Blackburn Rovers Robbie Savage. Six months earlier the news would have produced a twinge of disappointment on Wearside – a winger with only one season in the Premier League and an ageing midfielder of dubious popularity to supplement the over-thirty services of Yorke, Cole and Kavanagh. But the reaction from supporters was cautiously positive. They knew that pragmatism was the name of the game now. These players might offer steel to the team, Premier League ring-craft. Keane had talked about the need for his team to be more streetwise. Savage and Hunt were high-energy players typecast for that role.

Sunderland had indeed swung straight into action in the January transfer window with a firm bid for Stephen Hunt but not for Robbie Savage. It was strongly rumoured, erroneously as it turned out, that Savage had been in the boardroom at the Stadium of Light watching the Bolton game. These are the sort of rumours that flash across the Sunderland skyline, virtually by the hour, during transfer windows. It turned out Sunderland's interest in Savage had progressed no further than a phone call. The midfielder wanted a two-and-a-half-year contract and there was no way the club was going to give that to someone past their early thirties. Keane had learned it was easy to get players in when they were needed, but not so easy to get them out when they were no longer wanted. Sunderland were determined to strengthen, but equally determined not to be held to ransom. Keane wanted players brought in as quickly as possible, hence the swift move for Stephen Hunt. But January was not the best time to get value for money in an inflated market and Keane insisted there would be no panic purchases.

The manager entered the New Year with his attention primarily focused on the game against Blackburn Rovers, forty-eight hours into 2008. He wanted to right a wrong from earlier in the season. 'We felt we should have beaten Newcastle,

Blackburn and Villa this season,' he said, 'but we didn't because a lot of our players are raw at this level. They're learning though.'

The manager was learning too, and this was another chance to pit his wits against former teammate Mark Hughes. 'I speak regularly to Mark,' said Keane. 'He's been a manager longer than me and he's been very helpful. Really good coaches want to speak to you about things. There's no hiding their views; they want to give it up and I've enjoyed plugging into that. I didn't think, when I was a player, that Mark would necessarily become a manager. There were a lot of characters in the dressing room when I played that I thought would – the likes of Steve Bruce, Bryan Robson, maybe Paul Ince. Mark wasn't one of them because he was fairly quiet. But he's done an excellent job at Blackburn.'

That job of excellence continued as the Rovers did the double over Sunderland with a fortunate 1-0 win. Another of those matches the Wearsiders should not have lost.

Anyone who had watched Sunderland's Premier League travails over the preceding five years would have recognised the danger of the type of display they saw at Ewood Park. It was a game where Sunderland were on top throughout, but were still defeated. These were the sort of 'close, but never quite close enough' displays that see teams relegated. The game boiled down to a tale of two penalties: Whitehead's, saved; Benni McCarthy's, converted two minutes later.

The game got underway in freezing cold, blustery conditions, Sunderland starting impressively, backed by Wearside fans who had travelled in great numbers and who were to outsing the home fans throughout. It was one of the fans' very best away performances of the season and for so long in the game, Sunderland's players emulated their supporters. Blackburn had lost their previous three home games and had fallen away from their fine, early season form. So there was a tentativeness to their play, which forced them to wait until the 25th minute for their first sight of goal, David Bentley smashing in a free-kick from thirty-five yards out that was narrowly wide. Sunderland created better opportunities and their workrate and closing down was exemplary. It was as good a forty-five minutes as they had played away from home all season, and indicative of the head of steam taken from the Bolton victory.

In the 55th minute Sunderland earned a penalty, but Whitehead never looked confident. The low shot he placed, just a couple of yards to Brad Friedel's left, lacked pace and allowed the keeper to make the save look simple. Less than two minutes later, Rovers won a penalty at the opposite end when Christopher Samba drove a shot goalwards. It struck Higginbotham's raised arms and referee Rob Styles pointed immediately to the spot. Benni McCarthy stepped up and blasted a shot to Gordon's right. The goalkeeper guessed correctly but was beaten by sheer power. It was Blackburn's first and only shot on target of the entire game.

Sunderland took the game to Blackburn in the minutes that followed but Yorke's frustration at not being able to keep pace with the game saw him sent off for two bookable challenges when he could not reach the ball.

'No complaints,' sighed Keane.

Mark Hughes had given Keane sound advice earlier in the season when he warned him that before the season's end he would have issues with referees. If Hughes had wanted to offer more wisdom that night it would have been succinct – take your chances when you can. 'Sunderland closed us down really well and stopped us playing our passing game and they'll feel quite aggrieved they haven't got anything out of the game,' he conceded. 'The conditions didn't lend themselves to any kind of football being played and it was basically a situation where we had to get the ball into the right areas.'

It wasn't just the night air at Ewood Park that was freezing. There was a distinct chill in Keane's press conference too. This was as frustrating a game as Keane had known as a manager, and for his players to have done everything they needed to win, then contrive to lose, was hard for him to swallow.

'Two penalties were given,' he said. 'We missed, they scored, we lose the game. End of story. You get what you deserve in life. We ended up with nothing, and maybe that's what we deserved. You can talk all day about decent possession and doing okay. I said the same at West Ham United. I said the same at Manchester City. It's a learning curve for everyone and the penny has to drop.'

To compound the defeat Jones suffered a knee problem and Keane was to leave him out of the forthcoming FA Cup game against Wigan for fear of aggravating it.

Once again, other results combined to drop Sunderland back into the relegation zone and reinforce, in the manager's mind, the need for transfer window reinforcements. 'It's not nice to be in the bottom three,' said Keane. 'Opportunities keep slipping us by and I hope that by the end of the season we don't regret it. The Rovers game was the perfect opportunity for us away from home. We could all see that they were there for the taking but we didn't take it. In life you get opportunities and some people take them; some people don't and at the moment we're not taking them.'

Only two points on the road had been taken from a possible thirty-three, both gained courtesy of last minute goals, and if that didn't set the alarm bells ringing alongside those of the departing sleigh bells, then nothing would. It was so cold at Ewood Park that even Sunderland legend and style guru Gary Bennett was forced to wear socks – an attire the radio commentator was never fond of. Sunderland supporters, meanwhile, deserved medals the size of bin lids for travelling such distances and braving the elements over the Pennines to reach Ewood Park's freezing terraces. They certainly could not have been drawn out by the prospect of away-day glories. And, more than anything, Keane was conscious of letting down Sunderland's phenomenal backing on the night. 'Sometimes during a game I get a chance to look at our supporters. And they deserved better than what they got. When a result like this one happens it just makes you more determined to get things right.'

As 2008 got underway, the Wearsiders were one of six Premier League teams still to win away, a remarkable number, given the fact that more than half the season had gone. The previous season Sunderland had won the Championship on the back of twelve wins and three draws in Keane's twenty-one away games in charge. It wasn't easy for him to understand quite why there should be such a difference in their previously clinical approach. Travelling to away grounds was never something that gave him a moment's concern when he was a player.

'I actually liked playing away from home sometimes,' he said. 'Especially going away to a ground where you were up against not just the opposition but the majority of supporters too. When you go away from home and you're under the cosh it's an opportunity for a player to impress everyone. A lot of players I have seen tend to be what I call 'home players'. They are very good at home and are up for it but seem to go missing away from home. We don't want players like that in the camp. We can't afford it.'

Keane looked back over the massive crowds Sunderland had attracted in the last two home games and the tremendous backing at Blackburn and reckoned that one of the best cards in his hand, when it came to attracting new signings, was the huge and passionate support the Wearsiders attracted. Fans who stayed behind their team, even on nights of disappointment such as that at Ewood Park. 'If you're a club which can attract over 40,000 fans for all your home games and you have the potential to sell out a 48,000-seater stadium every week, then people are going to be interested,' he said.

'If you're a club which takes a passionate away following all over the country for every game, then that makes an impact on players. This season in the Premiership they've been reminding people of just what an impressive set of fans they are, and what a big club this is. I think it will have a bearing on how we do in the transfer market because the fans are selling the club to people each week by turning up in their numbers and supporting the team the way they do. Sunderland Football Club is not an easy club to manage by virtue of the fact that it is such a big and passionate club which people feel strongly about. But I wouldn't have it any other way. You go to some clubs and the fans are the same whether you're 1-0 up or 1-0 down but it's not like that at Sunderland and I think that's a great thing.'

Quinn knew that the importance of Keane at the helm was invaluable when it came to bringing players in, even though he accepted Sunderland wouldn't become a real draw until they had genuinely established themselves in the top flight. The manager might not bag the spouses of too many WAGS but Quinn felt Keane was increasingly being seen as someone who represented strong values and principles in the game.

'We are playing catch up again in a way,' he admitted. 'But we think that the idea of Roy Keane coming up and developing a career in front of 48,000 fans every week is big. It will be a big draw. Players in general get stick for always just going where the money is. But I think sometimes we do them a disservice. There are some great players out there who know where the best football clubs are, and I think we will have players who will come here because they want to wear this particular jersey with pride.

Roy stands for something and people in football know that, especially after last season.'

While fans' eyes were firmly fixed on the entrance door, they were surprised to see who was being shown the exit door. Supporters were shocked when they heard that tricky winger Wallace had been transfer-listed. They had not regarded the twenty-two-year-old left winger as one of the weak links of Sunderland's struggling squad. Nor had Keane. Wallace had been a regular in Keane's team, with the manager recently championing his international credentials. Questions were raised over whether there had been a training ground fall-out to precipitate such a surprise move. Rumours persisted that there had. But the move signalled the intent of the manager to remould his playing staff as he saw appropriate, making hard decisions, some of which involved allowing players to leave to help generate money to get others in. Wallace was one of a number of players the manager had spoken to, to let them know the club would listen to offers. The others were Halford, Harte, Kavanagh, Wright and the Championship season's top scorer Connolly.

The club's formal announcement on sales was part of an approach the Black Cats had adopted to raise money in the transfer market and balance the squad. Since Quinn's Drumaville consortium had taken over in July 2006 the group had invested heavily in the club. With no clear advantage discernible turning into the New Year, there seemed to be an air of financial prudence creeping into the club. The chairman and the board would back Keane again in the transfer market, but they would also demand that he try to regulate the squad, to look at shipping people out, as well as in. In January the club announced a pre-tax loss of £15.4 million for the 2006-2007 season. That was the price of promotion, a significant reversal on the previous season, when the Black Cats were relegated from the Premier League under chairman Bob Murray, but made a pre-tax profit of £7.5 million. In the Championship season the club's turnover had fallen from £39.3 million in 2006 to £26.3 million in 2007. Despite relegation to the second tier of English football, wages increased from £17.4 million to £23.7 million, which was a huge figure for a Championship club. On the way to promotion, £9 million was generated in gate receipts and a further £4.1 million in sponsorship and royalties, although the club's television revenue fell dramatically, from £18.5 million to £7.9 million. The money invested by Drumaville showed a desire to speculate, to accumulate, for there was no doubt that their spending had provided the platform for promotion and the access to television revenues, which would help the club grow further. They would provide more funds but would want Keane to work both ends of the equation.

'We're looking to bring in a number of players who can play a key part in our season and, as a result, we are having to manage the squad,' said Keane. 'There are some players who I would consider allowing to leave the club or go out on loan if it suited all concerned and I've spoken to the players involved.'

It had been known for some time that Kavanagh, Wright and Connolly could leave the club if agreement could be reached with interested clubs. The sticking point for all three would largely come down to wages. They were on the sort of contracts that were beyond the scope of pretty much every Championship club – a clear illustration of the growing gulf between the two divisions. The news that Halford, Harte and Wallace could also go was an indication that Sunderland were not going to allow the squad to swell indefinitely.

Wallace was an intriguing development nevertheless, especially since the manager had talked about the squad being down to the 'bare bones'. It also indicated a drive by the board to streamline the playing staff. From now on the players would all have a genuine part to play in the club's future. It must have been irritating to the board to be paying out large sums in wages for players who had hardly featured in the first team, or not at all.

Sunderland had added a touch of caution to their approach in the market. Their interest in Robbie Savage disappeared the moment it was known that a player, who would soon turn thirty-four, wanted a two-and-a-half-year contract. Sunderland took the decision that the player simply did not warrant that, despite Mark Hughes confirming the Wearsiders' initial phone call.

Keane had identified four players he wanted, but former Manchester United teammate Quinton Fortune was not to be one of them. When Keane was asked whether Fortune, who had been training with the squad for a few weeks, was coming in, Keane replied he hoped 'to get that sorted out by the end of the week'. It was a reply reporters took to mean that the deal would be done but the manager's words had been misunderstood. What he actually meant was that a decision would be taken, one way or another, by the end of the week. Fortune had spent a successful month training with Sunderland, an arrangement that had been beneficial to both. Keane made the decision not to pursue the signature of his former Old Trafford teammate.

'The four players we are after haven't changed,' he said cryptically, well aware of the intense newspaper speculation that is a wearisome feature of the transfer window. Two of those players were Stephen Hunt at Reading and Matt Taylor at Portsmouth. Keane had hit a brick wall with both clubs, but he and his board were hoping that pressure and persuasion would eventually win the day.

Jonny Evans arrived on Wearside just seventy-two hours into the New Year, to the surprise and delight of Sunderland fans. For the second time in successive years, Evans joined on his birthday, 3 January. Keane was delighted to get his man but did not want him burdened with the weight of expectation he knew fans had. 'We're really pleased to have brought Jonny back,' he said. 'He did a terrific job for us last season but I want to remind everyone that he's just turned twenty and a club like Sunderland can't be depending on twenty-year-olds. We can try to get the best out of him, but it has to be appreciated that he's a young man and not the Messiah.'

Most Sunderland fans disagreed.

It was heart-warming for them to know that their feelings towards the youngster were reciprocated. 'I built up a lot of affection for Sunderland,' said Evans, revealing he had gone to watch the Black Cats' game against Birmingham City back in August. 'I was just sitting at home one night and knew Sunderland were playing so I decided to go there with my girlfriend. She's a massive Sunderland fan, having watched all the games last season. When I got the chance my heart wanted to come back to Sunderland. And as soon as I knew Roy Keane wanted me to come, I couldn't wait. Everything happened in a couple of days, which was fine by me because I felt I had unfinished business at the club.'

Keane wanted to add further quality to the squad and one of the worst results of Sunderland's entire campaign, the FA Cup third round game against Wigan, emphasised that that couldn't happen soon enough. Sunderland fans who witnessed the crushing 3-0 FA Cup defeat to Wigan fled the Stadium of Light feeling angry, humiliated and embarrassed. Club goal-scoring legend and now radio commentator Gary Rowell confessed himself 'gobsmacked'. Keane said he was 'ashamed'. It was the worst third-round defeat at home in thirty-six years and the poorest way possible to mark the competition in the season of Ian Porterfield's death. It meant Sunderland had shipped six goals in crashing out of both cups at the first hurdle – three in the League Cup to lowly Luton, three in the FA Cup to a weakened Wigan.

Goals came from Paul Scharner, McShane and David Cotterill. McShane was particularly luckless, Evans having being dispossessed when, ironically, he was trying to bring calm to the back four. Not so much a messiah on this occasion as a very naughty boy. 'Jonny's been great in training but we should appreciate he hasn't played first-team football in a long time,' defended Keane.

In some ways the result mattered little, for it meant that at last the plot thinned for Sunderland. The romance of the cup was gone for another season. Now the mission was purely and simply to stay in the Premier League. But the manner of the defeat was the real talking point. Sunderland failed to muster a shot on target in the first sixty minutes and only three half-chance attempts in the remaining thirty, while conceding three soft goals.

Keane made six changes to the team squeezed out by Rovers. Nosworthy returned from a two-month injury lay-off. Evans and Kavanagh played their first Sunderland game of the season. Waghorn was given another shot up front. But Wigan, too, made almost as many changes and were playing away from home.

Though Sunderland were left to concentrate on the league. Steve Bruce felt they had cause for optimism. 'Roy's team will epitomise him, they won't give up, that's for sure,' said the Geordie. 'But when you come into the Premiership from the Championship it's a big struggle. Teams have got years on you. He didn't lose many games last year but he'll have to get used to it this season.'

Keane laid the blame for Sunderland's cup defeat squarely at his own door and it was breathtaking to hear his self-condemnation afterwards. 'The sole responsibility falls on my shoulders – 100 percent,' he said. 'I've brought a lot of these players to the club and I pick the team. We focus on the Premiership now, but there's been too many defeats. We've played Wigan twice now and over the two games they've beaten us 6-0. Now, I don't think there's that much difference between the two sets of players but we are losing too many of these games. So clearly I'm not doing my job. I'm determined to get it right, but eventually time runs out on everyone. I felt before the game that we'd be okay, but that was nowhere near being the case. I know there's no guarantees in life, and no guarantees in football, but I didn't see this coming. It's a major disappointment, so you have to step back and look at everything.

'It's not as though I picked a weak team; I thought the team was good enough to win. A lot of the lads we played were regulars in the side. We felt the game was there for us on the day but we didn't make it happen. We can talk all day and make excuses and play the self-pity card but that doesn't get you anywhere. We have to improve.'

He said he felt ashamed, reminding us once again that you couldn't accuse him of a lack of candidness. 'A Sunderland fan said towards our dugout that "you should be ashamed of yourselves" and I couldn't argue with that,' he said. 'I am ashamed.

'I'm very ashamed. Sunderland losing 3-0 at home to Wigan in the cup is very hard to take. Our fans are fantastic and I understand their feelings. I think they were spot on. We've had 20,000 odd fans come to see us who deserve better than that and as manager I take full responsibility. People say ashamed is too strong a word for it, but I don't. I think it's about right.'

Coming from some managers, that might have sounded glib; an easy shout. As usual with Keane it was direct, earnestly expressed and spoken from the heart. 'We've dressed up a few other results but not this one,' he said. 'We've lost 3-0 to Luton in the League Cup as well. We can't just shove that one under the carpet, because our fans certainly won't, and now we've lost 3-0 to Wigan in the FA Cup. Sunderland fans deserve the best, and they're not getting it at the moment.'

On the positive side, Sunderland would have a couple of free weekends in the fixture list, which would help them rest and recuperate as the season stretched towards its denouement. Immediately after the game Keane could take no consolation from that. 'We wanted to be in that next round,' he said. 'A lot of people have spoken about the FA Cup final and said it is not a priority, but they might think differently if they'd reached a final or won one. Personally, I would love to be in the next round now and not talking about free weekends and all that nonsense.

'When I was a footballer I always wanted to be involved in games. If I was sitting here saying I'd picked our kids and fringe players and came unstuck, it wouldn't be so bad. But that wasn't the case. We prepared for the game well and we thought the team we put out was good enough to get the right result.'

It wasn't looking too great in the transfer market either. The Stephen Hunt bid was increased several times, but all were rejected at a time when Keane was beginning to come under media pressure for the first time in the job. Growing discontent was expressed by fans in newspapers and on websites. There was an editorial in the north-east's Sunday paper questioning why it was that the Black Cats' boss, alone of managers, should remain immune to criticism from the terraces. Things were hotting up in the hotbed of English football.

In the game against Wigan, Sunderland had fielded two of the Latics former players against them – Graham Kavanagh and David Connolly. Both Connolly and Kavanagh would be bitterly disappointed not to be involved more in the club's Premier League campaign. Kavanagh played an important role in helping lift Sunderland out of the doldrums when he arrived on transfer deadline day. Connolly, who arrived minutes before the window closed, proved key to the club's success during 2006-07 with thirteen goals in thirty-five league appearances.

Both would feel they could do a job in the top tier. Kavanagh had recovered from a serious knee injury and was ready. Connolly believed he could increase Sunderland's goal ratio. But Keane had made his judgement call, and both had slipped down the pecking order at the club. After the Wigan result they would not be involved again.

With Kavanagh aged thirty-four and Connolly at thirty, both needed first-team football. Ironically the very money that was first used to persuade them to help the club get promoted now worked against them moving on. Both players came on wages that were the going rate in the Premier League but beyond the price range of most Championship teams, the division that would be their most likely destination.

How Connolly felt about the current situation we did not know because he had declined interview invitations all season. It was known that Kavanagh wanted to remain part of the Sunderland set-up but he was ready to accept that his stay could be over. However, it was hard to blame players for failing to find attractive moves that would potentially cost them hundreds of thousands of pounds in lost earnings. The financial generosity of Quinn's consortium enabled Keane to get in the players who were able to get the club out of the Championship, and perhaps it was part of the price to be paid that they would remain on the books for much longer than needed.

Keane meanwhile brought Marton Fulop back to the club. The Hungarian international had proven his worth on loan at Leicester, who had offered one million pounds for the twenty-three-year-old. While Ward had been prepared to play deputy to Gordon, Fulop needed first-team football to protect his international place and had impressed at the Walkers Stadium. Beleaguered Foxes manager Ian Holloway was determined to get his man and thought the seven-figure bid would be enough, but Sunderland wanted more money for him. A lot more. Keane might look at pruning his squad but he would not be selling players below what he considered their market value.

This was a testing time for the manager, off the field as well as on. He had been in management less than eighteen months but he was being forced to adapt rapidly. He was involved in a Premier League transfer window he had to get absolutely right, and he knew it. 'The big clubs do their buying in the summer and I can understand that because in January all the clubs are chasing a few quality players and you have to be careful you don't get pressured into buying the wrong players. It would be very easy to get players in quickly who you find you don't need, and end up having them on your books for a long time to come.'

The week that followed the cup exit proved to be difficult for Sunderland and Keane admitted he was intensely troubled by the cup defeat. 'I wasn't right until Thursday after the Wigan game,' he said. 'You are expected to suffer, that's part of the job, but that definitely needs to shorten.'

Fan unrest and anxiety had gone up a notch in the wake of the defeat. The abruptness of the League and FA Cup defeats made the pessimists more miserable, but hit the optimists harder. They had hoped, yet again, that this might be the turning point they were seeking with increasing desperation. Questions were being asked of Keane. Signings such as Halford, McShane, Higginbotham, O'Donovan, Chopra, Harte and Cole had come in for scrutiny. His failure to sign right-sided cover for Edwards was questioned. The problem of having no established right back until January, or central defensive partner for Nosworthy until the transfer window, was also a topic. People argued over tactics away from home, that were seen as negative. There was the question of having so few full backs at the club. Some thought he was too loyal to the ageing Yorke.

The real damage was only done the day after the Wigan debacle when the club was hit by another punch below the belt. An interview appeared in an Irish Sunday paper which, within forty-eight hours, spread to every local and national newspaper in England and represented the first real attack on Keane's management style by one of his players.

It was Clive Clarke.

The Irish defender, who had been sidelined since his heart attack but never really figured in Keane's first-team plans, had chosen a particularly vulnerable moment to attack his boss. Coupled with events later in the week, the effect was to produce the biggest examination of Keane's credentials as a manager. Clarke's words were damning.

These were not the surly murmurings of a disgruntled squad member or the ramblings of the disaffected. They were the frank views of a man who had plenty of time to let his opinions percolate. 'He's going around booting chairs and throwing things,' reckoned Clarke. 'He's never going to give you confidence behaving like that. He doesn't talk to the lads. If the lads at Man United couldn't reach the standards he wanted, and they're some of the best players in the world, then it's going to be a lot harder for the lads at Sunderland to reach them. I spoke to him a couple of times at the club and he rang me when the heart-attack happened, which was nice of him. We're not very pally so there's no real reason to speak to one another. But I probably speak to him more than the players who train there every day, even now. I was never really part of his plans, and that's not going to change just because something bad happened.'

Clarke was full of praise in the same interview for Quinn, who had organised a very generous deal for the stricken player. But

Clarke would get no thanks from the chairman for those kind words when they appeared next to scathing criticism of his manager. 'Niall has promised to honour the eighteen months of my contract, which sums up Niall really. That's the kind of man he is. An honest bloke. It's not just a business to him.'

The Wearside public were perturbed. They had silently borne the bad run of results but this was the first real sign that splits might exist internally, and that had to be a concern. The player was fined by the club.

'We had a talk about it,' said Keane at his next press conference. 'Well, actually, he didn't talk that much! I might have something to be worried about if it was from someone playing a lot of games. But I think Clive has played one, or two, for me? He hasn't been here a lot of the time – he's been away on loan and then off with his health problems – so I'm taking it with a pinch of salt but, trust me, it's being dealt with internally.'

The incident saw Keane sum up his own view of the manager/player relationship. 'Is it important for a manager to be popular in the dressing room? Most certainly not, no. I've never been involved in this game to be popular, whether as a player or manager. That's a dangerous road to go down. I'm involved to win. But you hope for loyalty.'

Loyalty however was in short supply in football, as events just nine miles up the road in Newcastle demonstrated. News had come through that Sam Allardyce had been sacked at Newcastle United just eight months into the job. This was a disappointment to Sunderland chairman Quinn, who was friends with Sam Allardyce. Quinn had envisaged a Tyne-Wear rivalry emerging under Allardyce and Keane which would continue putting both clubs in the spotlight. And the chairman also hoped that links like the ones he had with Big Sam would take some of the sting out of the bitterness in some quarters, which had increasingly bogged down the derby in recent years. Quinn believed that north-east rivalry was essential if the region was to become a focal point of the football world. He also felt strongly that quick-fire sackings were not the right way for football to go.

'I hope ourselves and Middlesbrough in the bottom half of the table stay up,' Quinn said when both clubs were still unsure of their Premier League futures, 'because ourselves and Boro are about the only clubs in the bottom half who have had faith and trust in their young managers. All the rest have sacked theirs and maybe if all three clubs that go down have changed managers, then maybe it will send a message out that that is not always the wisest way for a board to go.'

Sam Allardyce's sacking brought the number of changes in the Premier League hot seats to eight. Chelsea, Spurs, Wigan, Bolton, Fulham, Birmingham, Derby and Newcastle had all sacked their bosses. With just four wins in twenty-three games, and his team in the relegation zone, Keane's own job could have hung in the balance. It didn't. Quinn and his board showed their faith. 'We believe in Roy and we've always been prepared to back him.'

Even if they hadn't, it wouldn't have bothered Keane.

The Sunderland manager once defined happiness as the absence of fear, and the prospect of getting the axe held absolutely no concerns for him. He had watched managers quite literally go by the board – Jose Mourinho, Martin Jol, Chris Hutchings, Sammy Lee, Billy Davies, Lawrie Sanchez. 'The statistic about sackings doesn't concern me one bit,' he shrugged. 'If you get sacked, what is it? The end of the world, is it? It's not.'

He was far more focused on his day-to-day duties, which included his plans to offload players. 'We're talking about generating a few bob and I have to look at letting one or two go. We have got players like Graham Kavanagh and Dave Connolly who have not been getting games; then there's Stephen Wright who is due back; there's Marton Fulop and big Stan Varga returning. You can't just stand in their way if they want to play games. That's a natural thing and it's something we have to look at.'

If those players were to leave, they would leave with the manager's best wishes. Kavanagh, Connolly and Varga were three of the six players Keane signed within forty-eight hours of taking over the club and all played their part in the club's promotion. Wright remained Sunderland's longest-serving player and the last man at the club who was signed by Peter Reid, while Fulop was an able backup to Ward in the Championship-winning season. Keane said: 'They've all been good lads and good pro's.

'I'm looking to bring players in during the transfer window, but I also have to look at the ones who we might have to let go of during that process.'

Sunderland were not giving up on their pursuit of Stephen Hunt. It had, after all, taken three bids for Gordon before he came to Sunderland. But nothing was happening with Hunt. There were other sources of concern too. The club had had to pay Birmingham City £28,000 for Sunderland fans not taking up their full allocation of their overpriced tickets. With no win on the road so far this season and a game coming early in the New Year, when money was tight in Wearside households, 900 tickets were still left for the Spurs game at White Hart Lane on 19 January.

Quinn offered what looked like a veiled threat to fans when he said that they might have to review the club's ticketing policy unless these tickets were taken up. The club would need to consider requesting smaller allocations. For once it looked like the chairman's sure media touch had deserted him. It came over as slightly churlish on his part, given the fact that fans had had little to cheer on the road. The club statement did not impress many supporters, who could point to the fact that no victory on the road all season was hardly an inducement. Many were skint after Christmas and there was major disruption on the east coast rail line to London, which made even getting there an arduous journey. It was storm-in-a-teacup stuff but there were a lot of stormy teacups about for Sunderland.

CHAPTER SIX

The Road to Redemption

We're scrapping away and the aim still has to be to try topping our own mini-league. ROY KEANE

WHILE Keane considered what new blood he might bring in, he was also looking at his fringe players and was impressed with their efforts in the reserves. A two-goal blast from Stokes cemented a comfortable victory over Newcastle United's second string at Tyneside's Kingston Park, in blustery rain-swept conditions. He hoped his first brace for Sunderland would help fire him back into the first-team picture for the visit of Portsmouth. 'It was great to get a full ninety minutes under my belt because I can't remember the last time I played a full game from start to finish,' he said. 'It's the first time I've scored two goals in a game for Sunderland and it will do no harm to my first-team chances.'

Stokes' moment had passed though. The young Irishman, who had started the season with such high hopes, was to become a peripheral figure. Keane would recall him for the next game, against Portsmouth, but Stokes would gradually drift out of the picture. The youngster shared the same birthday as the club's goal-scoring legend Kevin Phillips but not, it seemed, his prolific ability in front of goal at the highest level.

Keane had asked to be convinced by his players. The arrival of Evans and the resurrection of his partnership with Nosworthy in central defence would also limit opportunities for the likeable Higginbotham and the enthusiastic McShane. It was tough for McShane in particular. He had looked well on his way to becoming a cult hero in the first quarter of the season, but his star had waned.

Sunderland faced a Portsmouth team enjoying a great season under 'Appy 'Arry Redknapp. What underpinned Pompey's success was their stunning away form. They had won eight out of nine – the best away record in the Premier League. It was a record Sunderland hoped to dent at the Stadium of Light and they could not have played them at a better time. Pompey were without four key players because of the demands of the

African Cup of Nations. The match was to bring a 2-0 win for Sunderland, a strained leg for Jones and the sight of Richardson celebrating a two-goal blast by being mobbed by teammates before throwing his shirt into the greedy hands of an ecstatic crowd at the final whistle. Richardson, a key member of an epic and successful relegation battle while on loan at West Brom – when the Baggies went from bottom to fourth bottom on the final day of the season – felt that for all the money Sunderland had spent, it was good old togetherness that would give them the best chance of staying up. 'Team spirit is the key really,' he said. 'We had a great team spirit at West Brom that year.'

Richardson and Jones stood out in the game and that could hardly have comforted the watching Portsmouth manager. Richardson had played under Harry Redknapp at West Ham United and Jones at Southampton. Sunderland had been searching for a saviour over the last few depressing months and in this game there were some obvious candidates. Richardson scored both goals, while his former colleague at Manchester United team, Evans, helped the Wearsiders keep a rare clean sheet on what was his first Premier League appearance.

If you were holding out for a hero there was targetman Jones. The big man had become such an important player for the club that the unfit talisman was patched up El-Cid-like and sent out to spearhead his team against Pompey. He was subbed half a dozen minutes before full-time – ten minutes after being reduced to a virtual walking pace with his aching knee. By then, not only had he set up Sunderland's opening goal, he had been a menace to Portsmouth throughout.

Sunderland made five changes to the team that lost in the cup, and all were aimed at improving the team; Portsmouth made four but all theirs were enforced, having lost key players to Africa. 'Too many quality players to be without,' rued Harry Redknapp afterwards.

Redknapp's media profile had rarely been as high as it was in this game, following a £20 million offer from Tyneside for him to boss the Magpies in the wake of Sam Allardyce's sacking. The interest that generated was reflected in the scrum of photographers surrounding the away dugout before kick off. But he was at pains to deflect attention from that issue afterwards, doing it in his usual heartfelt, earnest way.

Portsmouth's day might have been so different if Pompey's top scorer Benjani Mwaruwari had made the most of a great early chance, but he dragged his shot across the face of goal from the edge of the six-yard box and gradually Sunderland asserted themselves. They were helped by their 4-5-1 formation. Yorke sat in front of the back four, where his passing and tackling could shine. The energy of Miller and Richardson helped out in front of him. Jones played the lone frontman, aided by Murphy and Stokes on the flanks, pushing on when the home-team was in possession. This tactical system was often criticised by Sunderland fans who couldn't see the benefit from it. In this game they could.

Sunderland took the lead in the 33rd minute with a memorable goal. Evans pumped a long ball forward down the left for Jones to chase. Sol Campbell thought he had done enough when he shoulder-charged the Sunderland striker off the ball. But Jones kept on going. Chased a lost cause. And, to Campbell's surprise, just managed to keep the ball in. He added insult to injury by nipping back across the backtracking Portsmouth captain, passing a ball inside to Richardson at the near post. The midfielder kept his cool brilliantly to drag a low left-foot shot across David James into the inside netting at the far post.

The killer second goal came just before the break. This time Richardson started and finished the goal. He pressured Benjani Mwaruwari into conceding possession in the midfield, which allowed Miller to pass forward to Murphy on the edge of the Portsmouth area. Murphy could make no progress but Richardson, who had continued a diagonal run towards goal, picked up the ball and, running across defenders, shot from right to left as he held off Hermann Hreidarsson. A rising right-foot shot proved too much for David James. Richardson and his teammates were left to celebrate the first top-division brace by a Sunderland player since 2002. It could hardly have been better timed, once again the achievement coming for the first time since the days of Kevin Phillips.

Three minutes into the second half Richardson fired one over the bar from eighteen yards, and he went even closer just before the hour when he tracked across goal from right to left before smashing a superb shot off James's crossbar. But a hat-trick was not to come.

Minutes before that Benjani Mwaruwari should probably have scored when Portsmouth counterattacked on an excellent throw out from David James, which put him clean through down the left. With Gordon blocking him, his attempted square ball was intercepted by Evans, leaving the striker punching the post in frustration at the opportunity wasted. The inclusion of Evans meant that, despite playing three times for Manchester United's first team earlier in the season, his first Premier League bow was in the colours of red and white.

Keane's record-breakers had reached 20 points with this win. The highest Premiership total the club had managed in six years. It was a result that gave, perhaps, the clearest sign yet that they were not going the way of those abject relegation teams of 2003 and 2006. The win left Sunderland still in the bottom three, but not only was it a genuinely impressive performance, it also left the team three points away from Reading in 13th. It was hotting up at the bottom and this result put Sunderland right back in the race for survival. It was the Wearsider's first victory of the season over a team in the top half of the table, their third clean-sheet of the campaign. The comprehensive win sent fans away from the Stadium of Light in such a buoyant mood that you might have forgotten that this was one of the most fraught weeks of Keane's managerial career.

Harry Redknapp hailed Keane and Jones. He was asked about Jones but was happy to volunteer his opinion about Keane before the subject was even raised. 'I just think Roy is great,' he said. 'I think he's different class and I think he's going right to the top. He was a top class player and I feel he'll be a top class manager.'

On Jones, he said: 'I can't believe how much he's come on, but that's not to say he never had the makings of a top player when I knew him. He always had the attributes. He's great in the air; he's quick; he's got a presence; he's got the lot really, but the one thing I wasn't sure of was whether he had the desire to be a top player. Obviously he's showing that this season, but I think you probably have to credit Roy for that.'

In the wake of a week in which Keane admitted he could find no positives at all from the FA Cup defeat to Wigan, the manager was brimful of them after the victory which kept Sunderland in touch with the rest of the teams above the relegation zone. 'I asked for a response and I knew I would get it,' he said. 'People will rightly question us after the previous week against Wigan but I see the players in training and know what they're capable of. Kieran is one of the quickest players I've come across over the first four or five yards and I think we saw that in this game. We've been unfair to him since he came back from long-term injury because we've had to throw him straight back in. He's still not match fit yet but he's getting there.

'Kenwyne is a big player for us and him being involved was a big plus. I don't like to play anyone who is less than, say, eighty percent fit. I would say Kenwyne was no more than sixty or seventy percent fit, but you saw what a great approach he had to the game.

'Defensively I thought we did well. Jonny Evans and Nyron Nosworthy had a good understanding in central defence last season and it's nice for us to have a clean sheet. I think Craig Gordon will be happier for that. You ask any goalkeeper and clean sheets help you. He is looking more assured. It's not easy when you're playing Sunday and other teams have got decent results the day before. We knew before the game that, even if we won, we'd still be in the bottom three. That can be tough for some players but they showed the right attitude.'

Despite success on the pitch, transfer dealing wasn't straight-forward. Portsmouth's Matt Taylor, a Sunderland target, suddenly chose to join Bolton Wanderers, after apparently agreeing a deal with Sunderland, which was reported in the Sunderland Echo. 'I want to thank Roy publicly for his time,' said the diplomatic Taylor. The reality was that Sunderland had pulled the plug on their interest after a telephone conversation failed to impress Keane. 'I knew within ten seconds he wasn't a Sunderland player,' said the manager.

There was some good news with the signing on 15 January of Jean Yves Mvoto, a French U19 international from Paris Saint-Germain for about £300,000. 'A bonus signing,' Keane said, earmarking him as one for the future.

But it was securing senior players that remained his priority.

Meanwhile, there was good news on a different sales front, with Sunderland not only having sold out the troublesome Tottenham ticket allocation, but also the allocation for the Liverpool game that followed. It was typically amazing stuff from Sunderland fans who had seen only two draws and no wins away from home all season. Quinn commented: 'I know one or two people thought I was being a bit harsh but I want to make it clear that I wasn't giving out to our fans. It's simply that it breaks my heart to see us handing over money to other clubs for fresh air. I'd rather give it to charity.'

Keane also had his mind on money. 'If certain players are worth £20 million, Kenwyne is worth £40 million,' he said, deadpan. 'It's not as if he's getting four or five good chances a week, he's getting one chance every four or five weeks. But I have to say that Dwight Yorke has been a big help to him. He speaks to him on a regular basis.

'Transfer fees are big now but they'll be a hell of a lot higher in the next few years, trust me on that,' he said.

Keane still had his eyes fixed on the battle at the bottom. 'We're scrapping away and the aim has to be to try topping our own mini-league. That's why the Portsmouth win was so important in keeping us in touch. A week is a long time in football and I've got to say we are a touch happier this week than we were last week.'

Trips to White Hart Lane had proven the most punishing and unrewarding of all for Sunderland fans in the top tier: seven visits previously in the Premier League, seven straight defeats. This was to be the eighth. The same number of consecutive away defeats Sunderland had now endured over the last few months. No wonder the away tickets hadn't been flying off the shelves. And after Sunderland fans heeded the plea of chairman Quinn to buy, I wondered how many felt slightly foolish after a game in which their team produced kamikaze defending to gift Spurs all three points. Sunderland's problems were once again entirely of their own making and, despite a thrilling second-half fightback which would have yielded at least one goal on any other day, it was hard to argue the final result wasn't a fair one.

'Brutal' was how Keane described the Premier League after the game. Not as a criticism but as a compliment. He was saying that games aren't decided on artistic interpretation, presentation or overall play, but on seizing the moment when the game is there to be won and taking your chance when it comes. 'They did; we didn't,' was his frank verdict.

Sunderland's cause wasn't helped by the frustrating absence of in-form Richardson, who suffered a hamstring strain in the run-up to the game and would be sidelined for weeks. The formation that served Sunderland well in the 2-0 victory over Portsmouth was perhaps too defensive-minded against one of the most porous rearguards in the Premiership. 'We looked more threatening when we went to 4-4-2, and maybe we should have been like that from the start,' admitted Keane.

But it was basic defending rather than the formation that cost Sunderland. With barely 100 seconds on the clock, Nosworthy lost possession in the right back position, McShane's attempted clearance struck Lee Young-Pyo and winger Jamie O'Hara's cross was helped on by Dimitar Berbatov to Aaron Lennon, who scored from eight yards out. Sunderland did not crumble but Spurs held the whip hand. On the quarter hour Gordon's goal had to withstand severe pressure as the opposition queued up with shots from around the box. There was a danger Sunderland could be sliced apart by the pace of Aaron Lennon. In the 18th minute Spurs broke with the speedy winger, beating Yorke to the ball, and when Yorke clearly handled, trying to regain possession, he was very lucky to get away with it. Evans made a great tackle to dispossess Jermain Defoe a minute later, but Spurs should have doubled their lead in the 21st minute when Tom Huddelestone's raking long ball put Jermaine Jenas clear. He chipped a shot towards Gordon's right-hand post, which Dimitar Berbatov was a fraction away from steering in from a yard out. Five minutes later Berbatov's shot from ten yards out thwacked the crossbar. Before half-time Gordon was at full stretch to claw a clever Jermain Defoe lob wide.

Keane's patience with Stokes reached an end when the Irish youngster lost possession before the break. He was replaced by Chopra and the team switched from 4-5-1 to 4-4-2. Almost instantly, Sunderland improved. Jones and McShane went close; Murphy, having a fine game, began to torment the Londoners. Gordon at the other end kept his team in it.

Sunderland attacked. Collins had a shot cleared off the line, Chopra hit an 'air shot' from six yards out with the goal beckoning, then Whitehead fired wide with the goal at his mercy. The Wearsiders were desperately unlucky when goalkeeper Radek Cerny produced world-class form to deny Murphy's shot and Miller's follow up, but these were chances Sunderland could not afford to squander and Spurs sealed victory in injury time.

A booming goal-kick from Radek Cerny bounced twice in the Sunderland half before it reached substitute Robbie Keane. He kept his composure, driving a left-foot shot home which Gordon, having previously excelled, might have done better with.

Keane did not particularly enjoy his namesake's 100th goal for

Spurs; nor did his fellow former comrade-in-arms Quinn – especially after the chairman's plane had been subject to a two and a half hour delay, which meant flying down on the day was not an option. With the rail service still paralysed, he had made the long journey down by car.

The Premiership's longest run of away defeats continued, but not one of the half-dozen teams above Sunderland that weekend took real advantage and the club now turned its attentions to the six-pointer at home to Birmingham City. A home win would drop the Blues into the bottom three and hoist Keane's men out of the relegation zone. They would have to do it without the injured Richardson and the now suspended Chopra – the match-winner when Spurs and Sunderland met first time around – who picked up a fifth yellow card and a one-match suspension.

Keane acknowledged Jones had by now become arguably Sunderland's key player. He admitted a lot was being asked of a young footballer who had just stepped up from the Championship. The twenty-three-year-old was not only the club's leading scorer, with five goals to his credit, but was in the Premier League top ten for assists. His absence in the FA Cup game against Wigan had proved telling, with Sunderland never producing a real attacking threat. The striker missed that game with injury and Keane was determined to avoid burnout.

'Kenwyne has a knock to the back of the knee and we'll have to see how it is, but sometimes I think it's just the workload we've asked of him, which can't help his situation. I read all this speculation about different strikers in the papers who might be going here or there but there's no doubt in my mind that we have the best striker in the league at the moment. The shift he puts in every game is terrific and maybe we've put a lot of weight on his young shoulders. He's played up front by himself in a lot of games away from home and the workload he gets through in games is unbelievable.'

Difficult season or not, Keane – a Spurs supporter as a boy – 'people supported Man United, Liverpool or Celtic so I thought I would be different' – was refusing to abandon his principles of calling it as he saw it. 'Do I feel hard done by?' he responded in the wake of a Sunderland's spirited second-half comeback which had made Tottenham's one goal lead look too slender. 'No.'

'If you give two goals away, like we did, then you don't deserve to win any football match. I give credit to their goalkeeper, who made some outstanding saves, but when you give a goal away after 111 seconds it's not ideal. Lack of concentration is the story of our season and at the top level, it's concentration that wins you matches. A lot of what being a footballer, a top footballer, is about is what goes on between your ears. If you start a game like we did, a goal down at Tottenham in two minutes then you're going to have problems. The last goal – a straight ball upfield from their keeper that none of our players touch before it reaches Robbie Keane – well ...' his voice trailed away. 'I don't think our poor away record is preying on the players' minds because our last three games – against Reading, Blackburn and now Spurs – could have brought us points. But they didn't. That's the reality of the Premiership. We have missed the quality of our best players. But we persevere and perseverance is the most important word for our situation right now.'

Sunderland fans made the long return journey knowing that their first away win of the season would now have to wait until February. And that knowledge must have reminded many of Sunderland's 15-point relegation when the Wearsiders didn't win a single game until the very last match of that campaign. It was a dispiriting time. Four wins in twenty-five games to this point of the season simply wasn't good enough, and everyone connected with the club knew it. As I looked out from the first floor of the Spurs press room that evening I saw, in the middle distance, the tall figure of Quinn, unnoticed, cutting a solitary figure in the dusky gloom as he walked through a narrow and darkened alley towards the club car park. Having urged fans to make the long journey, he had made the long journey himself and found it equally as thankless. He looked lost in thought. And not one of the dozens of partying Spurs fans, in an outside bar singing 'que sera sera' and looking forward to League Cup glory on the horizon, either recognised or paid any attention to him at all.

The city of Sunderland was saddened in the wake of the Spurs defeat by news of the death of former Sunderland star Billy Elliott – a player for the club in the 1950s, who had gone into management and helped coach Sunderland's 1973 team. He was eighty-two and had been ill for some time. Another connection with the past broken. A member of England's Lion of Vienna team and Sunderland's Bank of England team in the 1950s, he was renowned as one of the toughest and most uncompromising of tacklers. So it was strangely appropriate that on the same day, Sunderland should sign tough-tackling fullback Phil Bardsley for £2 million.

Though the right wing had become 'the graveyard shift' after Edwards' loss, the right back slot had been a graveyard for a succession of players since no-nonsense Chris Makin had left the club in 2002. Bardsley, in the same mould as his fellow Mancunian Makin, was finally to bridge that gap. That was perhaps unsurprising, given his background. When Billy Elliott joined Sunderland for £26,000 in 1953, he came from Burnley, a top-tier club that was among the leading teams in the land. Bardsley's pedigree was even better. The twenty-two-year-old's career had been spent with Manchester United. Richardson and McShane were his teammates at youth level. Bardsley had made his debut for United in their 3-1 win over Sunderland in the 2005-06 season.

Then it emerged that Chelsea's Steve Sidwell had never been coming to the club, despite reports to the contrary, while Fulop was intent on going 'no later than the summer' and was keen to go out on loan again. Sunderland signed Rade Prica, the previous season's top scorer in Denmark, for £2 million from AaB Aalborg. He was a player the club had been watching for three or four months. Usually the grapevine flags up signings like this but Prica's arrival surprised everyone. It was an example of Sunderland's scouting network in action, with Mick Brown, Manchester United's former head of scouting, developing a European network.

'Mick Brown has been vital to us,' said Quinn. 'He has set up a system and structure looking at players Roy might look to sign. 'Roy trusts him implicitly and he's a vital cog in our wheel. He knows what our team needs and has to know what we're looking to do with the team and the squad. He sorts out a lot of the wheat and the chaff because you can't have Roy looking at 100 players a week. With Mick and his system, and the way the two guys work together, we are getting through decisions – be they yes or no. He's giving us a chance to make good, solid decisions. It's a great structure and it's bigger than that. It helps avoid panic buying. It's best practice. You have to take as much of the gamble out of signing a player as possible. Roy's big thing is character. It's vital. If you have something special like we did last year, we don't want people to come in and destabilise things and split the camp – because that's what happened before.'

Keane was delighted by the character shown by Bardsley and Prica and hailed them as 'no-maintenance players'.

'When they came in, there was no rigmarole with them,' he said. 'It was straight in and ready for training. Other players were asking questions like "who else are we buying?" and that's one question too many. I remember when I went to Forest I never asked Brian Clough one question. I met Alex Ferguson; I never asked him what the plans were for this or that. He told me. That was it. It's nice when you have a general conversation about the area and schools, but when they ask too many questions you just think, "no, just keep quiet, let me do my little bit". It made me change my mind. You can gauge a player.'

He was less happy about the reporting of the transfer window generally by his local press. For the second time in the season he raised the issue personally. He had been unhappy with an earlier match report, now he was concerned by some of the transfer nonsense appearing in the region's papers.

Since the beginning of football, football clubs have overwhelmingly had their closest media relationship with the local papers. There's nothing sinister in that. It's just a reflection of the fact that local newspapers are where people have always got local news, where the links between club and press have always been strongest. Clubs know that if they want to get their message across, and usually in the way that they want to get it across, then local newspapers are vital.

In their turn, local newspapers are usually happy to promote the interests of the club, especially if it means getting better interviews or exclusive stories. It's a symbiotic relationship. Nothing is set in tablets of stone though, they fluctuate depending upon personalities and preferences. Though Keane wasn't eager to develop a close relationship with the media, he was expecting his local press to follow high standards when it came to sorting the wheat out from the transfer chaff. And he was particularly irritated about reports in north-east papers that he felt were giving fans false hopes; the Sidwell story a case in point. This situation was a new challenge for him, something he had never really come across before. He insisted that the club had never tried to buy the player and found it hard to believe that stories were being printed saying he was on the way up the motorway or was in the north-east having talks. 'You'll give people false hope,' he said. 'You see reports saying Sidwell is coming, and then the next day he's not, and people think he's turned us down and it's not the case.'

We had an impasse here that was typical of the modern-day drift of football. In the days of just a decade gone, if a local sports reporter wanted to check out the truth of a story he simply phoned the manager, the chairman or a board member and was informed, on or off the record, what was happening. Everyone was in the loop and everyone was happy. The local newspaper was right every day, even if it couldn't print all it knew. And clubs avoided situations like the Sidwell one in Sunderland's case. The system worked well but it had its drawbacks for managers and, occasionally, for reporters.

When Denis Smith was in charge of the club in the late 1980s and early 1990s, he went along with the standard practice in the north-east at the time, which was to hold two press conferences a day! In the mornings he would see the Sunderland Echo for that day's news. In the afternoon he would see the morning paper journalists for the next day's stories. This was a recognition of the fact that publicity was the lifeblood of clubs like Sunderland, where the hunger for information was always great. But it had its drawbacks for bosses. 'I've been sitting here for the last hour, wracking my brains for some news to give you,' Smith once confessed to my predecessor, Geoff Storey. You had to accept that a manager spending part of his day thinking of news stories to give out was not necessarily the most constructive use of time.

In Peter Reid's day that had dropped down to a once or twice a week meeting, although he would always take a phone call. Sometimes it was unclear whether that was a good thing or a bad thing for a manager who was a human roller-coaster. I once rang him on a quiet news day on the off chance there was something he might have to offer us. 'Yeah,' he said. 'I'm transfer-listing Michael Bridges, Allan Johnston and Lee Clark. Is that a good enough exclusive for you?'

He hung up, leaving me wondering whether or not I could possibly break a story based solely on one sentence, delivered out of the blue. That was typical of him. It was a scary, if exhilarating experience being the local man with Peter Reid. A little bit like Keane, you never knew what you were going to get.

One day, as I was preparing to leave his office, Peter Reid said, 'oh, by the way, I've got one for ya. I think I can give it to you now. We're signing a new player.'

'Really?' I asked – nothing better for a local paper than a scoop about a new signing. 'What's he called?'

'Burnt Arse,' he replied.

'You can't seriously expect us to print a story on the back page of the Echo saying Sunderland are signing a player called Burnt Arse?'

'No, no, we are,' he laughed, looking a little taken aback that I hadn't been impressed by the exclusive he'd just given me.

'You're joking?'

'No, seriously,' he insisted. 'I'm not sure about the spelling though,' he admitted.

We checked the spelling. Swiss U21 international Bernt Haas signed for Sunderland from Zurich Grasshoppers in August 2001.

Phone calls disappeared under Howard Wilkinson and Mick McCarthy, apart from absolute emergencies. And Keane was not someone who would ever get involved in taking a call from a journalist. So we had a dilemma. The manager was great for us when we saw him on a Thursday or a Friday. He would give us – as much as he could – clear and truthful answers to transfer questions. But that was no help on Monday mornings when the editor was asking for a follow-up on Sunday newspaper speculation. Or for other days of the week either, for that matter.

When Reading manager Steve Coppell had said, 'on any given Monday, my local lads are usually busy refuting the stories that have appeared on Sunday,' I knew exactly where he was coming from; he was helping them correct or verify whatever had been claimed at the weekend. I'd spent a large part of my early years on the sports desk doing just that, working with the manager or someone else in authority at the club. The club you cover isn't the only source you have, of course. There are multitudes. Some good, some bad. Some reliable, some less so. In a good working relationship, the club is almost always the best source. And, while there was no greater comfort to a local journalist being confident of the accuracy of their story, it should also be comforting for a club to know they had an avenue to get out a balanced view of speculation.

195

With the Sidwell story, Keane seemed to think all we were interested in was ways of selling papers. But that wasn't the case. It's my editor's concern to sell papers. I'm only interested in getting the story right. It's genuinely not my worry whether the paper sells or not. It's not what I'm paid for. There's nothing worse for a local sports journalist, who is expected to get it right, than when he gets it wrong. It has happened a couple of times to me, and there's nothing more damaging to professional pride. I also had a decent editor in Rob Lawson who was happy to go with whatever story I offered and not exert pressure to sensationalise. The Sidwell story hadn't even been printed in the Echo. Suggestions that he was in the area had been mentioned in other regional newspapers. The Echo had simply said that he remained linked with a move. All of which meant it was an annoying time for both manager and reporter.

If there was a good thing to come out of the spat with the manager, it was that there was a desire to avoid the local papers being dragged too far off the mark. The manager would not be making phone calls to the Echo – or vice versa. But structures would be put in place to help restore a closer link when it came to transfer speculation. It meant the Echo were in the loop on transfer deadline day when Keane secured the last of his January signings and one of his most influential – Charlton Athletic captain Andy Reid was added to the squad for a fee of £4 million, while Halford went the opposite way on loan.

The arrival of Prica, Bardsley, Evans and Reid left Sunderland's players hoping for a boost similar to the one they had received the year previously. Nosworthy said: 'Last year Carlos, Jonny and Danny Simpson came in and made a big difference. Hopefully the same will happen again. I'm very glad we got Jonny back again because he's quite easy to play alongside. He's a talent.'

A few days before the window closed, Sunderland announced a series of events to honour the 1973 FA Cup squad – thirty-five years on from their original triumph. It seemed only appropriate in a year in which Ian Porterfield and Billy Elliott had been lost.

Yorke, who had never been relegated, would feel that staying in the top tier would be the best tribute the current team could pay to the past one. 'I don't want relegation on my CV,' he said. 'We need to realise, as a group of players, that it doesn't get any better than this.'

Edwards was back in training, but Keane didn't want him to come back too soon with injuries mounting before the Birmingham game. With the campaign past the half-way stage and reaching towards two-thirds gone, it remained incredibly tight in the bottom half of the table. Only two points separated six teams between 18th and 12th in the division and no one in the bottom half could feel completely secure. Everyone was expecting 12th placed Newcastle, with 26 points, to be safe. But their recent form – two points from eighteen – was certainly the stuff of relegation. The much-vaunted Kevin Keegan revolution had stalled, and all the teams below had their top tier status in jeopardy.

The Sunderland game against Birmingham City would be a test for fledgling Premier League boss Alex McLeish, who had taken over from Steve Bruce at St Andrews. Like Sunderland, Birmingham City had been promoted from the Championship the previous season and had their hands full trying to avoid an immediate return come May. Since taking over from Wigan-bound Bruce in November, the progress made under Alex McLeish had been steady rather than spectacular as he went into the quintessential relegation six-pointer between two clubs with identical records. Both had 20 points from five wins, five draws and thirteen defeats; Sunderland were still in the relegation zone, Birmingham hovered just above it. Sunderland went into the match pursuing a 50th competitive victory over the Blues, a first over them in the Premier League and the first at home in the top flight in twenty-four years. All those records were to turn in Sunderland's favour in a match that also provided the clearest signal yet that, this time, the team really was on the up.

It was one of the most pivotal games of Sunderland's season, though supporters were not to know it at the time. They were just happy to enjoy the Premier League table afterwards. Their team went up four places, from 18th to 14th, on the back of just one win. It was a sobering thought to reflect that, had Sunderland lost the match and the results for the remainder of the season had panned out just the same, Keane would have been relegated, Birmingham City saying up at their expense. Sometimes the line between success and failure is a fine one.

As encouraging as the victory was, it was the way Sunderland clinically disposed of a team that had been impressively resilient in games against Chelsea, Manchester United and Arsenal in its preceding three fixtures. Most pleasing of all was the immediate contributions made by new signings, Bardsley and Prica, who both had big roles to play in what was now the Black Cats' third home win on the bounce.

Sunderland's habit of beating opponents in 'six-pointers' had made all the difference to their survival prospects, and Birmingham could now be added to the scalps of Derby and Bolton. The two teams had been relegated together in 2006, promoted together in 2007 and met on this occasion in virtually the same position in the league. So it was no surprise when the two teams made identical changes for the match – one change each, both to accommodate a new signing while another new signing, a striker, was given a place on the bench with the intention of being brought on in the second half. For Sunderland, right back Bardsley came in at the expense of McShane, with Prica on the bench; for Birmingham, James McFadden started up front in place of Gary O'Connor, with Argentine new boy Mauro Zarate among the substitutes.

Right from the off, Jones – newly voted Trinidad & Tobago's Player of the Year – was in the thick of things, and it was no surprise when he had a hand in the opening goal on the quarter hour. Bardsley lifted a free-kick in from the right. Jones' giant leap on the left saw the ball nodded down and goalwards towards Murphy, who drilled a rising left-foot shot on the half-volley past the goalkeeper from six-yards out. It was a fine goal. The first shot on target of the game. Perfect for settling the nerves after Sunderland had made the better start in a high-octane opening.

Sunderland's players wore black armbands in memory of Roker Park hero Billy Elliott, and he would have appreciated the competitive nature of the match. Elliott was capped five times by England and was still playing with Sunderland at the time of the Munich disaster – the tragedy that was commemorated in the week of his death. He was the only ever-present in the relegation team in the 1958 season, but a prouder record was that England never lost any of his five internationals and he scored three times in those games. He had enjoyed long success as a coach too and had made his mark on Sunderland's 1973 FA Cup triumph. It was Billy Elliott who first turned striker Dave Watson into centre half Dave Watson at Roker Park. Watson would go on to win the man of the match award in that Leeds final and a host of England caps in the years that followed. So Elliott had made his mark both as player and coach. He was always famed as a player for his tough-tackling, and in the first game played since his death there was no shortage of commitment from Sunderland or Birmingham, but precious little composure until Murphy's classy goal. From then on, Sunderland were barely troubled as the home defence shone. In front of them Miller and Yorke broke up attacks to keep the Wearsiders on the front foot. The importance of the fixture was underlined by the fact that, despite Sunderland enjoying the lion's share of possession, Keane was an animated figure on the touchline demanding more discipline from his players.

His concerns proved well-founded in the 40th minute when Birmingham produced their best goal-scoring chance of the game – as well as their first shot on-target. The flag stayed down as top-scorer Cameron Jerome cleverly sprinted past Evans, down the right flank and zeroed in on goal. Nosworthy got in a covering tackle but not before the striker shot – Gordon making a vital block with a trailing glove to ensure Sunderland retained a deserved lead going into the break. This was a game when Gordon did earn his team points.

Yorke failed to emerge after the break, a calf-problem forcing him out. Sunderland brought on Prica, who made an immediate impact with a clinically taken goal. A ball punted forward from midfield by Miller down the left-hand channel reached Liam Ridgewell, and the defender headed back to goalkeeper Maik Taylor. Prica's anticipation was instant. The Swedish striker nipped in between the fullback and goalkeeper to clip a smartly-placed lob home for an audacious debut goal. 'He gambled for his goal and you can't coach that,' said Keane. 'Instinct and anticipation.'

The twenty-seven-year-old had chances of a hat-trick before the game was out; first he handled the ball before bundling an O'Donovan cross over the line, then he headed a cross straight at Maik Taylor from point-blank range. Victory momentarily took the heat off Sunderland at the bottom of the table, which was just as well with Liverpool coming up in the next game. Another real bonus for the club was that Bardsley looked the part in the problem right back position from the very first whistle.

Keane was delighted to see his new signing's no-nonsense style. 'It is so important for defenders to tackle,' he said, in danger of stating the obvious. 'Sometimes a strong tackle can be just as important as a goal and Bardsley did that very well.'

Now Sunderland moved on to Liverpool.

'An easy one for us,' smiled Keane.

Murphy had scored a vital goal against Birmingham, but admitted his head was still spinning from the knowledge that he had been expecting to leave the club just days earlier. 'The club accepted an offer for me from QPR and I was trying to get my head around it when the gaffer called me in and told me he wanted me to stay at the club!' He shrugged, confused. This was another sign of Keane backing his gut instincts when the crunch came. He had been ready to let Murphy go, but at the last minute it had not sat comfortably with him.

'You expect it is going to be tough when you come to Sunderland,' said Alex McLeish, the Birmingham City manager. 'But we shot ourselves in the foot. You can't win every ball against Kenwyne Jones. He is such a handful and such a threat from balls into the box. But you have to be there to win the second ball. In the second half we were pushing to get something out of the game but were always in danger of leaving ourselves exposed at the back.'

Suitably buoyed, Sunderland now faced a Liverpool team that had been struggling by its own high standards. You couldn't quite call Liverpool a club in crisis but, by their own standards, the season had all the makings of a flop. Out of the League Cup to Chelsea, failing to impress in the Champions League and FA Cup, and disappointing in the league. Drawing six of their eleven games at home had undermined their early title challenge, and manager Rafa Benitez had already conceded there was no way his team could catch up Manchester United or Arsenal. What was worse, their form had put a 4th-place finish in real doubt. Liverpool needed to do what the Liverpool of old used to do, which was to have a storming second half of the season to secure a top-four spot. Sunderland had to hope the comeback didn't begin with them. Unfortunately, it did.

The Wearsiders' dismal record against the Premier League's big four continued, even though the out-of-sorts Reds could only stutter their way to victory. Despite the hefty-looking scoreline, this was the least convincing display by a top club Sunderland had faced, and the fact Liverpool started the game in 8th place told its own story about the woes surrounding Anfield.

Sunderland were as concerned about the manner of their ninth defeat in a row away from home, as they were about the injury to Richardson, which left their squad wafer-thin in midfield again. Richardson was rushed back from a hamstring strain for the Liverpool game but the gamble backfired when he pulled up within seconds of the start and was replaced by Prica in the 17th minute. 'I turned to pass to him from just about the opening whistle and realised his hamstring had gone,' said a bemused Whitehead.

'He said he felt fine in training,' explained Keane wearily.

The injury meant Sunderland switching from a 4-5-1 formation to 4-4-2 but it made little difference to the flow of a game, which was scrappy and disjointed, and no advert for Setanta's choice of live coverage. Not that Keane's men would have minded. They dug-in for the long haul and looked to hassle and harry Liverpool out of any rhythm. The Wearsiders' approach was a physical one and Keane, from the sidelines, was urging it to be more so. Unattractive though the spoiler tactics were, they proved to be effective. Liverpool's one shot on target before the break arrived in the 38th minute when Jermaine Pennant crossed from the right, pulling the ball back to Fernando Torres at the near post, but the header from eight yards dropped neatly into Gordon's gloves. A far more threatening attack came a minute before half-time when a wonderfully precise touch from Steven Gerrard released Fernando Torres facing goal. But Evans produced a perfectly-timed tackle to deny the forward.

Draw specialists Liverpool were on their longest winless run in the league for five years and, as the hour-mark approached, there were rumblings of discontent around a ground echoing to the noisy travelling support of Wearside's finest. But, having defended stoutly, Sunderland's good work was undone in the 57th minute when a blocked Steven Gerrard shot was not cleared and was allowed to reach Jamie Carragher on the right-flank. Carragher nipped past Murphy as if he wasn't there and whipped over a ball to the back post where giant Peter Crouch rose above Bardsley to head downwards, the ball perfectly placed just inside Gordon's right-hand post. Up until that point you would have been hard-pressed to guess which team was fighting to avoid the drop and which was hoping for a top-four finish. But once Peter Crouch had done the damage, Liverpool began to cruise, their confidence boosted by the knowledge Sunderland had shown such little attacking threat that disappointing substitute Prica had been subbed himself before the hour.

As he had been in the first game against them this season, Gordon was excellent, denying Fernando Torres and Peter Crouch with great saves. At the other end, goalkeeper Jose Reina notched the 50th clean sheet of his Liverpool career – acquired at a faster rate than Ray Clemence's record for the Reds – and it must have been one of the least troublesome in the Spaniard's collection. 'You don't expect too much when you come to places like Anfield but I'm disappointed that we didn't do enough in the final third,' reflected Keane.

Sunderland slipped further behind in the 68th minute when Peter Crouch helped a ball into the path of Fernando Torres. The striker skilfully held off the challenge of Bardsley, then fired home a shot, which Gordon made contact with but could not stop crossing his line. Sunderland still had time to make it an interesting finish but referee Rob Styles shirked his responsibilities in the 73rd minute when he failed to give an obvious penalty to the visitors. A Murphy shot was clearly blocked by Jamie Carragher's elbow raised above his head but Rob Styles – demoted earlier this season for giving Chelsea a penalty, which never was, at Anfield – waved play on, much to the fury of Sunderland's players and manager. The Wearsiders tried to get back through open play and Chopra saw an effort cleared off the line, but Rob Styles added insult to injury when Jermaine Pennant surged past Nosworthy in the box and was brought down. Sometimes they're given and sometimes they're not. Styles, who had aggravated the Kop earlier in the season with the Chelsea decision, was in the mood to be generous to the Anfield faithful. Gerrard made no mistake from the spot.

Keane was to speak to a referee only a handful of times all season, but this was one of them. There was comic relief before that 'chat' though, during the half-hour cooling off period that every manager has to wait before talking to the officials. A policeman knocked on the referee's door on Keane's behalf at Anfield.

'Who's there?' came a voice from within.

A Liverpool steward shouted: 'It's the bizzies. They want to arrest you for impersonating a referee!'

Beating Sunderland at Anfield was one of the key games of Liverpool's season. They went on a run of five straight league wins immediately afterwards to regain their 4th place spot. Any chance Sunderland had of getting back into the game disappeared with Rob Styles' wayward refereeing, according to Keane, who again sailed close to the wind with his comments. 'I don't think we were ever going to get a penalty, no matter how long we played,' he said. 'I think Rob was demoted after not giving a penalty for Liverpool against Chelsea, so ...

'What's disappointing from our point of view is that we had a penalty awarded against us by Rob Styles at Blackburn Rovers for exactly the same offence, which was overlooked in this game. We even had meetings this week where officials spelt it out to us that if you raise your arms above your head and the ball hits you, it's a penalty. I know that people might say it doesn't matter because Liverpool would have beaten us anyway, but it does matter. Sheffield United were relegated last season on goal difference and these things add up – far rather 2-1 than 3-0 for us.'

At least there was some good news. The industrious Whitehead looked far more like his normal self after getting a string of games. Whitehead freely admitted his form has not been all that he would have wanted it to be after his return in November from the cruciate ligament injury. 'I've not been playing my best football and there's no getting away from that. No point denying it,' he said, speaking honestly, as usual. 'I don't know whether it's the after-effects of the injury or just a loss of form. Playing in different positions doesn't help but I felt in spells against Liverpool that I was getting back to much more like my normal self.'

Sunderland's loss at Liverpool was followed by a win over Wigan – a third home win in succession. The run of results re-emphasised what Keane had touched on during the preseason tour. Home form really could be the key to the campaign. The day that Sunderland faced Wigan for the third time in the season, only the top six teams had better home records than the Wearsiders.

The victory that was to come was also to prove a point that Keane made in his prematch press conference. 'Wigan aren't our bogey team,' he insisted. 'We just played poorly against them twice.'

Sunderland's spirits were raised going into the game by the news that Reid was nearing fitness again. He had been sidelined since mid-December with minor ligament damage, but that had not stopped Keane signing him. 'He adds something to the squad,' said his new manager. 'He brings creativity, guile and vision in midfield and I think he'll be a great signing for us.'

The deal had seen Halford go out on loan to Charlton Athletic and he was one of several players to head out the exit door in the transfer window. January closed with Cole joining Varga on loan at Burnley and Kavanagh rejoining Sheffield Wednesday on loan, a team he was to help escape relegation on the last day of the season.

Cole's exit marked the end of a gamble by Keane that his former teammate might produce a fairy-tale finish to his career for himself, and for Sunderland, by adding to his immense Premier League goal haul. Cole had cost nothing other than his wages and therefore was a low-risk gamble. But it was an example of the manager's hunch not turning up trumps on this occasion, even though on first glance it had been worth the risk.

A week after the transfer window closed, a purposefully discreet message from the club revealed that Clarke had gone. 'Clive Clarke has left the club following the termination of his contract by mutual agreement following medical advice.'

Sunderland had experienced both success and failure in their pursuit of players in the window, and the club's board were learning all the time about the nature of the game. Quinn hinted at the frustration felt at the time over the failed pursuit of Stephen Hunt, 'Drumaville understand now that we can't just go out and get the players we want.'

Halford's departure meanwhile had its own poignance. He had been Keane's first signing of the summer. The right back had been one of the very few players who really stood out in the Championship. Someone who made you sit up and take notice. Few fans would have bet against him locking down the position at Sunderland for years to come. 'He's got tons of ability,' Quinn said a few weeks after the defender signed. 'He's tall. He's good in the air, he's got talent and we're happy with the player we've signed. We found it really difficult against Greg when he was playing for Colchester and at one stage we had three players on him and were struggling to contain him even then, in a game we won. He's a quality player and in my opinion was one of the best three or four players who came to our stadium last year.'

After he moved to Charlton, Halford said that he felt hard done by. 'I didn't really want to move from Reading, but they made a quick buck and I was off. Yet it was more frustrating at Sunderland. I made a few mistakes and got punished. When you make mistakes in a team managed by Roy Keane, you don't get many chances.'

Keane though was fatalistic. He had given Halford more than enough chances to prove himself. The Premier League is an unforgiving place to ask for indulgence. 'The club can't stand still for any player,' he said. 'When players like Phil Bardsley and Jonny Evans come in, you can't stand still. Greg's got a chance to get games he wasn't going to get here. Players get opportunities. Some take them, some don't.' It was an example of just how difficult it can be to get things right in the transfer market. The Halford signing really should have worked out. And yet, it had not.

Though Halford had disappointed, other players were catching the eye at Sunderland and they came to the fore in the game against Wigan as the club's excellent burst of home form continued. While other home wins had been uplifting, the victory over the Latics would have fans streaming from the ground talking about only one thing. As defining moments of Sunderland's season go, Murphy's 75th minute screamer against Wigan was up there with Chopra's opening day winner against Spurs and Stokes' last-gasp goal over Derby County.

It was a moment which took the breath away, quite simply one of the best goals ever scored at the Stadium of Light. For Murphy, who might have been at Loftus Road had Keane not had a change of heart, it was a personal triumph. But the victory it confirmed had broad-ranging implications that extended way beyond private justification. The Premier League relegation battle was heating up. Newcastle United were finally dragged into the scrap. Sunderland were now four points clear of the drop zone with five teams below them and just two points behind the Magpies. Sunderland now had a genuine chance – midway through February – of squeezing out of the battle at the bottom.

Victory over Wigan was down to ten percent inspiration and ninety percent perspiration, but it was the inspirational moments which would live long in the memory – Etuhu's first goal for Sunderland, the quality of Reid's crossfield ball to Murphy and the striker's subsequent goal. Keane knew it was a game Sunderland really had to win. The last home match of the season against one of the bottom six, he started the game with four recognised strikers in his team, Jones and Chopra up front, O'Donovan on the right wing, Murphy on the left.

The breakthrough in the game came just before the break and it went Sunderland's way after Bardsley went down under pressure twenty-five yards out on the right of the Wigan goal.

'Couldn't see how that was a free-kick,' groaned Steve Bruce.

The Wigan manager's sense of injustice was heightened ten-fold when Whitehead curled the ball in for Etuhu to meet, left of goal, completely unmarked, for a bullet header that gave Chris Kirkland no chance. It was the Nigerian's first goal for Sunderland since his move to the club the previous summer and while it was a beauty and well worth the wait, his manager wanted it to be the start of a trend. 'Top midfielders get goals and Dickson has got goals in him,' he said.

Etuhu's season was to end soon afterwards. He had returned from the African Cup of Nations with a knock, which was to restrict his appearances for the remainder of the season. In the final weeks of the campaign he would be sidelined altogether. He was one of a string of players at the club who had had a mixed campaign. His ability to break up play was undoubted but whether or not he could successfully and consistently distribute the ball would be the key to how far he could go in the game.

Wigan should have equalised within seconds of Etuhu's superb opener. But Emile Heskey – who had sparked that bad day for Sunderland in the first week of the season – drove a shot across the face of goal from just eight yards out. A poor miss. But Wigan looked set to make instant amends in the second half and were desperately unlucky not to score with either of three chances they created within a minute of the resumption. Just eighteen seconds in, Marlon King was luckless with a shot, which Gordon did well to block, but the loose ball was almost sent over the line by Michael Brown only for Whitehead to surge in with a goal-line clearance. Just as Sunderland were drawing breath, ex-Black Cat Kevin Kilbane thundered in a shot from left-of-goal that smacked against the base of the far post. Emile Heskey then headed on to the crossbar. With just fifteen minutes to go, Murphy settled the issue with his third goal of the season – the trio all having come at home.

The goal-scoring opportunity owed everything to new signing Reid who had been on the pitch only a matter of seconds. Reid's entry had brought light relief to the game. Clearly overweight, the barrel-chested midfielder actually had fans bursting out laughing when he came on the pitch. Physically, he looked like a Sunday league footballer. Mercifully, he didn't play like one.

Earlier in the week Murphy had been waxing lyrical about the passing ability of his Republic of Ireland teammate and the striker proved to be their first beneficiary. Reid picked him out perfectly with a crossfield pass from left to right. It was probably the most incisive pass seen from a Sunderland player at home all season – Reid showing his worth as well as his girth. Murphy still had everything to do as he bore down on goal and the last thing expected was what came next – the striker working the ball onto his left-foot before rifling a shot goalwards from twenty-five yards out, which was past Kirkland in the blink of an eye. The ball crashed into the back of the net off the crossbar so spectacularly that the crowd reacted in disbelief and laughter at the sheer audacity of the strike. It was a goal that was to win February's Match of the Day Goal of the Month competition. No one in the 43,600 crowd would have argued with the verdict.

The game was far from over at that stage, but Sunderland's rearguard was in mean mood – Collins in particular not giving an inch. Even when the defence was breached, Gordon – sporting a new number-two haircut – was having one of his best games. No one could claim now that he wasn't starting to influence results. He tipped a Kilbane header acrobatically over the bar in the 81st minute before producing a world-class save to clear a goal-bound ball from the resulting corner.

A wearied Bruce said: 'We played well, but when a player scores a goal like Sunderland's second and their keeper makes a save like he did, you know it's not going to be your day. We came up here in the cup last month and won 3-0, yet we played twice as well in this game and lost!'

Tyneside-born Bruce, a figure of mockery on the touchline throughout from Sunderland fans, at least had the consolation of knowing things were getting tighter at the bottom after a Boro victory took them above Newcastle. 'Any team that goes six and seven games without a win, like Newcastle, can be sucked into it,' he said.

Whatever happened though, you felt Bruce, who took Sunderland fans' taunting of him in exactly the right spirit, was the man for the job at the JJB.

'I'm used to putting out fires,' he smiled.

Bruce, a good pal of Keane's, took everything in his stride, even the incessant baiting over his weight that Sunderland fans always handed out on his visits to the Stadium of Light. Breezing into the press room after the defeat, he spotted Bob Cass, veteran journalist of the north-east circuit and beamed, 'Was that you they were chanting at Bob? I think it's outrageous, them calling you a fat Geordie bastard!'

Sunderland's victory and results elsewhere changed the picture at the bottom of the table for the Wearsiders, who now lay 14th and had a fortnight's break to recover from injuries and strains. It was the perfect time for Sunderland to show such terrific home form. In fact four top-division wins in a row was Sunderland's best run in the top tier since the 1930s, when Raich Carter and Bobby Gurney were in their pomp and Sunderland were last winning the league. Bruce reckoned 38 points would keep any team up. Sunderland had 26 points with a dozen games left to get the dozen points the Wigan boss thought was required.

Keane, though, was concentrating on this game rather than the ones to come. 'We've got two good goals, a clean sheet and three points so we're very happy. I think the marine-style hair-cut suits Craig Gordon. It used to help me when I was a player. I used to feel leaner, sharper and even meaner. So I might shave mine again next week! Craig has started looking sharper in the last month, but I keep saying you have to remember he's a young man who is learning his trade. He was outstanding against Wigan. As for Daryl's goal, it was worthy of winning any game. He's been one of our better players, particularly at home.'

It had been feared Jones' international commitments on the other side of the world would ruin his performance against Wigan – he'd played in a friendly against Guadeloupe, which the club felt was hardly the most pressing of fixtures. In the event, he put in the shift that his manager had warned he better produce. 'It's a good sign that we've got some quality internationals at the club,' he said, 'and even though it can be a strain, I'm not in the mood for arguments after that result. I might have been if we'd lost!'

Victory strengthened Sunderland's position in the league, particularly with so many teams losing around them. Four wins out of four at home was turning the Stadium of Light into something of a fortress. 'Well, we can't rely on our away form can we?' said Keane. 'I know a lot of players prefer playing away from home when there's pressure on but I think our players handle it. There's tension there with the supporters, but that's part of football and it can be a good thing.'

Keane spent a small part of the fortnight's break in the league programme watching the youth-cup victory over holders Liverpool on Valentine's Day. His squad took part in a team-bonding exercise in the Lake District, with guitarist Reid making his mark with singalongs, while the manager remained away on other business. With no FA Cup involvement, there was plenty of spare time, and time enough to be distracted by a spat when the FAI finally hit back at Keane's regular criticisms.

Chief executive John Delaney said: 'The only criticism I'd have of Sunderland would be their manager giving his weekly report about Irish football, Cork hurling and all that he does. We don't comment on the players he's bought or where they are in the league. So I think he should get on with managing Sunderland and stop commenting on a regular basis about the FAI. He looks very good at deflecting from his own issues. We have been very supportive of Sunderland as regards the Irish connection. The inaccuracies that come out from him are what bothers me. He said we cut corners but Liam Miller was injured against Brazil, and he should remember only two or three countries insure their players against injury and we are one of them. So we do our business properly in that regard. It's the constant looking to the past and not understanding what we're about today. That's one simple example of where he gets it wrong.'

It was fair to say that Keane would lose no sleep over the criticism, later admitting, 'I think part of me likes upsetting people.'

Everyone was keeping their heads down at this stage in the Sunderland camp, and that included Chopra who was just desperate for a change in luck. 'My form hasn't been particularly good this season but I know that will change,' he said, seemingly more in hope than expectation.

In the week before the next game, Sunderland continued restructuring its squad. Summer signing Anderson went out on loan to Plymouth. It was no surprise that the defender was allowed to go, now that Higginbotham and McShane were struggling to get into the team with the Evans-Nosworthy partnership restored in central defence. Meanwhile youngsters Waghorn, Luscombe, Jordan Cook and Jordan Henderson were all awarded new contracts in recognition of their progress in the youth team. Fulop finally got his wish and got a loan to Stoke City, but it lasted all of five days. Ward picked up an injury and the Hungarian was forced to return to the Stadium of Light, much to his annoyance.

'I hope he enjoyed his trip,' smiled Keane.

Sunderland now faced their longest away trip of the season and a game Portsmouth boss Harry Redknapp identified Jones as the Sunderland dangerman. 'I've been impressed with him. He's a fantastic athlete with a great leap,' he said. 'I've seen him batter a lot of defenders this season and when I worked with him at Southampton I regarded him as a player you would be scared to sell, unless it was for big money, because it could come back to haunt you. I've heard some people are calling him the new Drogba – and that's possible. There's no doubt he's a real handful.'

Keane meanwhile called on his players to be at it from the off. 'We cannot be fearful,' he warned. 'We have to be at the races. There have been far too many occasions on the road when we have started too slowly and given sloppy goals away. You can't do that at this level.'

There was no doubt that form away from home had become a major cause for concern in the camp. The real possibility existed that Sunderland would not win away at all on their travels. It did not necessarily presage disaster. In 2000, Coventry City, managed by Gordon Strachan, Keane's former boss at Celtic, stayed up despite failing to win an away game. However, no club had managed the feat since.

'We have to keep believing that win will come,' Keane insisted. 'We hope to put it right and it will come. I know it will.

'Hopefully it will be in my lifetime.'

211

CHAPTER SEVEN

All at Sea and a Dose of the Blues

Man United, Chelsea and Arsenal are probably the exceptional clubs but Sunderland Football Club is still enormous. I knew the Mackems were mad but I didn't realise they were that mad. We've got 5,000 people following us around the country every week. It is unbelievable. DWIGHT YORKE

THE only victory Sunderland supporters could enjoy in Portsmouth was HMS Victory. Horatio Nelson's flagship lies in dry dock two miles from Fratton Park and though several Sunderland fans made it that far, there were no easy comparisons for reporters at the game about daring attacks or thrilling firepower. While the Wearsiders nullified Portsmouth with hard work and a 4-5-1 formation, the visitors struggled in turn to create meaningful attacks of their own. It made for a stalemate that left neutrals cold, and committed fans gripped only by the prospect of that one mistake or moment of brilliance, which was always likely to decide the outcome of a game with so few goal-scoring opportunities.

That moment arrived just twenty minutes from full-time when Bardsley, in such fine form since his transfer, stuck out a foot invitingly and Portsmouth's most dangerous player Niko Kranjcar twisted quickly to pirouette over it. Referee Phil Dowd bought the performance – ignoring previous evidence of the Croatian's willingness to go down under the slightest contact – and pointed immediately to the spot. Bardsley's interception was pretty innocuous but a second earlier Reid had clumsily half-tripped the Eastern European and maybe the referee awarded the penalty for the two awkward challenges following in immediate succession. Either way, Pompey's £9.5 million new signing Jermain Defoe made no mistake with an emphatic finish. The former Spurs striker drove his shot to Gordon's right as the goalkeeper moved left. From there, there was no way back. No team in the Premier League had a better record than Portsmouth for holding on to a lead.

All in all it was a match to forget for everyone except statisticians. They would duly note that Sunderland's tenth straight away defeat would take them to the brink of a new club record. Sunderland players reached the final whistle without a single shot on target, much to their manager's anger, for he appreciated how far fans had travelled, and in what great numbers. They deserved better. 'I would have taken a point,' Keane said. 'But you have to do more than we did in attack. You have to bring something to the party, and in this game we had absolutely nothing going forward. We've got thousands of fans behind the goal and we've got to give them something to shout about. If we'd played until midnight I don't think we would have scored.'

Keane's formation, which featured Murphy on the right wing and Reid, making his full debut, on the left, was intended to be strong defensively but positive in possession, with runners supporting lone striker Jones. It succeeded admirably in the former objective and failed utterly in the latter. With Sunderland lacking the pace of an Edwards or a Richardson in midfield, Jones was too often left an isolated figure up front. Balls punted forward to him were sometimes won by the big man, other punts dropped regularly into no man's land where Pompey shirts tidied up. Long before the end – even with the introduction of strikers Prica and Chopra – Jones cut a frustrated figure with Sunderland failing to click upfield.

That left Sunderland looking to their next game – the visit to Derby County at Pride Park – to avoid equalling a record of eleven consecutive away defeats set more than forty years previously. That record was news to Keane in the postmatch press conference, but the drabness of his team's defeat was not. In the cramped confines of the Portsmouth press room, just outside the main gates of Fratton Park's mock-Tudor entrance, he lashed his players publicly for not showing enough confidence or belief. It was a vitriolic attack that underlined the manager's occasional frustrations with his inexperienced squad.

'I think one or two of my players were a bit overawed on the day,' he started. 'One or two of them brought their autograph books and I don't like to see that. If they're going to be overawed by one or two of the Portsmouth players, what are they going to be like when they come up against the really big boys, the Arsenals, Liverpools and Manchester Uniteds? I'm pretty sure some of my players will be in Portsmouth's players' lounge, getting autographs now. No, I guarantee it. And that's a sad state of affairs. If you're a top footballer, you shouldn't get anyone's autograph.

'It's my job to change the players' mentality. Sunderland have been seen as victims for far too long. It was the same at Blackburn Rovers when we've had a penalty saved and they've had a penalty scored. All these points add up. I think David James must have had one of the easiest games of his career. Portsmouth didn't need a goalkeeper on the day! I do believe we've deserved a few more draws on our travels this season but not necessarily in this game.'

In the postmatch press conference it's pointless asking questions. If you're lucky enough to ask a brilliant question immediately after the match, you'll see the answer in the Sunday papers. Then in the Monday morning papers. And finally, you'd get to print it in Sunderland's evening paper on Monday afternoon. Because of that, you watch, and you wait, and look for a line that maybe everyone else won't use.

Keane is almost always scrupulously polite in terms of waiting for everyone to ask every question before he gets up to leave. Some managers keep it perfunctory, especially after a defeat. They answer a few questions and then they are already halfway out of their chair. Usually, the end of a Keane press conference is signalled by a few seconds silence, then the manager says 'okay?' and he's on his way. That was exactly the form at this press conference, but as Keane got up to go on this occasion, one of the veteran journalists on the southern circuit stopped Keane to ask if he could have his autograph on a piece of memorabilia.

Bearing in mind what had he had just said about autograph-hunters, it was an astonishing act of brass neck. 'Pardon,' said Keane staring in disbelief as the question was repeated. 'Could I have your signature Roy, please, for my son?' And then, by explanation, 'I covered your matches for Ireland.'

Putting aside the fact that the manager was unlikely to feel a debt of gratitude for having his international matches covered, it seemed almost beyond belief that anyone could ask for his autograph after what Keane had just said about his own players. For a second, I seriously wondered whether it would all be too much for the Sunderland manager. Instead, the dead eyes settled. He signed the item as though he wasn't even in the room. If you could have bottled cold, seething contempt, you could have filled a barrel from Keane.

His disappointment with the defeat had been compounded by the awareness that, just like that freezing cold night at Blackburn, fans had trekked so far for so little. Sunderland's fans certainly deserved better for their country-long haul. No matter how poor Sunderland were on the pitch, the travelling support was first-class off it. A week before the game, for one of the longest trips in English football, Sunderland had sold out their away allocation. 'That just says all you need to know about them,' said local hero Gary Rowell.

Gary Rowell – along with Kevin Phillips and Len Shackleton – was the only player to score more than 100 goals for Sunderland since 1945. Unlike those two other icons, he had grown up a Sunderland supporter. He had stood behind the net at Wembley in 1973, where Ian Porterfield had buried that goal, then went on to score 102 goals between 1975 and 1984 for Sunderland. Now a radio commentator for Century and a columnist for the Sunderland Echo, his love for Sunderland was genuine and far-reaching, never better illustrated than when he was marvelling at the supporters and the lengths they went to for the club. They still idolised him. If the FA Cup win had helped Sunderland fans through in the early 1970s, son-of-Seaham Rowell's goal-scoring exploits had sustained them through the 1980s. As Rowell said, Sunderland supporters' loyalty was a given thing.

Over 1,800 fans travelled the 700 mile round trip from Wearside to Portsmouth – even though their team had still to win away from home in thirteen attempts. The last time they had taken even a point on their travels had been at Middlesbrough – in September. There were nine straight defeats across five months after that. All of which made the journey to the south coast a long, long thankless task, and an even longer journey back. London supporters can get to a fifth of Premier League games by hopping on the Tube or a bus. A third of the north-west's games are in the same region, while Midlands fans rarely have to travel any major distance. But fans on the fringes of the north-east have become battle-hardened to making longer trips in larger numbers.

This time the journey had a poignancy, which would have been lost on almost every single fan who made the trek. For Fratton Park was the setting for what was, for a whole generation of fans, the worst moment of their Sunderland-supporting lives – the club's first relegation. And this was its 50th anniversary. Over the course of the following five decades, everyone had got used to Sunderland being a yo-yo club – the club promoted and relegated three times in the last five years alone – but in 1958, Sunderland's relegation shook football. It had quite simply never happened before and anyone interested in football would have regarded a top division table without Sunderland in it as almost unnatural.

Sunderland joined the old First Division in 1890, and stayed there longer than any other team. The match-day programme used carry the proud statement: Sunderland is the only top-flight club in English football never to be relegated. A lifetime in the top tier. One of the reasons why Sunderland was one of the biggest clubs in the land. The sort of stability Quinn and Keane were seeking to restore. The journey's end of that long arc was a relegation confirmed at Fratton Park in the wake of the payments scandal that ripped the heart out of the Bank of England club. A relegation on goal difference only. It took six long years for Sunderland to get back to the top. They were never to recover the pre-eminence they had formerly enjoyed. Their first season back after that relegation – the 1964-65 campaign – was tough. It was the season Sunderland set that record for away defeats. They stayed up. So the comparisons were obvious with Keane's team, a team that was hoping to avoid that previous team's record but match its survival skills.

The Portsmouth defeat would not matter so much if Sunderland were to get a win over Derby County, the team desperately trying to avoid eclipsing Sunderland's dreadful relegation records. Keane said: 'We can't settle for anything less than three points, especially when you look at our run-in. We equalled the record for club defeats last week and those are records I don't like to have.'

When the Black Cats and the Rams had met back in December, Stokes had been Sunderland's goal hero, but the young striker had not progressed and Keane went into this game talking about loaning him out to a Championship club, though the move never came off. 'We've had an inquiry from a club about taking Anthony on loan and that's something we are weighing up. I've got to pick the best squad possible on who's showing the best form, and that's one of the reasons why Anthony hasn't been involved of late. There's never been any doubting his potential, but from the day we signed him I said he was a young man learning his trade. If that means playing a few reserve games then that will only do him good.'

While Stokes' star had faded, in the run-up to the Derby game one player's light had been extinguished altogether. Keane bombed Miller into outer darkness for regular late timekeeping. The news came as a shock. But the flashpoint had been brewing for some time with Keane because of Miller's frequent lateness for training and when the player was late that week, again citing traffic problems, the manager took the same radical approach as he had done with Wallace – Miller was transfer-listed.

Keane could hardly have laid it on the line more eloquently in his press conference that week, that this was discipline rather than Draconianism. There wasn't a trace of self-doubt from the manager over the action he'd taken. 'If you're driving to work, then don't get in a car with Liam Miller,' he said. 'He gets involved in more car crashes than anyone I know. There's a different excuse each time and I'm sure Liam will find a few reasons for being late, but we gave him the benefit of the doubt five, six, maybe seven times. Believe it or not, I don't walk round here with a stick threatening people. I'm quite a nice guy and I don't go looking for trouble. But if trouble's there then you have to face it.

'If a player's late once or twice, all well and good. If he's late three or four times, well, maybe all well and good. When it goes beyond five, six or seven times, then you've got to draw the line. We can't wait for anyone. Liam's a Corkman like me and I've defended him on many occasions. I can tolerate a lot of things and I've been more than fair, but there comes a point when you have to say enough is enough. The problem is Liam's time-keeping, it's as simple as that. It's not about him as a player, or as a lad, because I've got a lot of time for him. We need every player we can get, but I've got to look at the bigger picture. We set a very high standard here and he's not been able to match that.

'So he's on the transfer list.'

Later in the same press conference, the subject of late winners for Sunderland was raised. In the Championship-winning season Sunderland had beaten Derby with a last-gasp winner, which finally put the Black Cats in the promotion picture. The all-important goal in that match, ironically, was Miller's. 'He wasn't late on that occasion,' admitted Keane straight-faced.

The month of March is synonymous in the minds of race-goers with the Cheltenham Gold Cup. Its approach was a reminder that it was at the horse race festival two years previously that Quinn and his prospective consortium members first began to progress with their plans to take over Sunderland Football Club.

When Quinn launched his bid for the club there was confusion over exactly whether Irish businessman Sean Mulryan was part of the consortium. There was uncertainty whether he was part of the deal, or whether he wasn't as the bid progressed. It was claimed that initially he was, and then had withdrawn. Certainly, his name was not on the list of the Drumaville members revealed in July 2006 although he had close business connections with fellow property developer Paddy Kelly, who is on the list. Quinn was rock solid in the conviction that his consortium had always been in a position to take over the club, whether Mulryan was on the list or not.

Just how close Sean Mulryan's involvement with the club actually was only emerged from a speech he gave in Roscommon town the month before Cheltenham 2008, prior to the Derby County game. In that talk he revealed how instrumental he had been in first putting together the partnership that was now driving the club forward. 'It is widely known that I am involved with Sunderland. I was responsible for bringing Roy and Niall together to work again.

'I had lunch with Sir Alex Ferguson in London and he told me that Roy would make an excellent manager and that, on and off the field, he was a genius. I told Niall that and he said, "okay, we'll go ahead". We met with Roy, but Roy didn't realise that Niall was going to be in the room. He walked in, took one step backwards and said, "what's he doing here?" After about twenty minutes, and this shows the strength of the man, he said, "we had better draw a line in the sand. You, Niall and myself should go out there and sort our differences". They did and it's all history now. So that is the Sunderland story and now you know that I was hijacked into it really!'

It was a scoop for the Roscommon Herald, where the story appeared. Like the Bob Murray bugging tale, it was an example of how big stories can take years to reach the surface. It's the iceberg syndrome again. In football only a tenth of what happens tends to be visible at any one time.

There was no hiding anything at Pride Park where two struggling teams scrapped their way to a goalless draw, in a game that was even less attractive than the one Sunderland had played out against Portsmouth the week previously. There were 11,000 applications from Sunderland fans for the 3,000 away tickets at Derby, and you couldn't help but feel at the final whistle that it was the 8,000 turned away who were the lucky ones.

Under Keane, games between these two clubs had produced classic clashes. But no one at this dreadful match would be boasting in years to come, 'I was there.'

County boss Paul Jewell was typically forthright. 'Rubbish,' he grumbled. 'Like watching paint dry.'

Keane was a tad more diplomatic.

'Not a classic,' he murmured.

In truth, it was the poorest quality game Sunderland had been involved in all season. A game full of unforced errors, dreadful passing and misdirected punts. County failed to produce a single shot on target, which explained why they had failed to win in twenty-two games. They did, however, frustrate Sunderland who created only three real chances.

Murphy came within an inch of giving his team a fourth minute lead when he hit the post from fifteen yards out; Chopra scored a perfectly good goal ruled offside; Higginbotham, playing against his former club, saw a late goal-bound effort blocked on the line by Hossam Ghaly who, in all honesty, knew very little about it.

Of the three efforts, it was Chopra's that was the cruellest and hurt Sunderland most. The goal came from one of the few well-worked moves by Keane's team and culminated with Reid curling in a great low ball from the left-wing. Chopra sprinted ahead of a static defence to drive home from the edge of the six-yard box. The Tynesider had timed his run to perfection but it was almost too perfect. Replays showed he was fractionally onside but that did not help the linesman who only saw the striker suddenly burst ahead of the County defence before reaching the ball. The official instinctively raised his flag.

Sunderland's defence was rarely tested, which was unsurprising. Derby were scoring their goals at a rate of one every three hours and ten minutes. It was a statistic that helped the Wearsiders notch their first clean-sheet away from home.

The linesman's error went into a catalogue which now joined the officials' mistakes at Reading and Aston Villa. It was something to reflect that, had the correct decisions been made on each occasion, the Wearsiders would have had six more points and be lying 12th in the table.

At least Sunderland finally ended that awful sequence of ten consecutive away defeats. That was no consolation to Keane, who entered the press room in particularly grim mood and got straight to the point. 'We should have won,' he said. 'We scored a goal but it was taken out of our hands by the officials. Chopra was onside so that makes it a case of two points dropped.

'Goals change matches and we ended up huffing and puffing with Derby. They say luck evens out, but I haven't seen much of it going our way so far. We have had some massive decisions going against us and we have to hope the man upstairs is going to give us the benefit of the doubt, because we're certainly not getting it from the officials.'

Later he was to point out that despite his criticisms of referees, he was not in the habit of continually knocking on their doors. 'I've only seen three referees since I got the job, which I think is not bad going. I made a point of seeing them this game and I have to say I'm not satisfied with some of the responses. I've been very disappointed by their attitude to Sunderland Football Club. It seems to be pushed under the carpet, particularly with this club. The attitude seems to be "it's only Sunderland, it doesn't really matter" and that can't be right. Chopra timed his run perfectly and it's hard for him, and for us, that the goal doesn't count.'

His mood was not improved by inquiries in the postmatch press conference from an Irish journalist over his decision to transfer-list Miller. The gist of the questioning was that Sunderland might have beaten Derby with Miller in the team and it might have been wiser to keep the midfielder in favour. As Keane turned his gaze on his interviewer, he gave him a look that called to mind a description of the Sunderland manager as 'the only person who could look menacing drinking mineral water'.

'Are you allowed to turn up late for work?' Keane growled. 'Do you think it's okay to turn up late for work?'

The questioner did his best after a pause.

'I suppose it depends on what the reason is. Whether there's an explanation,' he replied, not looking too convinced himself.

Keane shot him a withering look and looked away.

'I don't think we missed Liam Miller,' he said. 'His agent has said a lot but I'm 100 percent happy with my decision. We created chances in the first half and I can't fault the players for their efforts. It wasn't a good game but the goal should have stood.'

Though his inquisitor had faded away quickly at Derby, this wasn't the case in Dublin, where Eamon Dunphy, the journalist who had ghost-written Keane's autobiography, was unimpressed with the manager's conduct. 'Every time Roy Keane opens his mouth these days, he lets himself down,' he wrote, going on to criticise the manager's openness about the Miller situation.

'Keane has publicly humiliated his fellow Corkman and I think he has done so to enhance his own public image as a hard-nosed manager. I think that it is simply wrong that Keane is using Miller – and Anthony Stokes before him – to put a spin on how he wants to be perceived. To abuse such a hard-working player by making such crass remarks about his driving – as Keane did last week – is frankly unbelievable. He seems to think strong management involves embarrassing and humiliating players in public. He did the same with Stokes, mentioning a nightclub that he is known to frequent and talking last week of him going on loan to a League One club.

'All these melodramatic gestures by Keane means that Sunderland have become a soap opera. Keane has become a drama queen, playing to the gallery to get a few cheap laughs. Sunderland has become "The Roy Keane Show" and that is sad to see. If Alex Ferguson had taken a similar stance on the many occasions that Keane stepped out of line at Old Trafford, then his Manchester United career would have been cut very short.

'Ferguson, Don Revie, Brian Clough, Bob Paisley, Jock Stein, Arsene Wenger – all the great managers have been disciplinarians, but there is a massive difference between imposing discipline and making players look stupid. Keane has become a bullshitter. Sunderland made it into the top ten spenders in Europe last summer but their form this season has shown how questionable Keane's judgement is. It was just showboating to the media. Maybe he's hoping they'll compare him again to Ferguson or to Clough.'

The column sounded full of spite, Miller offering Dunphy a

handy tool to beat the manager with. If Keane was perturbed by the criticism, he never showed it. He was smiling in his next press conference when he said: 'Eamon has had an outburst, has he? I think in future if I'm asked a question then I should ring Eamon before I give my opinion. I think he'd be happy with that. He's obviously a good friend of mine. I think I last spoke to him about four or five years ago. Maybe I need to give him a call. He's clearly upset about that.' Dunphy's words must only have re-emphasised to Keane his own comments earlier in the season, that it was unwise to cultivate friends in the media.

Having failed to overcome Derby away, Sunderland faced a far more difficult task in trying to avoid defeat by Everton at home. McShane could be forgiven having nightmares at the very mention of Everton's name. But he felt he had learned from the experience and perhaps felt a little that he had been unfairly scapegoated for the game. He might have won his way back into favour by now. Certainly he was giving everything he could on the training pitch. But Keane preferred the Evans-Nosworthy axis and that left the Republic of Ireland a frustrated figure. A cult hero to Sunderland fans in the first third of the season, he was now associated with the Everton game more than anything else and with fans going starry-eyed over Evans, there was a danger that McShane's early contribution would be marginalised. He had, after all, been the man-of-the-match in that very first game of the season, against Spurs.

'The Everton game was an interesting game for everyone, but especially me,' said the twenty-two-year-old, with understatement. 'It was a great learning experience, a wake up call if you like: Welcome to the Premiership. It was an interesting day because you could say I was to blame for maybe three of the goals but I tell you what, I stopped five, like. You expect your mistakes to be highlighted. That's the Premier League for you. You have to accept that the positive things won't be shown as much as any errors. But it was a strange sort of game and I seemed to be involved in almost everything. I never stopped seeing the ball from first minute to last. I made mistakes but I also made blocks too. It was a hard pill to swallow afterwards but it happens in the game and I feel that I've become a stronger player because of it. I've played twenty-odd games in the Premiership and it has been a great learning experience coming to Sunderland. A good step up for me.'

You could feel sympathy for McShane, a player who wore his heart on his sleeve. Fans usually love a player with his style of commitment, his long hair flying as he slammed into another bone-crunching tackle. But the Premier League is about finesse as much as it is about fight. And McShane had yet to fully win supporters over after being high-profile in some costly errors. In the first third of the season, he would have been pushing for Player of the Season in many fans' minds. Now supporters weren't so convinced.

Reputations can take a lifetime to earn and an instant to lose. That's never truer than in football, but while the unfortunate McShane's star had fallen, increasingly Gordon's was rising. Keane thought his goalkeeper might have an important part to play in the game against David Moyes' men. For, although Everton goalkeeper Tim Howard was in the running for the season's Golden Gloves award, Keane reckoned his £9 million man was definitely one for the future. 'Watching him in training, he is outstanding and he will be a top, top goalkeeper,' he said. 'One of the best in the world. I have absolutely no doubt about that. Our goalkeeping coach Raimond van der Gouw says he would not swap him for anybody.'

Sunderland had come truly unstuck against the Toffeemen earlier in the season and Keane was determined that would not happen again. He would adopt a more measured approach at the Stadium of Light than he had done at Goodison Park. But once again, he would later admit, he didn't quite get his tactics right. The first forty-five minutes was pretty much excitement-free at the Stadium of Light, and best forgotten. The second half – Andy Johnson's 54th minute goal and a late flurry from Sunderland aside – was largely the same. You had to feel for a crowd of more than 42,000 that deserved more for their admission money. Not for the first time in recent weeks, Sunderland rarely posed an attacking threat.

With Evans and Bardsley strong in defence, Keane knew he had to turn his attention to what might spark his team into life in attack. This was Keane on a learning curve. He admitted that one of his mistakes at Goodison Park was being too gung-ho in chasing the game. This time he wanted to be solid. Get a draw, or nick it. But don't go in with caution thrown to the wind and risk another hammering. It almost worked too, but it couldn't be called entertainment.

An excellent Everton following, the biggest at the Stadium of Light that season, took to relieving the boredom by playfully chanting 'we stole your stereo' at rival fans.

Everton got the goal that counted ten minutes into the second half. Collins gave the ball away cheaply in the left back position and the resulting cross went straight through the area where Mikel Arteta picked it up and crossed back to the near post. Tim Cahill and Andy Johnson challenged for it together in a bundle of bodies, and replays were to show the ball came off the top of Johnson's arm and rolled past the helpless Gordon. The goal shouldn't have stood but you could hardly blame the officials for not picking it up.

'It wasn't the formation which cost us. It was sloppy play,' Keane argued afterwards, knowing that the system he played had put attack at a premium. 'I was less concerned about the ball coming off a player's arm than I was about the cheapness with which we gave the ball away initially.'

Substitute Reid came close to conjuring an equaliser on the stroke of full-time, taking a superb free-kick from thirty yards out, which Tim Howard stretched athletically to tip over his crossbar. It was the only time that Sunderland had really threatened. By the final whistle they had given Everton a good game. The fact there was only one goal in it would give Keane some heart.

David Moyes was just relieved to ease past Keane's men in his pursuit of a top four finish. 'It wasn't an easy task coming to Sunderland. Not many teams come here and win matches, so I've got to be pleased.' Moyes had impressed Keane with the classy way he handled the 7-1 win over Sunderland earlier in the season. The Everton boss offering sympathy and support rather than gloating, and the Black Cats boss' had appreciated that. Keane had enjoyed his meetings with pretty much every Premier League boss. It had been a pleasant surprise. In preseason he had expected top-tier bosses being colder and more ruthless than the Championship. Those suspicions had proven unfounded.

'They have all been excellent. Arsene Wenger, Rafa Benitez, Martin O'Neill and so on and so on – all excellent. These managers are very keen to help out a young manager and give good advice. That's a part of the game I've really enjoyed, meeting managers after games. You see different sides of people.

You have a drink, glass of wine or cup of tea and most of them have been very good. They give you advice without realising it, just general chit-chat. I've had to go in to different managers on the back of a defeat and that's not easy, but its part of a tradition.

'The good managers are quite happy to give away their experiences, because if you don't give it out, you don't get it back yourself. I've made that many mistakes this year you wouldn't believe, but my players have got me out of it sometimes. But if you're not prepared to make mistakes you're not going to get anywhere. Hopefully I will learn from it, and I will.'

Keane was not to realise that, occasionally, managers could be star-struck just to meet him too. One London manager and his backroom staff were thrilled to find Keane such good company. 'Just like a normal fella,' one assistant manager said, as though Keane had just landed from Mars.

Plenty of Keane's signings from the previous summer had just not worked out, but Sunderland fans in the Everton game were able to see an impressive run-out from substitute Baines – the fullback Keane had chased with such vigour the previous summer. Five bids had been made by Sunderland to Wigan for Baines and the Scouser revealed how flattered he had been by the club's interest. 'When you know someone wants you so badly, you owe it to them to go and speak to them, to sit in front of them,' he said. 'Roy Keane was very impressive and not what I expected. He was very relaxed. I came away thinking in different circumstances I would have loved to have played for him, but the more I thought about it, the more I wanted to play for my home club.'

Keane had taken no umbrage over Baines' decision, despite putting so much work into the prospective deal. Unlike the WAGS players who chose boutiques over balls, Baines had chosen to go with his heart in his football career. 'When I left Manchester United, I had plenty of offers,' he observed. 'I had always wanted to play for Celtic and I understand it that Leighton wanted to play for Everton.'

Of the game itself, he said: 'We were very open earlier in the season and were heavily beaten on occasions, so we went with a solid formation. People will look at our shape and say, well, it didn't really work out but it was our own mistake that cost us, not the formation. We were punished for sloppy play. It was a cagey type of game and on another day we might have got something out of it. We lost to one goal but I can show you the stats. There was nothing in it.'

Keane was later to admit that he had got his tactics wrong for this game. He said he should have had more of a go. But it was wholly understandable at a delicate stage of the season that he should have erred on the side of caution against a team that had taken Sunderland to the cleaners previously. 'I got it wrong, picked the wrong team, picked the wrong shape, and I should have changed it.

'It has changed my mentality because I was naive. It is just a case of getting the balance right away from home. You have to be solid but you have to have a goal threat. At Goodison we had a goal threat but my God we were open at the back.'

The second defeat to Everton dropped Sunderland to the fringes of the relegation zone again. And it was even more depressing to see Quinn admit in his club programme notes that he had formulated a Plan B for what would happen if Sunderland were relegated this season. Worryingly, it was quite conceivable that he might just need it. Sunderland's woes were to be deepened by the replication of the same scoreline against Chelsea at the Stadium of Light the following week.

Before then, though, they had the disappointment of going out of the FA Youth Cup at the semi-final stage in controversial style, losing to Manchester City at the Eastlands Stadium. It had been a terrific run by the young Wearsiders and the midweek game had real atmosphere, with a good crowd turning up. Sunderland felt confident they would overturn a first-leg deficit.

As the players come through the tunnel at Eastlands, they look at the sign which stretches over their heads which reads: Pride in Battle. Sunderland certainly showed that. But they lost when a late goal, which would have taken the game into extra time, was chalked off by a linesman. 'Another one goes against us,' said a disbelieving Keane, who watched from the stands and put up with the occasional boo from City fans.

It was a theme he was to return to in press conference during the week. His damning indictment being all the more powerful for being softly-spoken. And, as he examined the whole issue of refereeing, it was almost as though he was discussing the issue as much with himself as the assembled press corps. 'We are not getting the rub of the green against any club and this week even the youth team had a good goal ruled out in the last minute,' he said. 'What is going on? I haven't got a clue, but it worries me. Don't fall for this nonsense that things will even themselves out. There is no way anything can even itself out for us. If you are talking about the Liverpool defeat, the same referee gives the same decision against Danny Higginbotham at Blackburn but not against Jamie Carragher in an identical situation. I would love to say the big four get all the decisions. But we are getting it against any club. I can get my head round ones where it was fifty-fifty, a bit close, but we have had decisions go against us that aren't even close and I am left going, "where has that come from?"

'Villa, last minute, we score, Steve Bennett disallows it. It was clearly a goal and no one was even appealing. Reading when it was over the line, surely you give the benefit of the doubt, but the guy gave it who was fifty yards away, other side of the keeper. These are vital incidents.

'Chopra's goal against Derby. We were told the benefit goes to the striker. He was onside anyway and they disallowed it.

'The theory that things even themselves out. Sparky [Mark Hughes] said it but I have abandoned that theory now, at this stage of the season. I cannot remember one decision where we have thought, "we're a bit lucky with that one". None.

'I was watching the kids the other night in the Youth Cup and they had one disallowed in the last minute. Nothing wrong with it. And they disallow it. It was not even a decision where you could look at it and get your head round it. Everyone is scratching their heads.

'We had 4,000 fans on the motorway that day for Derby County. I went to see the officials because we knew at half-time the goal was fine. I said "listen, the goal was onside" and the referee said "well Smartie told me at half-time that I got the call right". I said "excuse me, who is Smartie?" and he said "oh, it's John Smart from Sky". I said "he's dictating your decisions?" and he said "he told me I got it right".

'Then the assistant who gave it offside said "a Derby official said I got it right at half-time and why would he lie to me?" And I said "maybe so that when you went out in the second half you wouldn't even things up".

'Trust me lads, the fourth official had the cheek to say "I will watch it tonight on television and if I feel I have got it wrong I will be upset". I said "well, you won't be as upset as our supporters". There is no way he would be upset.

'On top of that the assessor is standing there listening to this and he rings me on the Tuesday night and says "yeah, actually it was a goal. It wasn't even a close call". What do we do? Say "great, crack open the champagne?" If the referee is being influenced by Smarties, and the assistant by Derby officials, what chance have you got? I haven't got a clue if they have it in for me or the club. Ask Smartie.

'We are not getting the benefit of any sort of decision. Trust me, I have enough evidence to show that. I am very tempted to register an official complaint. I was watching Italian football the other week and found Juventus had written to their federation saying a lot of decisions had gone against them, but what would happen if I did that do you think? If the FA ask me to go down there I could sit down with Keith Hackett and show him the evidence. There has not even been a doubt about the decisions. It is nothing to do with bad luck, it is about officials getting the decisions right. What would an official complaint be seen as? Sour grapes? What would change? It is unbelievable. It is costing clubs dear. I referee games in training all the time. I have sent off loads. It's not easy. It's a hard job. I am not here to crucify referees but you are on about our situation and my situation at Sunderland, and we have had so many decisions go against us it is unnatural.'

Phew. Vintage Keane. And this time, no national papers portraying his comments as those of a raving lunatic.

Going back to that FA Youth Cup semi-final, what struck me most was the professionalism behind it on Sunderland's part. The youngsters had travelled down the night before, stayed at a hotel and approached the game on the day, exactly in the way the first-team would. This might not seem a big deal but in former days, there were times when young players travelled as far as Charlton and Southend on the day of games. This was Keane's and Quinn's regime wanting professionalism at every level. And it said a lot about Yorke's contribution too, that he spent time with the youngsters and gave them pep talks. His image was of a playboy, but at Sunderland he had actively taken on the role of football mentor to many. As Keane was to point out many times, Yorke was as important to Sunderland for what he did off the pitch, as much as on it.

These might seem like little things but they all add up to big things. It was something that Keane had been particularly passionate about when he was a player at club and international level – attention to detail.

Evans mused: 'I've been really impressed by the way that the club has taken care of me and my family. My grandmother was over, and her two sisters and her brother, for a game and they were all saying how brilliant Sunderland were in the player's lounge. They were saying the staff were great – how well they'd been looked after and made to feel welcome, and that's typical Sunderland. A real homely club. They've been like that ever since I've been here.'

Attention to detail.

Keane even wanted input into the club's proposed new strip. 'No team ever won European trophies with a poor strip,' he pointed out. Attention to detail.

Sunderland had a batch of promising youngsters who would get over their cup disappointment and go on to win their league. There was no doubt Sunderland had excellent prospects – players like seventeen-year-old Conor Hourihane, the Cork lad who had been lured to Sunderland by the cachet of its manager. 'Roy Keane is a hero in Ireland, but in Cork he's like a god. There is a strong regional identity and the people back home love to see someone from Cork do well. He was a massive influence on me. I was a Manchester United fan too and used to go to Old Trafford to watch him when he was a player. He is one of the best players the Premier League has ever seen and when I knew he was interested, that was it.'

There were others too, like Waghorn, Luscombe, Colback ... but this was not their time as far as the first team went.

In that direction, the good news for Sunderland was that Edwards was on the verge of yet another return as the club's long-standing injury crisis finally began to subside. It left Keane to reflect a little on what might have been had fate not been so cruel in that first week of the campaign. 'You're not going to go through the season without injuries, but losing three key players before a ball was really kicked was a major setback for the club. I expected three or four players to have a big influence this season, but that was taken out of our hands. It would be nice if we could get our strongest side out for a few games and now there's a chance that might happen. How many times have we lost by the odd goal and how different might it have been had those players been available?' Such speculation was driven home by the way a strengthened Sunderland handled themselves in their next game, the match against Chelsea at the Stadium of Light. If only you got points for moral victories ...

For the first time all season, Sunderland really pushed a top-five team all the way. It was no surprise at all when they were applauded from the field of play, seconds after Whitehead's injury-time snapshot had fizzed just the wrong side of Carlo Cudicini's post. Yet a second consecutive home defeat left them vulnerable to dropping into the bottom three again. And a further cause for concern was the fact that it was now more than six and a half hours since Sunderland had scored a goal. Against the Blues it was that lack of clinical finishing that cost them dearly.

Edwards made his first start since December and immediately brought width to the midfield. It was Sunderland who created the first real chance of the match when striker O'Donovan – given a rare start as reward for training ground industry – burst into the box in the 6th minute and was sneakily pulled down from behind by Chelsea captain John Terry. Claims for a penalty appeal were waved away. How that might have changed the game was interesting to speculate but Sunderland never had the chance to sit on a 1-0 lead, or see Terry dismissed. And in the 9th minute, they were behind to what was to prove the only goal of the game – Frank Lampard's inswinging corner from the left nodded home by ... John Terry.

Chelsea's football was a delight to watch but it was a shame their approach to the spirit of the game didn't match up. Like the first time the teams had met this season, Chelsea behaved like Sunderland had no right to tackle or challenge. Carlo Cudicini ludicrously overreacted to a challenge from O'Donovan. Joe Cole flew into a huff with Whitehead over a nothing tackle. And early in the second-half Didier Drogba fell over with such embarrassing theatricalness that the crowd burst out laughing, and the striker had the good grace to sheepishly pick himself up and carry on. The closest Sunderland went before half-time was a Reid free-kick that forced Carlo Cudicini into a spectacular save, diving high to his left to claw the ball away from his top corner. Chelsea sat back on their lead and Sunderland pushed intelligently for an equaliser – Leadbitter and Collins carving out chances. The class of Chelsea on the counterattack, saw every one of Sunderland's defenders forced to make excellent tackles. But the game really turned in Sunderland's favour with Yorke's introduction a quarter of an hour from time.

The veteran was making his 450th English league appearance and, coincidentally, his 50th for Sunderland and he rolled back the years with some vintage play. Within minutes of getting on, he wafted a perfectly-weighted forty-yard ball onto the head of powerhouse Jones just outside the six-yard box.

The quality of the ball seemed to surprise the striker so much that all he could do was head tamely into the gloves of Carlo Cudicini. Not so much a shot as a back-pass. He was given another bite of the cherry a minute before full-time with Yorke once again finding him with a brilliant delivery from distance. This opportunity was a little further out but an even better chance, given that Jones was facing goal, but his header flew a yard over.

Remarkably it was the first time Sunderland had lost back-to-back home games since Keane had become manager. The final whistle left him with mixed emotions. 'I'm disappointed with the result. It was a sloppy goal from a needless corner and we never quite recovered,' he said.

'But I thought my players' reaction over the ninety minutes, performance-wise, was brilliant. What really pleased me was that when we won the ball back we showed quality and created chances. Jones and Whitehead were outstanding, Dwight Yorke came on and really contributed.

'It's very rare you lose a game at home and get applauded off the pitch, so great to our supporters for that. That was credit to us. I look around the dressing room afterwards and I couldn't see a player who could have given more than they did. Perseverance is a massive thing in football and if we keep on persevering like that for the rest of the season then we'll be fine.

'Kenwyne had a couple of chances which didn't go in. But the best strikers in the world keep getting in there and that encourages me about him. There's a bravery element in that because you've got to be prepared to miss.'

Keane went on to rubbish claims circulating that three of his players had been dropped for disciplinary reasons and called for an end to the internet rumour-mills, he said, could ruin lives.

Allegations on internet websites suggested that Richardson, Chopra and Murphy – who turned twenty-five that weekend – had been excluded from the squad as a punishment. It was the second time that season that internet sites had caused concern for Sunderland. In January there had been other allegations against players, similarly unproven.

And Keane insisted it was all lies.

'It's absolute nonsense. Three or four players supposed to be involved in something wrong? I don't know what the rumour is but for them players to be labelled, whatever it is, well it's wrong. I've been in football a long time and it seems to be something about this area that rumours go around about different players. Trust me, if they had not been included other than for the fact that I left them out for footballing reasons, then I would be prepared to tell you about it. Anthony Stokes has been ill for most of the week and wouldn't have been involved anyway.

'I put Liam Miller on the transfer list, and told you about it. I left three players behind last season when they were late for the bus, and mentioned it. The four players this weekend were just unfortunate to be left out but they have every chance of being involved next weekend. I think we should stop the rumours because it's unfair on them and their families. Trust me, they have done nothing wrong. If I leave another four players out next week, I hope there's not rumours about them, because it's nonsense.'

Rumours of a different kind surfaced when the first hint of transfer talk started in mid-March. A year to the day since Athletico Madrid's Diego Forlan was linked to Sunderland, he was linked again. The second instance proved to be as unproductive as the first.

The manager was looking to the future and players like Leadbitter, who was now getting into England U21 squads. Keane said that his team against Chelsea was based purely on the performances of his players in training. 'I use my eyes to pick my squad. I don't rely on agents or reporters or players' girlfriends. I go on what I see in training. For the first time virtually all season, I had a squad of twenty to choose from and that means that some players have to miss out. It's upsetting for them, especially when they are good players but I am looking for them to respond in the right way. I used to be left out at Manchester United and my attitude was that I would not be left out again. Andy Reid was left out last week and he got himself on the pitch this weekend because of what I saw in training. He was probably our best player in training by a distance. He reacted as I expected him to react. I'm not interested in picking my teams on price tags. It's all about training. These four players were just unfortunate to be left out. They have done nothing wrong. Nothing. Trust me.'

Edwards, meanwhile, had relished his return, regretted his own disjointed season and was happy to invite pressure on himself by stressing his desire to make an impact. 'I don't mind people expecting a lot of me because I expect a lot of myself,' he said. 'I still have a lot to prove but I know I can compete at this level. I had thought this was the season that I would make a name for myself in the Premiership but it hasn't worked out for me personally the way I planned. Not for the team either, but I'm sure we will stay up, I know it. We will have to regroup next season but we will come back and have a great season in 2008-09.'

Edwards' countryman Yorke, meanwhile, was already looking forward to going to Aston Villa for Sunderland's next game, hoping for an appropriate swan song. His long career had started at Villa Park, in 1989, and his family and newborn son would be there to watch him play. Yorke was representing a football club whose power and history he now fully understood after more than a year on Wearside. 'Man United, Chelsea and Arsenal are probably the exceptional clubs, but this club is enormous,' he said. 'You've just got to look around you – at the stadium, the training ground, the facilities we've got. And of course the fans. The Mackems are fanatical. I knew they were mad but I didn't realise they were that mad. We've got four or five thousand people following us around the country every week. Unbelievable.'

Yorke was a player Keane had never regretted getting in to Sunderland and he felt that he added a gravitas to the football club. 'When I first got the job we had to make a statement. It was important we got someone like Yorkie, who had been there and done it. The question was, could he be a sub? He doesn't exactly kill himself when he gets warmed up! But when you look at what he has contributed, as much off the pitch as he has on it, he is probably the best signing the club has made so far in my time here.'

233

Despite Jones' failure to capitalise on his good chances against Chelsea, Keane was lavish in his praise of a player who produced a towering performance up front. He knew how big the striker's efforts had been in terms of the overall performance of the team. 'The stats showed he won something like twenty-four headers against Chelsea and his overall play was great,' he said. 'And against a good defence like Chelsea's, that's really something. Some players don't win twenty-four headers in a season. So to do it in one game takes some doing.'

Even Chelsea captain John Terry was fulsome in his praise of Jones afterwards. 'We were all talking about him in the dressing room, his strength and his pace,' he enthused.

But in Sunderland's next game it was the big striker's partner who was to win all the plaudits.

CHAPTER EIGHT

Villains and Heroes and Mission Accomplished

The fans were colossal. Even the seagulls were happy. NIALL QUINN

I do believe I've not really got started yet in this job. ROY KEANE

SUNDERLAND'S long and increasingly desperate wait for an away win finally ended at Villa Park – ironically, never a particularly easy place for the Wearsiders to go. This was their first league victory there in quarter of a century. A game settled by a couple of moments of real quality. Chopra's goals might not have been as plentiful as he would have hoped, but each one had helped earn Sunderland points. His four goals directly secured eight points. The twenty-four-year-old's winner against Aston Villa brought not only the first away win of the season but also a four-point cushion from the drop zone, which would soothe the nerves of the players, and ease the relegation fears of the fans. When he signed him the previous summer, Keane spoke of how he hoped the Tynesider would be his 'fox in the box', and in this match the striker relished the role of the goal-poacher who makes a difference in a tight contest.

Sunderland were forced to start the game without flu victim Jones. They should have been the poorer for the loss of their star man. But they weren't. Maybe that was down to the positive 4-4-2 system employed away from home. Maybe it was the growing fitness of midfielders Richardson, Reid and Edwards, or an increasingly convincing defence. As much as anything else, though, it was the sheer diligence with which Sunderland stuck to their task, from first minute to last, which won the day.

The Black Cats' defence was in mean mood against one of the most physically testing frontlines in the Premier League. And the excellence deserved to be acknowledged of a rearguard which, since the arrival of Bardsley and Evans, had now produced five clean sheets in ten league games, compared to two in the club's preceding twenty-two. It was a transformation twenty-five-year-old Gordon was relishing. For the young Scot was finally beginning to make that £9 million price tag look reasonable. The arrival of Evans in particular had made a difference.

'Jonny is an organiser, and for someone so young to come in and do what he has done is remarkable,' said the goalkeeper. 'It looks as though he's been playing centre half in the Premier League for ten years, he looks so settled and composed. He fits in well and obviously knows quite a few of the lads from last season so it has been quite an easy adjustment for him, but it is still a great effort on his part. You can see these guys know each other's game very well and they are comfortable together. That's made life a bit more comfortable for all those players around them.

'It has been hard for me this season, like it has been for other players at the club who have come in. Obviously the quality in the league is very good and no matter who you are and what position you play, it is going to take time to adjust. I've come down here at a fairly young age for a goalkeeper and I know that it is going to take time. Now I've started to get clean sheets though.'

It was right that Sunderland's defence was praised for handling the pace of Gabriel Agbonlahor and Ashley Young, and the presence of John Carew. But it was Chopra's composure in front of goal that ensured three points were taken, rather than one. After an open game with chances for both teams, the match looked increasingly as though it was heading towards stalemate when he struck an 83rd minute winner. Sunderland had been under pressure when Reid took possession ten yards outside his own box and passed forward to Richardson on the left.

The ex-Man-United man glanced up and instantly hoisted a fifty-yard ball forward from his own half in the direction of Chopra, who cleverly exploited the gap between Villa centre halves Zat Knight and Martin Laursen. He was helped by out-of-form goalkeeper Scott Carson, who dithered over whether to stay on his line or come for the ball, and was caught in no man's land as the Sunderland striker athletically steered a rising ball over him from just inside his area. The goal – Chopra's first in open play since the first week of the season – was enough to give the Wearsiders that first Premier League away win under Keane.

Last time at Villa, Sunderland fans had been doing the conga on the terraces on the day they were relegated. With many of them in fancy dress, it was a colourful act of complete defiance in the face of national humiliation. They could have done the dance again, to keep themselves warm in the coldest Easter in forty years. But the celebrations at the end of this match were emotional in a way rarely seen in football and in complete contrast to that relegation day. Sunderland fans celebrated as though they had just won silverware, in the wake of the club's first away win at the 17th attempt that season, and their tired players gravitated naturally towards the terraces in an emotional union at the final whistle.

A proud Quinn, opposite them, stood and applauded. It was good to see him so high after he'd been so low just two short months ago, trudging off down that alleyway following the Spurs defeat. He's a genuinely self-effacing person, but the one thing he will take credit for is rebuilding that connection between club and players, which is so continually under threat at every top-tier club in the modern era. One of his proudest achievements since taking over had been helping the fans and the club reconnect. He regarded it as absolutely vital in Sunderland's rise over the last couple of seasons. He was passionate about the need for supporters to be genuinely united behind the club rather than break into bitter splinter groups, as they had done during his own last days as a player under Peter Reid, the manager he so admired.

'I always point to the Plymouth home game in the very early days when I was in charge and we should have won easily, but didn't. The players were nervous as hell and that was the first time I really witnessed, as a manager, how players can fold. The opposite of that was this Aston Villa game where we had the best part of 3,000 fans there and you could feel what was happening. Our fans outsang the Aston Villa supporters all day making the players feel taller and, at the end of the game, the players went straight over to the fans and there was a connection. A real, honest, emotional connection.

'The manager didn't tell them to do that. Every one of the players ran over automatically. That tells me we've got a chance. It made you really want the next game to come. That's the power of football. When everyone's doing it together, you've a great chance. We've been around the lower half of the league all season but they've been right behind us all the way. They've bought into the idea that this club could be roaring again. The club was in a terrible place and the only way to sort it out was to have everybody rolling their sleeves up and starting to do the right things, starting to work hard again. Including the fans. The fact they get behind us means so much. It's the little things, like Andy Reid, who's been here a couple of weeks and already they're singing a song about him. Okay, so it's not the most flattering song. But it's good because it tells you they're getting heroes again. The fans are starting to see things happen and they all add up.'

Quinn was later to reflect: 'It is nothing less than mind-boggling that a club which has won only one proper trophy since the Second World War can attract the support we do, despite spending the season in the bottom half of the table. People outside the club are constantly astonished by the numbers we get, compared to where we are in the table. At the start, people questioned my return to football with this club. They didn't see the potential. But I think most of them see it now. Some people think our support is unnatural. I just know it is incredible.'

For the second away trip in a row, the home team reported their biggest gate of the season. And rarely had there seemed such a bond between those on the terraces and those on the pitch for Sunderland, as at Villa park.

It had been a long wait for that away win.

In Leadbitter's view, it was the most important win of the season, while Nosworthy was to regard it as the best team performance of the campaign. No one could argue Sunderland hadn't been full value for money. Without Jones, Sunderland had beaten a Villa team undefeated at home in 2008. A team that had previously scored in every home league game.

Quinn was thrilled with the victory, knowing exactly what Sunderland were edging closer and closer to. 'If we stay up this year, it would rank as a better achievement than getting up last year. I know it would never happen, but I think an open-top bus-ride to celebrate staying up would be more appropriate than one for winning promotion! It would be Year One in the Premiership – job done. Then we'd be ready to go on and attract the kind of players who can take us on another step. Those kind of players would look at us in a different light because they'd see that we can stay in this league.'

After the Villa victory Keane was full of praise for his players, but at pains to point out that they'd been close to getting the win long before now. 'Let's keep it in perspective, we've won 1-0 away from home. It's nothing to get carried away about. It's not as if the away win hasn't looked as though it was coming because I can name half-a-dozen away games where we might have won but have been a bit unlucky. Against Villa, we just about edged it. Rode our luck a bit. Made the most of our one good chance. There's been plenty of games where we haven't done badly but just not managed to get over the finishing line. At Villa we did get over the finishing line and it's a nice feeling. Nice for the players and for the fans, who I hope will have enjoyed their journey back home this time.

'I only got involved in football to win and we've lost too many times this season. Sunderland is a great club and that's why we're striving so hard to keep it in the top flight. We know if we can stay in the Premiership then, in the year coming after that and the year after that, we can look further forward. We're all impatient to get there. We all want results now and sometimes it doesn't happen, but even the best managers take time to build a club and that's my aim.

'I thought my two centre halves were outstanding,' he said. 'Nyron was great – a real warrior for us. And Danny Collins put in plenty of decent blocks, while my keeper made one or two good saves. Overall I thought we looked a Premiership team. Especially defensively.

'We'd lost Kenwyne Jones to a virus, which was always going to make it difficult for us. But, ironically, it probably made us play better football because, obviously when you've got a player like Kenwyne in your side, the tendency is to go long because he's so good at getting on the end of things. Carlos Edwards has a slight groin problem, he picked it up in training the day before, so we didn't want him playing the full game. Neither of them will be fit enough to travel on international duty this week.'

Keane had been perturbed at the prospect of losing both Jones and Edwards to another poorly-timed friendly international for Trinidad and Tobago. But though Trinidad and Tobago's federation were unhappy and FIFA official Jack Warner made his protests known, they relented after a phone call from Keane explaining the injuries were genuine. Islands hero Yorke also intervened. 'I don't know what Yorkie had to do with it,' smiled Keane later. 'I just think he likes to get involved!'

For Yorke, the Villa game was an emotional experience. In what was almost certainly his last season in the top tier, he had been looking forward to his return to the club where it had all started for him in English football. And his fervent hope was that his current club could emulate his former one.

'I have great affection for Aston Villa' he said with his trademark grin. 'I was there from 1989-98 which were successful years for the club, and it was the platform for me moving on to Manchester United as a result. I have some great friends in that neck of the woods and I think they appreciate how important the game was to me. They're a club which Sunderland can look to copy because they are an established Premiership club who always seem to be there. That's what we have to try to do now.

'If you look at Sunderland, Sunderland are just as big a club but they have that reputation for coming up and going back down again. We have to cut it out because people are getting sick and tired of getting the promotion and celebrating that and then the next season they're back in the Championship. It's such a shame for such a great club to have had to go through that so often.'

Yorke took his position as role-model seriously and no one was more focused on Sunderland staying up. Consistently, throughout the season, Keane would talk about the excellent influence that Yorke and captain Whitehead had on the rest of the players at the club.

Chopra, though, was the hero of the day against Villa and his goal justified Keane's decision not to let him leave in the January transfer window. Cardiff City boss Dave Jones had made a cheeky loan bid for Ninian Park's former star player. 'It wasn't speculation in the papers that Michael might be leaving,' he revealed. 'I did receive a phone call. I admire Dave Jones for chancing his arm and giving it a try. You don't know what you might get until you ask. I make similar phone calls myself to other clubs, and there's nothing wrong with that, but he got a very polite "No".

'Before any game you ask which of our players is likely to get us a goal and Chopra always springs to mind. To be fair, we haven't created enough chances in games and he has been playing quite a few games on the right-wing, which doesn't do him any favours. We've got no doubt that if you give Chops chances he'll score you goals.'

Chopra meanwhile was happy to forget his unexpected

exclusion from the squad in the previous game. 'I wouldn't say it was a wake-up call. It's just keeping the players on their toes,' he suggested diplomatically.

The Villa win was a bonus for Sunderland but it was important not to let their home form slip and, besides, Sunderland felt they owed West Ham one after the disappointing defeat at Upton Park back in October. Full of confidence at the Stadium of Light, Sunderland were a different proposition to the team which had succumbed to the Hammers first time around. You sensed that they had already stopped looking over their shoulders. Since the return of Richardson and Edwards to the Black Cats' midfield and the introduction of Reid, Keane's men had looked a proper Premier League outfit. Two of them were involved in scoring the latest goal of Sunderland's season of late goals. In fact, at ninety-six minutes into the game, it was the latest goal scored anywhere in the Premier League all season.

Sunderland had gone into the game knowing that they could record back-to-back wins in the Premier League for the first time in a staggering 126 games. 'Were you in that side Danny? Deano?' Keane had joked to Collins and Whitehead in his prematch team-talk. But Sunderland just didn't get out of the blocks and were lucky to survive a poor first half, which left Keane fuming. Sunderland were mouse-quiet as the Hammers dominated. Mark Noble rifled a long-range shot wide. Dean Ashton's crafty, curling effort struck a post. Then the visitors took the lead. Freddie Ljungberg was allowed space on the right of the Sunderland box and the ex-Arsenal man fired a low shot into the opposite corner, the ball taking an unfortunate deflection off Nosworthy's backside to squeeze past the goalkeeper. Sunderland responded, raising their game. They equalised on the half hour.

Reid pulled the strings with two excellent passes, the second of which found Richardson on the left and he drove the ball across the six-yard box. Murphy at the near post backheeled past two defenders, allowing Jones the simplest of side-footed finishes from a couple of yards out. Mercifully the linesman's flag, correctly, stayed down. It was Jones' sixth goal of the season. His first in goal in ten games and three months to the day since his last one.

'I was particularly pleased it was a tap-in,' Keane said. 'It seems to me that we've had to work very, very hard for almost every goal this season. They've either been spectacular shots or great headers.'

The goal didn't unsettle West Ham. Carlton Cole forced a world-class save out of Gordon, the goalkeeper acrobatically tipping the ball over the bar, and an angry Keane was off down the tunnel before the sound of the half-time whistle had even died on the referee's lips. 'I was pretty vocal,' he admitted. 'I just think the team needed that. Sometimes I have a bit of a chat with Ricky Sbragia or Tony Loughlan about what sort of angle we're going to come into the players at, at half-time but I didn't need to chat with them. I hit the players before they even sat down. Well, I didn't physically hit them!

'But I think that's what I'm paid to do – to try getting it right in terms of my team-talk. I very rarely lose it with the players, and I wouldn't say I lost it in the West Ham game, but sometimes you have to remind the players where they are. In the first half we played like a team that was middle of the table with nothing to play for. We had a lack of urgency and we were so sloppy. It cost us one goal and it almost cost us a second when Craig Gordon was forced into an unbelievable save. So you just have to remind the players about what's expected of them. That's what I'm paid to do.'

Keane regarded his team talks and team selections as arguably the most important part of his work with the players. 'Sometimes I feel I get paid for a two-day week. Friday and Saturday are the two days I have to be focused. That's particularly true of my team-talk and my words at half-time. That's my job. It's usually spur of the moment but sometimes you can have a stat in mind. Like not having back-to-back Premiership wins in 126 games. Sometimes you just have to let a stat like that sink in.'

The Hammers injury-jinx struck again at the break and former Sunderland fullback George McCartney was replaced by John Pantsil – a move that signalled the visitors' decision to try seeing the game out for a useful away point. John Pantsil himself had to be replaced after a clash of heads in the 71st minute and in the 87th. West Ham were reduced to ten men when Freddie Ljungberg pulled up with a hamstring strain.

Sunderland almost completely dominated the second half with Murphy tormenting the Hammers from the off with shots, runs and crosses. Collins was desperately unlucky not to get on the scoresheet when his header was cleared off the line by Noble. It was ironic for Murphy, who had had such an excellent spell, that the best chance of the second half should fall to him and that he should waste it. Evans, once again a shining light at the back, flighted a ball down the left channel and Jones did superbly to bring it under control under pressure before squaring to the unmarked Murphy. But with an open goal at his mercy, the striker blazed over the bar from twelve yards out for one of the misses of the season. 'Probably the worst miss of my career,' he said afterwards.

It looked as though Sunderland's chance of the three points had gone with that blunder, but in the lengthy spell of time added on Sunderland got their killer goal. Substitute Edwards lifted over a quick cross borne of desperation in the 96th minute. Anton Ferdinand got up to it, but could only glance the ball down and on to Reid who swung a sweet left foot at the dropping ball. He caught it on the volley and left goalkeeper Robert Green with no chance as it flashed across him.

It was the first time Keane's evolving team had managed a Premier League victory after initially falling behind. Murphy was the first player to celebrate, leaping from the bench, the first to embrace the goal-scorer when he came off the pitch. There were scenes of ecstasy on the terraces, with the importance of the goal not lost on the delirious crowd nor on Keane, who turned and raised both fists to the chairman's box behind him like a prizefighter who knows his battle is all but won.

Quinn enjoyed the celebrations, as did the fans. 'When I left the club at 8 p.m., the bars were still full,' enthused the chairman.

If they were minded to, those fans could celebrate more than just Sunderland's victory. In the Midlands Derby County had just been relegated at Pride Park after only managing to draw against second-bottom Fulham, and the Rams' relegation had been confirmed. Derby went down on 29 March – the first time a Premier League club had been relegated before April. That result helped erase Sunderland from the record books and, before the season was over, the Black Cats' 15 points and 19 points campaigns were eclipsed by County's spectacularly awful haul of just 11 points from thirty-eight games. It meant that whenever the media looked for a yardstick to measure failure in the future in the Premier League, they would reach for the name Derby rather than Sunderland. Another small step forward for a north-east club in the business of rebuilding its reputation.

Hammers boss Alan Curbishley was the first to acknowledge just how important the weekend's result was for Sunderland Football Club. 'To win two games on the spin – from where they were previously – it's massive at this stage of the season,' said a boss who knew all about battles for Premier League survival.

Sunderland produced a game of thirds, said Keane – unacceptable for the first thirty minutes and then more than impressive for the hour that followed. 'We were poor in the first twenty-five to thirty minutes,' he insisted. 'Shocking. I could have played central midfield for West Ham United on the day. No, honestly, I could. I could have pulled on my boots again and done well because we were standing off so much. Then we conceded a goal you wouldn't expect to see in Sunday morning football.

'The players were told about it at half-time. They were reminded of the history of this club. The importance of this game and what's expected of them and they produced. They have always listened to my strong words. Sometimes you have to remind footballers of where they are at. This is a big, big season in the history of this football club and people shouldn't forget that.

'It has been a big, big yo-yo club. We don't want that to be the case anymore.

'In the end there was no getting away from the fact that we deserved the win. Just like we did against Aston Villa the previous week. Getting back-to-back wins is great. Can we get three in a row now? Well, miracles do happen.'

It was still a damn close run thing, though, as Keane was the first to admit. 'The last kick of the game,' he smiled. 'We were just hoping for one opportunity and thankfully we got it and took it.'

Keane was quick to praise a matchwinner who, observers had been quick to point out, did not look like your modern-day athletic footballer. 'I knew Andy was a good player from my own playing days although I did have to carry him a few times! When we brought him in, we knew he wouldn't be fit straight away but we wanted him to produce later on in the season. He's worked extremely hard to get fit and we've asked him to come into a struggling team so it hasn't been easy for him. He wasn't at his best in the West Ham game but he can always produce something and that's exactly what he did. Carlos put a half-decent ball into the box and if you want it to fall to anybody you want it to fall to Reid. In those situations you just have to make sure you get your effort on target and he scored a really good goal. A really important one. I think he's one of those type of lads who is laid back, he enjoys a few drinks and likes a singsong but he's got the confidence to play in front of our crowd and not many have that. He's a Premiership player and every day since he's come to the club, nine times out of ten he's been our top player in training. It was a big goal for the club, Andy Reid's. We had situations like that last year where you just knew that could be a significant goal.'

The result went a long way towards ensuring Sunderland's Premier League safety and avoiding a third relegation on the bounce. But Keane was taking nothing for granted. 'We can't relax now. We have to keep believing, but in our position we can't assume everything's going to be fine. We want to build a proper football club here and eventually we want it to run itself, so we have to look to build and build. But we're a million miles from being a top football club. I think we are getting there but we might not get there for another year or two. We have made a lot of changes in a short space of time and that's difficult for any club. A lot of our lads have not played many games in the Premiership, and that showed early on in the season, but I think the players are learning from the mistakes they've made and that's encouraging.'

Also encouraging was the clean-sheet as Gordon began to go from strength to strength. Looking back over the campaign, he said: 'We brought in an awful lot of new players at the start of the season and it was only natural that it would take time to gel all that together. The experience we've added in January has helped as well because we didn't have an awful lot of Premier League experience at the start of the year. But we are learning as a team and I think that it is noticeable, that we aren't getting caught out by certain things that we might have been getting caught out by earlier in the season. Everyone was thrown into the situation as Premier League new boys, but good players will adapt and I think that's how it is shaping up with ourselves this season. The £9 million price tag is never something I've looked at. I've got no say over how much is paid for me but the job is the same no matter how much you cost. If you were a free transfer, £! million player or £9 million player, it's irrelevant really. All you have to do is concentrate on your job and do it to the best of your ability. That's what I've tried to do. Roy Keane has been supportive, he's shown his faith in me and stuck by me and I appreciate that.'

At the opposite end of the pitch, Keane was appreciative of the contribution of Jones and excited about his potential. Could he really be the heir of the Drog? 'Whether he's a twenty to twenty-five goal a season man, we'll just have to wait and see,' he said. 'But of course he's got the potential and we keep on reminding everyone that this is his first season in the Premiership.'

Curbishley was right about the mini-burst of form turning Sunderland's season around. The following week virtually put the seal on it when Sunderland once again produced on the day against fellow strugglers. Before then, Keane sent his players away to a training camp in Spain. The weather conditions at the Academy had frequently been a source of frustration for the players and training staff, and the break was one of a whole series of moves that Keane would try to keep his players fresh physically and mentally.

'Some of the windy weather has been unbelievable but we're not going away on holiday, it's a training camp and sometimes a change of scenery does everyone good. We'll do anything to get even one more percent out of our players, and that's the thinking behind talks from people like the long jumper Steve Smith and sports psychologist Bill Beswick. Anything which helps, even marginally, can make a massive difference.'

Keane had wanted to keep the use of Beswick – formerly Steve McLaren's assistant manager at Middlesbrough – in-house. But when the news came out, he shrugged: 'We try different things on different occasions. We're always looking to bring in people who we think can help the players and we don't force the players to go to talks. Sometimes it's just a case of thinking outside the box.'

The main talking point of the week, though, emerged when Keane – back home to publicise the Guide Dogs for the Blind Association in Cork – revealed in interviews that he thought Sunderland would need to spend £40-£50 million in the summer transfer window to get to the next stage. He had spent £40 million during the course of the current season – spending unheard of for Sunderland. The idea that Keane would be pushing for the same, or more again, in the summer took everyone by surprise. When the subject was raised on his return he was amused at the uproar he had provoked.

'It caused a bit of a stir,' I suggested.

'Apparently so,' he replied deadpan before pausing and bursting out laughing. 'I don't think Niall's been seen since! Maybe he's gone to Spain. Or he's been seen on the top of Black Cats House calling the Samaritans.

'No,' he added on a serious note. 'What we're trying to do is to signal that the club is serious about competing. We believe it is. I've been lucky in that I've had great support since I got the job as Sunderland manager, but the summer will be another important period for the club. I had that support last summer and we're hoping to get good support from the board this summer. If you look at the players we'd got on our books when I first came here, there's been a massive change around. And, yes, we've invested heavily to bring that about but we have to look to do it again.'

Keane also raised a smile in the wake of a week in which he had criticised other managers. He argued some managers risked charges of hypocrisy when they called for players to show respect to referees but then those same managers ended up either being fined or sent to the stands. 'I spoke to my staff in my first week in the job about respecting referees,' he said. 'I can't be telling my players one thing and then get sent to the stands week after week. If you're going to tell your players to behave then you have to behave yourself.'

Wasn't that rich though, considering the way he had bullied and badgered Andy D'Urso when he was a player – the famous picture showing him surrounded by his teammates and snarling into the face of the referee? 'I was 100 percent out of order in that incident and I still feel bad when I see that photograph,' he replied. 'People keep going back to my mistakes as a player. I never said I was an angel. But you have to learn.

'And I still say they superimposed that vein on my head in the photo,' he smiled.

Victory over West Ham hoisted Sunderland into 13th position in the table and, in the minds of many, put them almost out of the relegation issues. The perception of Sunderland as a club was slowly changing on the back of victories that drove them towards mid-table. They were being seen less and less as a lame duck flapping to get out of the mire. By now Keane's own image was reaching a new configuration in the public mind. That change was never better illustrated than by an article in the Daily Telegraph from John Inverdale discussing the metamorphosis of Keane as a public figure: from snarling, battling player to composed, statesmanlike manager. Inverdale's point was that he had become a convert to Sunderland and Keane's cause by the nature of the dignified way the manager had conducted himself in public in prematch and post-match interviews since his appointment.

I was one of several journalists John called to double-check whether his gut instincts were based on solid foundations, though as grown men we had to negotiate his tricky question what colour Keane's eyes were.

'Hazel,' I volunteered.

We laughed at the idea of a mutual Keane appreciation society. But Inverdale put his finger on the pulse, when he talked about changing perceptions of Keane. Since he had arrived at the club, the manager had set about changing the image of Sunderland both in terms of how it saw itself and how others saw it. And part of that transformation involved himself.

When he had first arrived at the club he had wanted photographs of former Sunderland players and their triumphs splashed over the walls of the Academy where training took place. A reminder of the pride players at the club should have in Sunderland. An appreciation that it stood for something greater than themselves. It was one of the moves that prompted Quinn to remark: 'He has an eye for the methodical. His standards are incredible.'

The paint-balling trips, assault courses, orienteering trips and go-karting sessions, were aimed at team-bonding, yes, but they also projected a sense of the place as a good, healthy place for players to come – work hard, play hard. Keane was also projecting a healthy image for the club. And, of course, the club's image was changing, simply by virtue of its Premier League membership.

Anyone who has reported, supported or played in the Championship is aware that no matter what happens there, it creates barely a ripple on the public consciousness. As Keane had said on the opening day of the season – the Premier

League's the place to be. The spotlight of the top tier was giving Sunderland enhanced status. Increasingly, Sunderland were being regarded as a Premier League club and Keane as a Premier League manager of substance. His move to stop caricature portrayals in press articles had been a shrewd and important one. And articles like Inverdale's showed the manager was starting to be taken seriously as a character, with something to say and a persuasive way of saying it.

The feel-good factor around the club was boosted even further by the next match. On their last away trip they had ended a twenty-five year run without a win at Villa Park. At Craven Cottage, they had the joy of ending an unlikely sequence of Premier League defeats in London, which was bordering on the bizarre. Typical. You wait all season for an away win and then two come along at once.

Not that Sunderland fans, who took the pleasant sun-filled walk through Pimlico Park on their way to swelling the ground's Putney End, were complaining. A mad March end and awesome April start had pretty much banished relegation fears at a stroke.

Quinn had enjoyed the trip down too and had popped into a betting shop before the game to place a bet on the Grand National, which was being held the same day. A group of young men watched the big man and his entourage enter the shop, trying to work out who he was, before finally the penny dropped.

'Mr O'Leary, Mr O'Leary,' they called.

Quinn had backed a winner when he brought in Keane and he backed a winner that day too. He put his money on Comply Or Die – which seemed, tongue-in-cheek, like Keane's approach to football both as player and manager.

Three wins in a row – the first time Sunderland had done that in the top tier in seven years – took them ten points clear of the drop zone. And if Sunderland had had to ride their luck a little bit in those last three victories, well, it also needed acknowledging they had made their own too. Earlier in the season, Sunderland had given their all and frequently found it was not quite good enough – a familiar pattern for those who had watched the club over the last few years. Now, though, they were giving their all and were good enough for this level. So when they were below par – as they were for much of the game against Fulham – they had enough in the locker to get the desired result.

In the early stages of the game there was no area of

Sunderland's team which looked particularly on song. Key Fulham midfielder Jimmy Bullard was at the heart of everything good about his dangerous team. Against the run of play, Collins – denied a perfectly good goal against Villa in December – scored again when he headed home Reid's free-kick, only for the goal to be disallowed by referee Mark Halsey for an infringement action replays could not clarify. It was still Fulham's half but for all their fight, the second-bottom Londoners looked as though they had the death sign over them – just as Sunderland did in their previous two relegations.

Just like Sunderland in those doomed campaigns, Fulham played the better football only to go down to a sucker punch. The Cottagers' thoughts must already have been on the half-time break and discussing how they weren't ahead in the game, when Murphy took advantage of space on the right of the Fulham goal and clipped in a left-foot shot which Collins, totally unmarked on the edge of the six-yard box, headed emphatically home. This time the flag stayed down and, at the third time of asking, Collins had his first goal of the season. It was the 100th Sunderland goal scored under Keane.

'If Danny can get on the scoresheet, anything is possible this season,' beamed his manager, who was to point out importantly, 'We scored goals at exactly the right time in the game.'

After the break, Fulham came out all guns firing, determined to make up for the injustice of the opening half. Diomansy Kamara forced Gordon into a desperate last-ditch save with his shins. But just as it looked as if Fulham might get back into it, Sunderland once again scored. Gordon's goalkick was headed on by Jones towards Chopra, who took charge of indecision between former Newcastle teammate Aaron Hughes and goalkeeper Kasey Keller to nip in and shin the dropping ball over the Fulham goalie. The perfect way for the striker to bring up his 50th career goal. Owlish boss Roy Hodgson blinked despairingly afterwards: 'That second goal ... It was a poor, poor goal for us to concede.'

Fulham did superbly to pull one back, thanks to substitute David Healy who produced a top quality goal. He took a knock-down from fellow sub Clint Dempsey and, from right of goal, curled a delightful left-foot shot into the top right hand corner of Gordon's goal. It was a genuinely spectacular strike and it gave Fulham hope for all of 120 seconds before their defence

251

committed its third criminal error of the game and handed the win to the visitors. Whitehead's persistence paid off when he chased a Murphy ball into the box down the right and, under pressure, managed to squeeze it across goal to the unmarked Jones. The striker's first touch was not great and the ball bobbed up in front of him, but his volley of the dropping ball was utterly clinical and left neither Keller nor Hughes a chance on the line. It was Jones' second goal of the season against Fulham and confirmed Sunderland's first top-tier win at Craven Cottage since 1952 – a season which ended, ominously with Fulham being relegated.

The goal was just reward for Whitehead in his 250th league start. He was the driving force, chasing down and tackling, and getting his team back into it, his cruciate ligament injury now seemingly fully overcome as he produced as energetic a display as he had against Villa in the last away game. Victory finally got rid of an amazing record of fourteen straight Premier League defeats in London. Sunderland had taken only two points from the capital out of a possible 66 in the top tier, but the win over Fulham thrust the Wearsiders to the very edge of Premier League safety. The result was harsh on Fulham but, in fairness to Sunderland, the visitors showed quality when they needed to and their defence proved far more solid than the home team's.

Keane was not letting up. No matter how favourable the table was looking after the win – Sunderland now 13th – he was assuming nothing. 'We are in a much better position than we were three weeks ago but I don't see us as safe. I'm sure last season there were teams who thought they were safe until West Ham put together an unbelievable run and got out of it. You have to remember that Birmingham, Bolton and Reading are all more than capable of winning games, so we just have to keep going.'

Keane admitted, though, it was another important victory on the way – the first time Sunderland had got three back-to-back victories in the top tier since the year 2000. But he was not being fooled into believing his team had become world-beaters overnight. 'Our passing wasn't up to scratch but we always scored at the right time. It's nice to win football matches. That's what we're in the game for. No other reason. But I don't think we should be dancing in the streets just because we've won three in a row. It's perfect timing but I think it's no coincidence that we've done this when we've had our full squad to choose from.

We've had serious injuries to important players but they're coming back now.'

Sunderland received tremendous backing from a sizeable away support from first minute to last, and the manager was glad they could travel back to the north-east having enjoyed two away wins on the trot and the breaking of the London hoodoo. 'The fans have got to enjoy the victories because they haven't had that many. They were probably celebrating the night before the game, never mind the night after, because they seem to like enjoying themselves! They are brilliant supporters I have to say. They travel a long way away from home and spend their money and they deserve their good times. Having said that, I haven't seen a supporter score a goal so our priority is to make sure we're in the Premiership for them next season. That's the challenge, but I'm a lucky manager who has had great support from the board from day one and a lot of managers don't get that.'

The second away win on the trot certainly put the Sunderland manager in the best of moods. Leaving the ground, he signed a string of autographs before getting on the team bus and then, a few seconds later, come back off to sign more autographs. Truly a red letter day!

In contrast to Keane's easy demeanour, Roy Hodgson bore the hallmark strain of a Premier League manager who knows the game is just about up, in every sense of the word. 'I'm devastated by the result and I just want to get out of here without saying something really stupid that makes me look like an idiot,' he sighed in the post-match press conference. 'I'm really, really saddened. Sad we couldn't win the game because we really believed we could win it and much of our first-half performance suggested that we would. But the game is all about goals and we conceded some poor ones.'

It could have been the words of Mick McCarthy in any given game in the season Sunderland were relegated with 15 points and the comparisons continued.

'We didn't create enough clear-cut goalscoring chances and unfortunately we made bad mistakes for the goals and paid the price.'

The one difference between the two managers was that while Mick McCarthy's team inevitably went down, Hodgson somehow stayed up with an incredible run of form and last-day survival.

In contrast to Fulham's problems, Sunderland were now going for their fourth win on the trot and things looked in their favour. They had home advantage, out-of-form Manchester City visiting with little to play for. But it was not to be, with inconsistency and refereeing decisions again at the heart of their woes. When Keane conducted an end of season review, Manchester City would be at the top end of the list marked 'biggest disappointments'. Twice Sunderland played them. Twice City had been nothing special. Twice the Blues emerged as narrow winners, more through Sunderland's failings than City's excellence.

City's record against Sunderland in recent years was outstanding. This was their eighth win in eight games; their fourth successive double. Yet in those games, City had rarely been anything other than what they were; a competent, efficient Premier League outfit. Which was why Keane was so angry in the wake of the loss.

For the second time in a row, there was no reason why Sunderland could not have beaten Manchester City, if only they could have raised their game a little. That they did not was, in the manager's mind, down to the fact that the players had mentally relaxed a little, felt that three wins in a row had assured their Premier League status. There was no doubt Sunderland lacked the urgency, the energy, the precision with which they'd fought their way to the preceding wins. Yet for so long they were still largely in command – as they had been in their first encounter – just unable to land the knock-out blow.

It looked like it had the makings of a good game and a near capacity Stadium of Light was in good voice as the game kicked off. The first half was largely incident-free and best forgotten, with Sunderland carving out one real goal-scoring opportunity and City, none. Sunderland in charge but squandering their domination. Jones being denied by a Joe Hart save in the one clear-cut chance just before the break. Richardson was substituted at half-time and Murphy was removed just after the hour, but even when the Irishman left the pitch City had still to test the gloves of Sunderland goalkeeper Gordon, so ineffective had the visitors been. Both teams' defences deserved credit. City were under most pressure but Richard Dunne – the man with the most defensive blocks in the Premier League, was outstanding as he brought up his 300th appearance for the Blues in style.

For the second home game in a row, Keane had gone down the tunnel early, waiting for his players at the break. Whatever he said seemed to have an effect. But the Wearsiders could not produce composure in front of goal and just when it looked as though they would have to settle for a draw, the visitors took the lead.

The goal came through the most fortuitous of circumstances. Nosworthy was chasing down young substitute Daniel Sturridge in the box when he made the slightest of contacts and the young striker flung himself forward theatrically. Referee Mike Riley gave the penalty. It was a decision referees' chief Keith Hackett was to ring Keane personally about the following week, to apologise for. Top City scorer Blumer Elano stepped up to the spot and drove a low shot to Gordon's right as the goalkeeper went left.

Sunderland hit back immediately. Leadbitter drove a low diagonal ball to the left-wing and Reid, the hub of Sunderland's creativity, lifted the ball into the area. Whitehead met it with a perfect right-foot volley at the near post. Hart had no chance. At that stage you thought another grandstand finish from Sunderland beckoned. But City hit Sunderland with the classic sucker-punch four minutes from time when Leadbitter was robbed of possession and Blumer Elano fed substitute Darius Vassell, who scuffed a bobbling ball goalwards with just enough strength to beat the backtracking Bardsley on the line. Keane's renowned contempt for anyone who takes things for granted in football surfaced after the game when he savaged players and pundits alike, who assumed Sunderland were safe – seven points clear of the drop zone with 12 points still to play for.

'If I said it once during the week, I said it five million times – that we've still got a lot of hard work to do. We've maybe slackened off two or three percent and it's cost us, but I could have predicted it in the morning. I felt it in my bones. People need to start listening to the right people. They need to listen to me, rather than the nonsense they read in the papers. Sunderland safe? I've never read so much rubbish.'

Keane's mood, in his 75th game in charge, was not improved by the feeling that so many of his players were each waiting for a teammate to make it happen. 'It was a poor afternoon,' he said. 'The game wasn't great and we gave some bad goals away. I didn't enjoy watching the match and I'm sure the supporters didn't either. Clearly it wasn't a penalty, but there's no point in complaining about it. It won't make any difference and I'm more concerned about the fact that we never really got going. I think the last thing managers say to their teams every single week, every single week, is, "let's start well". But I might just as well have been talking Japanese. You can talk all you want in the dressing room, but I do believe that one or two people took their eyes off the ball.'

The City result was a disappointment for Sunderland fans who had loved the three-game winning run and hoped a quartet would push the club up to the heady heights of solid mid-table. A victory which would have taken them above rivals Newcastle United. But the very next game was the eagerly anticipated derby match at St James's Park. Sunderland's very own cup final fixture. A victory would have seen Sunderland leapfrog Newcastle anyway and the fixture had real spice with the teams so close to each other in the table.

In the run-up to the match Keane hinted with a half-smile that he was hoping for a surprise advantage in the game, the possibility that Sunderland's refereeing injustices would be put right in those ninety minutes. He revealed he'd had a midweek phone chat with the referees' boss, Keith Hackett, in which he'd received an apology for the decisions that had gone against the Black Cats. 'I don't know where he got my mobile phone number from but Keith Hackett rang me to apologise for some of the decisions that have gone against us. I have to say, though, that was little or no consolation. I didn't expect him to ring me and he might never again, but he felt the Man City decision was such a bad one he had to make the call. That penalty was clearly not a penalty. There was no logic to the referee giving the penalty either – the assessor told me the same thing. Their player should have been booked, and we should have been awarded a free-kick. People say these mistakes even out. So that means we'll have five penalty awards at Newcastle!'

The Newcastle game at least offered a fantastic opportunity for Sunderland to take the fans' general mood of positivity to a whole new level – especially as whichever team won would not only be above the other but would also be mathematically safe from relegation. Though it was almost a decade ago now, Sunderland fans travelled to Tyneside still cherishing memories of consecutive 2-1 wins over Newcastle under Reid – games in which Quinn had helped establish himself as a Sunderland legend.

He travelled to the ground this time as chairman, hoping above all that his players would give him local pride; that, perhaps, new Sunderland heroes would be found; that they would record a victory which would allow the small contingent of away fans allowed at the ground to celebrate with the joy they had done in his own day.

But in the end, fate, formations and poor form combined to leave Sunderland fans feeling as sick as they had done at Christmas time when they were lying second bottom in the table after that record-equalling thumping from Manchester United. Unlike the game against the red United, the black and white United never looked like world-beaters as Sunderland slumped to one of the most unedifying derby defeats of the modern era, in a game that rarely raised itself above the mediocre.

To Keane's list of disappointments – Wigan away, Everton away, Manchester United at home – the manager could certainly add Newcastle United at St James's Park. For the defeat, and the manner of it, would take a long time to fade from the memories of fans for whom the derby means everything. Keane had talked all season about the importance of character, but in the one game where he needed his players to show that quality more than any other, they let him down. It was the one game in which Sunderland needed to be at full-throttle from the start, showing fire, fight and sheer bloody-mindedness – passion their fans would have lapped up. But they failed to convince from the off.

To be fair to the Wearsiders, morale had been dealt a devastating blow before kick-off by the double-whammy of Bardsley (knee) and Evans (hamstring) being ruled out of the game after training ground injuries. McShane was recalled from the wilderness at right back and his second-minute foul on Michael Owen was typical of too many challenges from Sunderland throughout the game, showing ferocity without finesse. Bone-crunching tackles can turn derbies in a good way, but ill-judged clumsy ones rarely do. Michael Owen posted the perfect riposte in the fourth minute when he left McShane for dead to head home his team's opening goal. Though the young Irishman was at fault for losing Owen, he could also look askance at his teammates. Somehow Sunderland's five-man midfield allowed Ndjitap Geremi, in Newcastle's three-man midfield, the space and time to look up, compose himself and drill over a cross, which the England striker nodded wide of Gordon's dive to his right.

It had become unusual to see Sunderland's defence breached so simply but this was not the usual rearguard. Bardsley's and Evans' absence was keenly felt. They had been key to Sunderland's recent defensive meanness. Without them, Sunderland's defence looked a different proposition. McShane had the return game from hell, while Higginbotham could also be forgiven ring-rustiness, having had so few first-team opportunities since the turn of the year. They were no better further up the pitch, with neither Murphy nor Edwards distinguishing themselves on the wings on a day when a string of crosses were kicked harmlessly behind Steve Harper's goal.

It was an unusual-looking Sunderland team, with many players coming in after long spells out: McShane's first game since 19 January; Higginbotham's second game since 2 January; Miller back in for the first time since 2 February. Miller was a surprise recall to the team, although Keane had dropped hints in press conferences that the midfielder had shown the right attitude since his transfer listing. His return did not produce the sparkling performance his manager must have hoped for. Fortunately Newcastle were too lacklustre to capitalise on Sunderland's failings. The Wearsiders produced as poor a first half as they had all season and threatened little up until the break. The only real clear-cut chance they got was when McShane crossed in from the right, only for Whitehead to sky his shot over Steve Harper's bar at the near post. Newcastle, by contrast, were being gifted opportunities. Gordon was forced to fling himself full-length to palm an effort from fullback Habib Beye around his right-hand post. Collins needed to make a stunning dispossession of his former youth-teammate Micahel Owen to deny the striker a shot on goal inside the box. Then the offside flag stayed down on an Obafemi Martins surge down the left-flank but the striker's eventual shot was easily saved by Gordon.

Sunderland were awful but, just when thoughts were turning towards half-time and the difference Keane's team-talk might make, Newcastle scored their second and crucial goal, from a penalty. The visitors had no one to blame but themselves. There was a series of lapses before Higginbotham was unlucky to go in on a challenge with Michael Owen and see the forward's shot strike his arm. Referee Mike Dean pointed instantly to the spot.

Owen made no mistake. He fired a low shot under the body of Gordon, who dived to his right and made contact but could not stop the ball squeezing under him. Sunderland conceded nine penalties in the 2007-08 season. More than any other team. But it was possibly Owen's penalty which took the wind out of Sunderland more than any other spot kick. It was a psychologically devastating blow for the team just before half-time and it meant they now had a mountain to climb.

It was a surprise that Sunderland made no changes at the break – so many players had proved ineffective – but their manager gave them a shot at redemption. It looked as though it might happen too. The visitors won two early corners in quick succession, from which Collins had a header blocked at close range and Whitehead saw a shot deflected wide. At this stage Newcastle were sitting on their lead and Sunderland were enjoying the lion's share of possession, but seldom looking to threaten. Keane acted on the hour, bringing on Richardson and switching to 4-4-2. Sunderland became more threatening. Reid lifting a long-range shot just over Steve Harper's bar. The game opened up when Gordon was forced to make a terrific save from Martins in the 68th minute. The striker played a one-two with Michael Owen before driving his close-range shot into the goalkeeper's chest. But Steve Harper made an even better stop a few seconds later when he blocked a powerful Jones' header low down around his knees from a Miller cross from the right.

It could hardly be called a pivotal moment. At no stage did Sunderland look like a team which could score two goals on the day. When Chopra was brought on ten minutes from time it was a case of too little, too late. Sunderland were a spent force. The last few minutes dragged on interminably and everyone connected with Sunderland was relieved when the referee finally put the game out of its misery. Once again, Sunderland had failed against their bitterest rivals.

It was a dreadful performance but Keane's post-match press conference didn't reflect that. He took all emotion out of the situation, preferring to concentrate on the technical aspects of the game. 'I'm disappointed with the way we started the game and disappointed we couldn't get into half-time just 1-0 down. At this level we can't afford to give the goals away that we gave away. We made it very hard for ourselves – particularly with the second goal just before half-time. We need to stop gifting teams goals. Newcastle will look at their first goal as a good goal but from our point of view we have only ourselves to blame.'

There were no arguments there. Sunderland produced as unconvincing a display as they'd produced all season. That was bad enough as it was, against a team which were no great shakes. But in the derby, of all games, it was bordering on the inexcusable. 'My players understood how important the game was,' Keane insisted. 'I'm not going to question my team's desire. It's just that we just gave away bad goals. The injuries didn't help. We lost three players in the two days before the game – Rade Prica was also injured as well as Jonny Evans and Phil Bardsley. But you can't make excuses. Liam Miller has trained well and that's why we thought he deserved his chance.'

Keane had rarely sounded unconvincing all season but he did after this game and all the fans could hope was that perhaps he was biting his tongue for fear of what he might have said. The reality was that Newcastle had cruised past Sunderland without ever looking convincing themselves. Sunderland fans were bowed by the defeat. They're proud people and worse than a defeat was the knowledge that when the test came, their team were found wanting. Their pain was reflected in the chairman. Quinn was to describe his personal low of the season as watching fellow chairman Mike Ashley and his entourage coming into the boardroom dancing the conga.

The spirits of Sunderland fans had sagged when the team sheet was produced with no Evans or Bardsley on it. You had to fear the worst when the team was deprived of their talents. But Sunderland didn't help themselves with a formation that left Jones as a lone striker against a team whose defence had been their Achilles heel. Playing Reid behind him didn't pay off. Meanwhile local lads Leadbitter and Chopra looked on impotently from the bench – Leadbitter not involved at all; Chopra given ten minutes at the end.

The criticism players and manager received in the wake of the defeat might have seemed harsh to neutrals – especially, as Keane was to point out, Newcastle had a lot of years on Sunderland in the top tier. But there is no room for neutrality on Tyneside or Wearside in this fixture. Win, or play well, and you're a hero. Lose, or play badly, and you're a villain. It remained eight years waiting for a win in any Tyne-Wear derby for Sunderland and, astonishingly, more than quarter of a century for a home win. It was just too, too long for Sunderland fans.

Sunderland's players were criticised and Keane himself was questioned by the fans as much as at any time since taking over. Losing to Newcastle had strained their faith. Maybe it was a first sign that they were looking towards higher things than simply Premier League survival. A positive, if there was one.

Sunderland's next game was another derby, but in fans' eyes not in the same league as the one they'd just lost. The derby for Sunderland fans means Newcastle, and the match against Middlesbrough generates nowhere near the same intensity among supporters.

Sunderland's players however did all that could be asked of them in the circumstances. They shrugged off their disappointments and they won. It was Sunderland's ninth home victory of the season – in total, 27 of their 39 points gained at the Stadium of Light.

The victory over the Teessiders did not make up for the defeat to the Tynesiders. But the beating of the Boro delivered the best tonic of all for fans after a week wallowing in Magpie misery. It delivered Premier League safety to Sunderland.

Those who see the big picture in football – managers mainly – would point out to a Wearside mourning over its Tyneside loss, that although a win over the Teessiders didn't compare when it came to tribalism, there was no escaping its compelling significance.

Sunderland were safe.

A full three games before the end of the season. Safe. Bye-bye to the yo-yo.

Mission accomplished.

And Keane wasn't kidding afterwards when he said this particular game was Sunderland's season in microcosm. How often had fans seen his team start slowly and ship an early goal? How often had they fought so hard not to let a game go? Strain every sinew to claw their way back into it? And how often had supporters seen them score a goal right at the death through sheer never-say-die defiance?

If football games had lasted only eighty minutes in the 2007-08 season, Sunderland would have been 15 points worse off, pegged back on 24 and lying between Fulham and Derby County in the relegation zone. But they were not a team to lie down easily. On almost every occasion, they'd fought to the final whistle – a credit to the mindset of their manager. Statistics would show that, in terms of effort expended in a Premier League game, ground covered, Sunderland would be in a Champions League position compared to their peers.

They might not be able to match the top four for skill and ability. But they matched just about any team for miles covered or tackles made. Perhaps it was appropriate that Murphy – so poor at Newcastle and written off so many times – should score the winner that guaranteed Sunderland's Premier League status. Although his goals had been few, they tended to be important ones. And this was the most important of all in the Irish striker's Sunderland career. No one had been more of an enigma in a Sunderland shirt in the campaign than him. The scorer of great goals rather than a great goal-scorer. A player who frustrated and delighted in almost equal measure. Keane remained intrigued by the striker's potential, though he had been an ace of sanctioning his transfer to QPR in January. A player who could look a liability in one game, yet prove a matchwinner the next.

How ironic it would be if Murphy's goal allowed his manager the power to recruit the players who would replace him. For Keane signalled, in the immediate aftermath of this game, that he was already thinking what new blood he might be able to bring in, now that Sunderland could plunge into the summer transfer market as a Premier League team.

It is one of the enduring ironies of football that every success a footballer has tends to move him nearer to the exit door, one step closer towards being replaced by a better player. That could have proved to be the fate of all three of Sunderland's goal-scorers in the Boro game – Higginbotham, Chopra and Murphy. But the chances were that the trio would still be part of the squad next season.

The manager had signalled that having constructed a squad successful enough to stay in the Premier League, his intention was to supplement it, rather than scatter it. All three of those on target against Boro made their contributions but the manager was eager to stress afterwards that this was a genuine team effort. He reeled off one name after the other: 'Kenwyne, Nyron,

Deano, Daryl, Chops, Danny Collins, Grant ...'

Keane believed it was that sense of unity, that team spirit, which had been the key to the club staying up this and no one would argue with him. But as much as that had been vital, they owed just as much to one of the newest and ugliest words in the dictionary – 'bouncebackability'. From every setback in every game they had tried to bounce back. And nowhere was that more in evidence than in the Boro game.

Fresh off the back of that dreadful derby defeat at St James's Park, they once again started a game poorly, and conceded early. Hardly the best omen against the team with the best away record in the bottom half of the table.

The poor omens continued – the previous week it had been Newcastle striker Michael Owen who scored in just the 4th minute of the game. This time it was Boro striker Tuncay Sanli who scored at precisely the same moment. He took advantage of a clever chip over the defence from Afonso Alves to surge past Sunderland's back-tracking defence and drive a left-foot shot across Gordon from left of goal, twelve yards out. Unlike at Newcastle though, Sunderland reacted this time. Within two minutes they levelled. Higginbotham was making a habit of derby goals. Having scored against Newcastle with a header on this ground, he repeated his heroics when Collins crossed from the left in the 6th minute, skilfully nodding the ball back across goalkeeper Brad Jones from eight yards out.

'A striker's goal,' he grinned afterwards.

Sunderland took the lead in time added on at the end of the forty-five minutes. Miller prodded the ball down the right-flank for Chopra to run onto, and the striker cut inside centre half David Wheater, took advantage of a favourable drop of the ball and lifted a shot across Brad Jones with his weaker left-foot, the ball going in off the cross bar. It was the Tynesider's sixth goal of the season and the perfect way to go into the break – the complete opposite of the preceding derby when Sunderland had conceded a second goal just before half-time.

Just after the hour, the fading Edwards was replaced by Leadbitter with Sunderland still retaining the upper hand. Gradually though, Boro crept into it and levelled in the 74th minute. Former Sunderland hero, Julio Arca, had a quiet game on the occasion of his 200th appearance in English football and his first return to the Stadium of Light. But he made a telling contribution when he cleverly threaded a ball forward to Afonso Alves, who swivelled on a shot on the edge of the six-yard box, the ball striking Gordon, and eluding Higginbotham, as the defender chased it despairingly over his line.

That was the end of Boro as an attacking force. They could see that Sunderland were set for a charge and dug themselves in to resist a siege. It looked as though they had succeeded too, but in the second minute of time added on at the end of the ninety minutes, Sunderland produced yet another trademark late goal. It was created by the substitutes after Jones had won a corner. Leadbitter put the ball in from the left and Murphy – on for Richardson in the 85th minute – pulled away at the near post to glance a header past Brad Jones and over the line from close range.

It was the first time in the Premier League that Sunderland had scored two goals in a game from corners, and Murphy's header meant Sunderland were safe with the 250th goal they'd scored in the Premier League. For the eighth time in the season, Sunderland scored goals after the 89th minute. Nine goals scored in the last five minutes had earned Sunderland 11 of their 39 points. Victory also meant the Wearsiders had recorded the highest number of wins in the second half of a Premier League season.

But those stats were irrelevant as Murphy's header sparked scenes at the Stadium of Light as ecstatic on the touchline as they were on the terraces. The Sunderland bench leapt towards the pitch dancing a jig of delight. Boro coach Colin Cooper turned away in disgust as Gareth Southgate alongside him stared blankly. It was the Black Cats' first home win over Middlesbrough in eight years – a measure of the falling away Sunderland Football Club had endured between Quinn hanging up his Sunderland shirt and returning to take over the boardroom.

It meant Quinn, Keane and their players had achieved the club's overriding goal of the campaign. From the lowest of lows to an intoxicating high in the space of two games.

Always the gentleman, Gareth Southgate paid tribute to Sunderland. The Middlesbrough manager had struck up a friendship with Keane and his best wishes were genuine in the post-match press conference. 'The fact Sunderland got another late goal tells you a lot about their spirit. The way they are and the way their fans are. That's a credit to them. They're staying up and they have shown over the course of the season that they deserve to.'

A delighted Keane meanwhile had nothing but praise for his players. 'We've had a good dressing room and if we didn't have that, we'd have been knackered,' he said. 'That kept us going and my players deserve unbelievable credit for keeping this club in the Premiership. They've been brilliant. In terms of desire and attitude they deserve to be top of the league. It was a very good day for the club. Better than last weekend!'

As much as anything, Keane had enjoyed the sense of occasion. When Murphy's header went in, everyone in the ground knew something hugely significant had been accomplished. 'I'm glad that we stayed up this year in front of our fans,' he said. 'Last year, when we got promoted I was out walking my dog! It was a scorcher so I took it out for a swim. And when I switched my phone on at twenty-past-three there were a few messages on saying "well done" so I knew we were up. That was it. Our promotion confirmed when we weren't playing. So I think it's important for the club that we've done it as a result of a game we've played in. It was great for the fans to be able to celebrate together at the end.

'At the end of a game it's a balancing act, deciding what to do. We saw that with Manchester City in our previous home game when we got back to 1-1, but then lost 2-1 chasing the game. You get very annoyed when you concede late on. But I thought the fans helped with the decision in the Boro game because they were wanting us to go at them at home and I thought we were looking confident, especially in time added on.'

Keane, though, signalled there would be no resting on laurels now. Not next week and not next season. 'You are always wanting to take the club forward,' he said. 'I felt this season was one of the biggest seasons in the club's history and I really mean that. The club has been promoted before but it has tended to be very quickly, and unfortunately, relegated. It needed stability and if you are going up and down, up and down and up and down you are never going to get that. We've all been united in our desire to make sure we didn't go down again and the players have been up for that challenge. We've stayed up now with this victory.

'But if we'd had to be ready to do it against Bolton Wanderers in our next game, then we would have been ready for it. We still want to go down there and get a positive result because you still want to finish as high up in the league as you can.

'It's all part of the master plan. The first part was to get promoted. Staying in the Premiership was another challenge. I've got another year left on my contract and the next challenge will be to improve the squad and hopefully finish higher up the table and be bigger and stronger next season. But I really do believe I've not really got started yet in this job.

'Things that have been on hold are now pushing forward. We've had scouting reports and we've had to wait because we didn't know for sure which division we would be in. But I can tell you one thing for certain – we would never have bagged some players if we had been relegated again. The players that we are after now wouldn't go to a team in the Championship. So it's a vital summer for us now. Last summer we might have been a bit tentative but hopefully I'll be coming to the table in a stronger position in terms of recruitment this time around.

'As a club, we've got to keep going forward and we've done that this season. We've made progress. It's not perfection but it is progress. It has been a massive learning curve for myself and the players. No one has made as many mistakes as myself this season so I have to learn from that, and learn fast, if I want to be a decent manager. I'm just pleased for the football club after the weekend's result because, my God, we've had to fight for everything we've got this season. I don't remember a single game where I felt we've got out of jail there. Not a single game where we've been lucky. Even the Boro game was a cracking game where we had to give absolutely everything.

'It has been a roller-coaster, a proper roller-coaster. There's nothing at Alton Towers to touch this job. It is up and down and you are learning all the time.'

He joked that Quinn and the Drumaville Consortium had disappeared because they knew he would be after their cheque books now. He was deadly serious, though, about wanting to bring in top quality new players and left no one in doubt that his ambition for the club no longer stopped at keeping it in the top flight. 'We would like £60- or £70 million to spend now. I know, I know, it keeps going up every week! It was £40 million a while ago. Then it was £50 million. No wonder the board have gone into hiding! But my job is to make sure we're higher up the table next season. We want to challenge the likes of the teams just above us. Maybe we got too carried away last year with our expectations when we got promoted, but it has been tough for us. We don't know what the future holds but I can't imagine we'll have the same decisions go against us, or have the same injuries as we've had this time around. But then, if it does happen, we should have a stronger squad to deal with it. To succeed at this level you need a big squad and we've certainly been short of that. You have to remember that Evans is not one of our players, for example. When we got promoted, we got promoted with Jonny and Danny Simpson in the side. Two of our back four weren't even our own. In the Middlesbrough game just gone, our central midfielder Whitehead, was our right back. There are big gaps to fill. Not that long ago, we were second bottom of the Championship. I think we have to appreciate how far we've come.

'But I've been very lucky. Everything I asked of Niall and the investors has been fulfilled. We've had to change our mindset on a lot of things and now we have to do it again. If we want to get to certain top players, then we have to look at our pay structure. If you want the very best players they want to know where their fifty to sixty thousand pounds a week is.'

Keane once again reaffirmed his commitment to the challenge of helping a great football club realise its undoubted potential, even if he had yet to extend his contract beyond the one year which remained. No one would take that to mean, though, that he was anything but totally engrossed in the challenge at Sunderland. But the board would know that, if they wanted to keep him, they had to keep pace with his desire. 'I've got another year on my contract and that's okay by me. I can't guarantee anything, but I've said it once, I've said it a million times, that I'm very, very happy here. I'm very contented with the job in hand and I can understand the importance of continuity. The phone rang a few times with offers when I retired from football but none of them excited me. Sunderland excited me. And, as I said at the very start of the season, it takes a lot to excite me.

'Now we want to push on from here.

'You are looking at years and years down the line before we're challenging the top four. Look at what a great job David Moyes has done and how long it has taken him, and they're fifth in the league. But we want to keep moving forward. It's important for me before signing a contract to know that we're prepared to go to the next level. If not, there's always going to be question marks. I didn't ask them last time because I'd only been a manager two minutes. This time, though, I might ask the board if they're ready to go to the next level. Then I will look at what they put in front of me. But when I was first asked to come here I was asked to sign a five-year contract and I said "no chance". I've never signed a five-year contract in my life. I could have been sacked after the first year and walked off with a load of money. I'd probably have needed a wheelbarrow! But I do feel very happy here. Very comfortable.'

The season's mission had been accomplished with the win over Boro but with two games remaining, there was still the opportunity for another six points which, if secured, would take Sunderland up to mid-table, probably over Newcastle United. A Cock of the North award to make up for that derby defeat.

As ever, Sunderland's fans travelled in numbers to the Reebok – they sold out their allocation for the 15th time in 19 games. Sunderland's following at Wanderers was higher than those of any club that had been to the Stadium of Light. Par for the course. Few felt after the Boro game, with so many of players back in harness, that the Wearsiders would not finish the season strongly but they were to head to Bolton the following week and perform so badly that Keane's patience with his players snapped only a week after he'd been hailing them.

And in the ruins of a calamitous performance, he signalled the immediate start of a new 'Roy-volution'.

CHAPTER NINE

Beginnings at the End

Every new beginning comes from some other beginning's end.
SEMISONIC (AND SENECA)

SOMETIMES as a sports reporter you see a truly dreadful performance and your first thought at the final whistle is what the manager is going to say in the postmatch press conference. Will he try spinning it? In the case of Keane, I had found that, generally, he called it exactly as you would expect. On occasion he'll dress up a defeat or draw more than you would have thought. Every now and again, though, you could be exasperated by an awful display and Keane would put your condemnation into perspective by going far further in his criticism than you ever would.

That was the case with this game, and Sunderland's players knew they needed to beware strong words softly spoken to the press afterwards. Keane left no journalist in any doubt with his criticisms that not only was the shambolic display unacceptable but that certain players could pay for it with their jobs. It was hard to argue with him on a day in which so many Sunderland players let themselves down so badly.

Nor could watching chairman Quinn have been impressed with his team's defeat to a hardworking, but limited, Bolton team. The defeat dropped Sunderland from 13th to 15th and cost the club's transfer kitty the thick end of £1.5 million in prize money. After such a heart-warming display in the victory over Middlesbrough, which confirmed Premier League safety, Sunderland produced a performance against relegation-threatened Bolton that was even worse than their no-show against Newcastle United.

Keane made only one change – fit-again Evans returning at the expense of Edwards, who had largely been anonymous since his comeback, his season undermined by those constant injuries. Bardsley's season, like Ward's and Etuhu's, had been ended prematurely by injury, although none of their ailments were long-term.

Evans' inclusion at centre half saw Nosworthy going to right back, allowing Whitehead to return to central midfield. If there was to be a criticism of the manager's selection, it might be that he was too soft-hearted in trying to include all three centre halves in the team. Higginbotham had been excellent at Boro and did not deserve to be dropped, but Keane was naturally eager to get the outstanding Evans back in the team and shifted Nosworthy to full back where he proved a real disappointment. Maybe Keane should have been more ruthless and left a centre half out in order to keep the dependable Whitehead filling a position where he'd been excellent the previous game.

If sentiment had come into it though, it was unlikely to again. For this was a game in which too many players were given chances, and too many chances were squandered. The defence was unconvincing going forward but generally solid on the back foot. The real area where Sunderland lost the game was midfield.

Richardson, who had argued for a central midfield position all season, was given it at Bolton and promptly disappeared down the same rabbit hole that fellow midfielder Miller did. Neither made any real contribution to the game. Whitehead was below par in his passing, Reid had his poorest game for Sunderland since his arrival, Edwards was anonymous, Chopra buzzed around to little effect while Jones got neither the service nor the support, which might have brought the best out of him.

Evans was one of the few Sunderland players who was to have a half-decent game. The young defender had played a key part in Sunderland's improvement since the turn of the year, though he admitted that it had been a lot more demanding than the Championship. 'These games are more intense,' he said. 'Last season we were quite comfortable in most games. We always felt like we were going to get a victory because we were on a really good run. This year has been a lot tougher. Losing games has not been nice and the challenge has been a lot different from what it was last year, but I've enjoyed every game. Every time I've pulled on a Sunderland shirt I've taken a great pride in it. I definitely feel more comfortable here; feel more part of it. I've been lucky to play quite a number of games and the fans have taken to me.'

Former Sunderland star Gary Rowell said Evans was the only player to emerge with any credit from a game he considered possibly the club's limpest display of the season. The first real chance on goal did not come until the 28th minute and went the way of a domineering Bolton. El Hadji Diouf found space against left back Collins and curled a cross to the far post, which the irrepressible Kevin Davies headed inches over from the edge of the six-yard box. Sunderland's reply was almost instant. Jones jinked his way inside the Wanderers area from the left before striking a low right foot which goalkeeper Ali Al Habsi saved at his near post. Wanderers took the lead in the 42nd minute and no one could say it hadn't been coming; so many challenges had Sunderland lost, so needlessly and so regularly had they squandered possession.

The goal was created by Bolton captain Kevin Nolan who took advantage of space on the right of goal to cross to the far post. El Hadji Diouf pulled away from Nosworthy, and the Senegalese – who had scored against Sunderland when the two teams met earlier in the season – clinically lifted a shot from a narrow angle through Gordon and into the goalkeeper's top left-hand corner.

Sunderland proved little better in the second half and Keane's annoyance manifested itself just after the hour when he made a triple substitution. Chopra, Miller and Nosworthy off; O'Donovan, Leadbitter and Murphy on. 'I made three substitutions but I could have made ten,' the manager grumbled.

Sunderland improved and the pendulum slowly swung their way. They should have equalised in the 70th minute, when Reid curled a ball from left to right, which O'Donovan headed back across goal, but Jones somehow failed to connect, missing an open goal from five yards out. Wanderers had more chances before the game's end but took only one. From an 82nd minute corner, Kevin Nolan put in a terrific ball from the right and Murphy – Sunderland's goal hero the previous week with a glancing near post-header – became the villain this time with a glancing near-post header through his own goal. A typical week in the life of the Sunderland striker. Reid might have cleared it, for he was perfectly positioned when the ball came to him at the far post, but he had stepped a yard inside the goal when he made contact.

Victory cost Sunderland Football Club both in terms of points and positions. But with Keane so understandably angry at the final whistle, it looked as though it had also cost players their places. The season's end would now come as a relief to Keane, who admitted he had become frustrated at the limitations of his squad.

While he was delighted Premier League safety had been achieved he had already moved on. He had wearied of self-inflicted defeats like this one. He wanted change. Perhaps after such a long, hard push everyone was feeling the strain. In the press conference afterwards it looked as though Keane was mentally shuddering at just how badly wrong this season could have gone had there been many more performances like this one. 'We are short and it needs to be sorted. Twenty-two matches to lose in a season is a lot,' he said. 'We got late equalisers and late winners, but we needed them. I think someone's looking after us up above. If we hadn't scored so many late goals, we would have been adrift with Derby. Twenty-two defeats is the figure you need to know this season – twenty-two. Not where we finish in the table. Just the number twenty-two. The number of games we've lost; and if we lose to Arsenal in our last game it will be twenty-three.

'For a football club like ours, it's not acceptable. I'm lucky to still be in a job.

'We had prepared well, trained well. But then they go out on the pitch and play like that. I was looking at my players in this game to see how they would respond. It was a challenge and an opportunity for them. They knew how I felt before the game, how important it was and what I expected and if they weren't, well they were sure at half-time and full-time. I've learnt a hell of a lot about my players from this game and it just confirmed what I was thinking. Which was that we are short. Maybe it's a good thing.

'Maybe if we had won against Bolton and then beaten Arsenal we would have gone into the summer thinking "we're not bad are we?" but we are not great and this result confirms what I've been thinking.'

The Sunderland manager wanted to take a step back from things now. He had developed a clearer vision of how much needed to be done to take the club on further. 'I'm ready for a break,' he admitted. 'I've had enough after the Bolton game. Really had enough. To lose that many games in a season – and it's not as if we've been on a fantastic Cup run. We can't kid ourselves. We are talking about Premiership level here, not non-league. How many times do you have to say the same things over again?

'People are getting fed up with me saying the same things, and so am I. There's no question of the players' commitment and desire and their attitude. What we need at this level is quality and we saw, in this game, particularly in the first half, constantly giving the ball away when there's nobody near them and they're under no pressure, that the quality wasn't there. That was the case with a number of players. I can't accept the sloppiness I've seen. So there will be changes in the summer, big changes.

'Seven or eight?' he was asked.

'At least,' responded Keane. 'I need to get the right people in, but whether I can remains to be seen. I'm not going to say we need ten to fifteen players but we need major changes.'

Keane had wanted to finish the season with a flourish, starting at the Reebok. 'It was a sloppy performance and for players to give the ball away willy-nilly under no pressure whatsoever drives me absolutely mental. We can defend a lot of stuff that happens on the pitch. But sloppily giving the ball is not one of them. We're Sunderland, not a non-league team! It hurts to be saying every week that we need to improve.

'But you see the performances in this game and you have to learn from them. I'm not taking anything away from Bolton, they played to their strengths and made it hard for us. They've been in the Premier League a long time and they made the most of their experience. We gave the ball away so cheaply, especially around the middle of the park, and you look at certain players. People say we achieved our goal the previous week, so is that it for the season?

'This game was an opportunity for players to make their mark. I thought it was a big test for us and I wanted to gauge them. Would they go into celebration mode, would they switch off? And we were sloppy. There will be changes, plenty of changes. Trust me.'

'Any positives at all from the day?' he was asked.

He paused to consider the question for a few seconds. 'It was sunny.'

Sunderland had been dreadful, but many managers would not have taken the line that Keane did. They would have probably accepted that it had been a long hard season for their players and that this game proved a step too far. Sunderland fans had got used to being content to get across the finishing line.

Keane's mentality was completely different.

The Monday after the Bolton game a new book to review crossed my desk at the Echo. A Fan's Guide to European Football Grounds. And as I flicked through it, I began to understand where Keane was coming from. European football stadiums had been Keane's stamping ground for much of his career. That was the direction in which he was hoping to take the club eventually. Sunderland had last graced that stage, for the first and only time, in 1973. Keane's eyes were fixed on much higher slopes. He simply could not tolerate performances that did not show the drive and desire he required to take Sunderland to a higher level than merely staying up. Now he knew that his current squad needed revitalising for the challenges he had in mind.

Keane was as good as his word in the days that followed, as the first of his squad headed towards the exit doors. Five players whose contracts were at an end were thanked for their efforts and politely shown the door. None of them had been involved in the Bolton game. The club's longest-serving player, right back Wright, had not featured in the first team all season. Neither had centre half Varga – along with Wright one of the last two players at the club signed by Peter Reid – although Varga had been re-signed by Keane. They had known they would not be offered new contracts.

Veterans Cole and Harte had made only cameo appearances and their one-year contracts were not renewed. Young defender Peter Hartley had improved over the course of the season and had spent a productive end to the campaign on loan at Chesterfield. But Keane was focused on taking the club to a new level and the twenty-year-old Hartlepudlian was never going to have the ability to make that journey. Like fellow youngsters Jake Richardson, Billy Dennehy and Gavin Donoghue, this season was to be Hartley's final one at the club as Sunderland looked to the future.

Other youngsters had a chance. The teenagers who had impressed in youth league and cup finished their season with a flourish, playing their final game for the reserves against Gateshead in the Durham Challenge Cup. Eight of them were handed contracts for the following season. They won the game 2-0 – Sunderland's one bit of silverware of the campaign. That came only after a half-time team-talk from Keane, who had watched the first forty-five minutes from a corporate box and been unimpressed. Given the fact that Sunderland were 1-0 up at the break, that might have seemed harsh. But Keane was getting in that zone of getting serious now. There would be no coasting or showboating from anyone. At the final whistle, when they were presented with the trophy on the pitch, it appeared as though none of the players wanted to celebrate too much – just in case their manager judged them as slacking off.

The night before that game, the remaining members of Sunderland's 1973 team had gathered again at the Stadium of Light for a celebration dinner to mark the 35th anniversary of that famous day. Bobby Kerr, Jimmy Montgomery, Dave Watson, Denis Tueart – all the heroes who had brought the FA Cup home. At midnight, as 5 May arrived again, the 1973 team took the stage and Bobby Kerr and his old teammates raised the trophy again. They were given the applause and appreciation they deserved, half a lifetime after their original success. For more than a generation since that Wembley moment there had been little to suggest that such glory days might lie ahead again.

Now it seemed different. Keane blazed with the desire to take the club on further, faster. Admittedly Sunderland's mere Premier League survival this time around was hardly the stuff of legend – hardly the evidence that successful days were just over the horizon. But with Quinn and his consortium's backing and Keane's fierce ambition you sensed Sunderland could be embarking on an era when the success, which seemed the lot of so many other clubs, might finally come within their orbit again.

Ian Porterfield gone. Billy Elliott gone. Bob Stokoe gone before them. Their time was remembered. But it had long passed. The 1973 team had carried the torch across decades during which several Sunderland teams flattered to deceive. All the ingredients, though, seemed to be there for sustained improvement under Quinn and Keane.

For now though, the Sunderland manager was focused on ensuring the Bolton performance was not repeated against last-day opponents Arsenal, who would tear them apart if they reproduced that quality of display. The manager was looking to sort the wheat from the chaff. He had said that he was looking for his players to respond appropriately after Bolton. Even though it was clear that he was looking to bring in a whole raft of new signings, his players still had a chance to make a point. If they had been in any doubt that they were playing for their futures at Bolton, they were under no illusions when the Gunners came to call.

Sunderland's season ended as it began – against north London opposition at the Stadium of Light. Sadly, there was to be no repeat against Arsenal of the scoreline against Spurs. Sunderland had never won a final game of the season in the Premier League and this match never looked like breaking the mould. Despite the defeat, it was a day when the future seemed bright, even if Arsenal did put Sunderland in the shade. Curiously, the result seemed almost a side issue for so many in the vast crowd compared to the collective joy of knowing their Premier League adventure would continue.

Arsenal were expected to win; which they duly did. Sunderland were expected to be a whole lot better than at Bolton; which they duly were. But the sell-out crowd that thronged the Stadium of Light, came not so much in expectation of seeing Sunderland prevail but in anticipation of celebrating their club's top-tier survival. If that seemed an unambitious aim on their part, well, clearly you had to have lived through the broken-hearted 15-point and 19-point relegations to see where they were coming from. They wanted to pay tribute to the players of course, but not as much as they wanted to hail the chief architects of the new era – Quinn and Keane. And the terraces were buzzing over what Sunderland might achieve next season compared to the current one. It had been a long time since there was such optimism or excitement around the place.

Quinn and his consortium had provided the all-important backing, but it was Keane who had given the club direction and rival manager Arsene Wenger was the first to acknowledge it. 'When you come up into the Premier League with as little experience as he had and manage to keep a club up, then you have to say congratulations to him. It is remarkable.'

The Arsenal boss fielded a youthful, but still dangerous, team while Keane made five changes. Goalkeeper Fulop got his moment in the shop window and Yorke was given what looked to be a sentimental farewell appearance as the manager went for a 4-5-1 formation. That meant Chopra dropped to the bench, alongside Miller and Higginbotham, who had also started in the Bolton Wanderers reverse. Two of their other teammates weren't even that lucky – Richardson and Murphy didn't feature in the squad. Leadbitter and Edwards came in to fill the resulting gaps.

Later it was to emerge that Richardson, such a disappointment at Bolton, had been late for training in midweek because of a delayed train. He wasn't doing himself any favours. 'I knew as soon as I was late I wouldn't be playing,' he said glumly.

In complete contrast to Richardson's plight, Wallace was called back for the last game of the season. He had overcome his transfer-listing, a ligament injury in January and a prospective approach from Toronto in March, to come back into the team in May. Wallace, like Miller, like Murphy, had flirted with the prospect of leaving the club but had fought his way back into contention.

Though Gordon missed out on the final game, his thirty-four starts for Sunderland completed a successful debut season at the club. Only long-serving goalkeeper Thomas Sorensen had carried the first-team gloves more for Sunderland in the Premier League. And Gordon represented the future. He had improved in confidence throughout the campaign, especially since the turn of the year.

Keane's changes of personnel for the club's last game sparked an immediate response from the team, and Sunderland went for goal in the first twelve seconds with Edwards arrowing a bold shot from distance which was blocked and gathered at the second attempt by goalkeeper Lukasz Fabianski. Arsenal hit back a minute later through Emmáanuel Eboue's surging run down the right flank, and low shot which Fulop clung on and the fans settled in for an incident-packed first half-hour's play. Arsenal got their breakthrough in the 26th minute with an exquisite goal. Brazilian midfielder Gilberto Silva picked his pass perfectly from the halfway line, and Theo Walcott timed his run superbly to bisect Collins and Evans, sprint in on goal and drive a low shot beyond Fulop from the edge of the box. It was Theo Walcott who had broken Sunderland's spirits in the dying stages of their game at the Emirates and he showed again the quality that the Black Cats had to aspire to in the seasons coming up.

The home team had to be careful not to get caught out as they pressed for an equaliser. But a more crushing blow came just before half-time when the well-shackled Jones took a blow on his right wrist from an attempted clearance and headed down the tunnel in obvious pain. 'It's a cracked wrist,' revealed Keane afterwards. 'He'll have to wear a cast for the next few weeks.'

Jones was replaced at half-time by O'Donovan, who was to have the chance of making a lasting impression with a string of openings, but failed to finish off any of them. He was to head over Collins' left-wing cross, fail to make the most of a great through-ball from Yorke and then drive a shot off target from the edge of the six-yard box. It seemed a long time since O'Donovan had first had that phone call in Cork. But though he had not set the Premier League alight, Keane saw the twenty-two-year-old as one for the future. 'This season was always going to be a chance for Roy to bed into the club,' said the manager. 'Kevin Doyle and Shane Long at Reading had a year in the Championship but Roy has not had that. We've thrown him straight into a struggling team, but next year he'll be better for it.'

The final minutes of the season were not a damp squib. Fulop had to be off his line instantly to make a fine save from Emmanuel Adebayor, and Sunderland had to survive a bizarre free kick just six yards from goal when Whitehead was penalised for a back pass to Fulop. Theo Walcott got the better of Collins in the dying stages and had the ball in the back of the net through substitute Mark Randall, only for it to be harshly ruled offside. Then Fulop produced a world class save to deny Randall on the stroke of full time.

In the final seconds, there was the promise that Sunderland might yet have the most romantic of ends to their season with another trademark late goal. It would have been a fitting finale. But a great centre from Whitehead from the right, which brought a deft and dangerous goal-bound touch from O'Donovan, saw Lukasz Fabianski get down well to save.

Sunderland subscribers to Setanta TV would not have been impressed. This was the fifth Setanta-televised game of the season. Each one had ended in defeat.

The final whistle brought acclamation from buoyant home fans who had spent the preceding twenty minutes involved in Mexican waves and chants saluting Evans' quality defending. 'The fans aren't daft,' said Keane. 'If Jonny has decisions to make this summer, they'll hope he'll remember things like that.'

Evans had been named Sunderland's Young Player of the Year by the fans for the second year, despite having played only half a season on both occasions. 'I'm thinking about growing a beard next time around so I can go for Player of the Year, rather than Young Player,' he joked.

His words revealed that he had no qualms about returning. Sunderland fans had taken him to their hearts and he had delivered for two seasons in a row. A Manchester United fan since he was a boy, Evans would return to Old Trafford to see what the close season held. But Sunderland were very much a part of him. As the season came to a close, a season-long loan seemed the most likely option for the twenty-year-old. 'I've had two half seasons at Sunderland so far, and maybe next season I'll get a full season. I missed both derby games, which is a real disappointment because I was looking forward to them, but I'm glad we stayed up and are back in the Premiership next season. The manager at United said around Christmas-time that I could go out on loan again, and when he asked me where I would like to go I was always going to be coming back to Sunderland. I loved my time here first time around and I was glad just to get back. It would be nice to play for a full season and show the fans over a longer period of time what I can do. I think the move to Sunderland was good for me, Manchester United and Sunderland.'

Other honours went to Jones who was voted Player of the Season in a poll on the club's website, and not a bad choice in the view of his manager; but the Sunderland Supporters Association Player of the Year went to Collins – a remarkable comeback from that first week of the season when Keane had originally looked to offload him.

Sunderland's opening and closing games had been decided by a solitary goal. And if the last day did not match the euphoria of the first, there was still the pleasure of celebrating the fact that the agonies of one relegation after another had ended. Keane had rumbled darkly after the Bolton defeat that he didn't think staying up deserved a lap of honour at Sunderland; just as he had rejected the idea of an open-top bus when the Championship was won. But in the event, he, his staff and his players rightly returned to the pitch.

It had been a season of struggle, with so much to learn from; so much to absorb.

But the struggle had been a success.

Defeats to Bolton and Arsenal could not wipe that away. A walk around from the players and staff saw the efforts of those on both sides of the pitch perimeter applauded. Players appreciating fans; fans appreciating players. Keane went with them but remained almost as close to the centre circle as he did the touchline. Nipping in and around them among them, getting pictures for Monday's paper, was Sunderland Echo photographer Tom Yeoman. Only one Harry Hill! Many players brought their children on the pitch to give the youngsters a day they wouldn't forget. Whitehead, though, didn't go through with his prematch threat to bring his pet dog Saffy onto the turf! Nosworthy, an Arsenal fan as a boy and Sunderland's fourth different right back in as many games, insisted: 'Staying up for Sunderland this season is bigger than getting promoted.'

Watching from the stands, a proud Quinn could reflect on a journey's end of sorts. It was in the final day game of the 15-point campaign, ironically a match also against Arsenal, that the seeds of his takeover had been sown. His potential backers that day had been impressed not only by the scale of the venue and the size of the crowd but the sporting way they treated Thierry Henry after he had put Sunderland to the sword – applauding the Frenchman on his substitution.

Quinn clapped his players around the pitch but he, like his manager, was already looking to the future. 'Now our long range aim is to have a solid Premier League club with a strong foundation and look to stay in the top flight throughout the next decade,' he said. 'Just under two years ago Arsenal came here in the final game of the season, and I watched it with some of the people who were looking to join me in taking over the club. It was the end of a catastrophic campaign, but Sunderland fans showed what the heart of the club is all about by turning up in vast numbers and saluting Henry. That really made an impact on my people, who could appreciate what a great club this must be for fans to have been through what they had but still be able to respond like that.'

Keane was not fooling himself about the quality of his squad as things stood. After spending £40 million Sunderland finished with 39 points. Quinn himself was part of a Peter Reid squad relegated from the Premier League with 40.

Relegation can be a close run thing.

Staying up had been a great achievement for Sunderland Football Club. But Keane was hungry now to ensure the next step was taken.

Sunderland had finished the season having lost every single game – home and away – against the Premier League's top five teams. That wasn't fazing Keane. Disappointing though it might have been, things could have been a whole lot worse. 'We know it's an area we have to improve on and we have been close on a couple of occasions to getting something. But Birmingham took a point off Liverpool and Fulham took a point off Chelsea, and those two teams have gone down this season so it doesn't count for everything. The fact is, our results against the top teams were never going to be decisive. What kept us in the Premiership this season is our results against the teams around us. The two teams that came up with us have gone down, so we have to reflect on that.'

The manager was now intent on a summer of rebuilding to ward off the danger of a relegation battle next season – although he did intend to take a little 'chill' time before that process began. 'I want to step back a little this summer,' he said. 'I wasted a lot of time and energy last time around. It was very tough for us last summer and we have to expect it to be the same this time too. But this time I have to identify the players and just let the chairman and chief executive do their bit. I can't really get away from everything because I've got young children and responsibilities, but I want to try and switch off for a while. I'm due a meeting with Niall Quinn and Peter Walker so we'll have a better idea of what we have and how many players we can afford to buy, but everyone's chasing quality players and I think it's going to get harder for all of us.

'The Arsenal manager is in the same boat as me. There's not a lot of quality players available. The way things are, we know we want players to improve the team. They don't have to be world superstars – just better than what we've got.

'We finished fifteenth in the table and I think that's about right. We probably are the fifteenth best team. That's why I always felt deep down we would be fine, but you still need the points on the board. As long as we improve on fifteenth next season, then that would be something. We're told teams that stay up in the first year can struggle in the second, so we're taking nothing for granted. We have big challenges ahead but we have to look to improve the squad first. We are close to the teams above us, but not close enough yet. We saw nearly 48,000 here for the Arsenal game and I think we've just about kept them happy this season. I think they'll be wanting a bit more next season, exactly the same as me. You get a bit greedy. You always want a bit more.

'Promotion last season, fine.

'I knew it was going to be hard to stay in the Premiership but we've managed it. That's fine too.

'Now we look to move on.

'We've asked the supporters to be patient. But supporters are entitled to say "well, hey, we've been patient for quite some time here – now we want to see something".

'We still have a lot of work to do.'

ANYONE who tries to climb a mountain needs to set up a base camp. That's what Sunderland Football Club did in 2007-08 – no more, no less. In the wake of the goal being achieved, there was the feeling around the club that eyes were immediately being fixed on greater heights.

There was a purpose about the place.

Sunderland had enjoyed a renaissance. They were the fifth best supported team in the Premier League that season. For the first time in the club's history it had sold all its corporate boxes out. Before the new season arrived they would be sold out again.

'It's great,' said Quinn. 'It shows the business community is buying into Sunderland as much as the fans.'

The Drumaville Consortium had found forty million pounds for Keane to spend on new signings over the course of the season, many of which did not come off. Enough did to ensure the club was not relegated. In that context, the investors would see it as money well spent.

Of the two teams Sunderland were promoted with, Derby County spent £12 million and Birmingham City £20 million – both went down.

The money found for Keane was perhaps the most decisive element in ensuring the club's survival, but it was an investment in Keane as much as it was in the club.

He had been on the sharpest of learning curves but it had not cost him or the club too dearly, and he and Sunderland stood to benefit hugely from the experience. Already at Sunderland he has been through as much in two seasons as some managers experience in ten. He would be better for it. He had said he was a fast learner. He needed to be.

The days when promising young managers served their apprenticeships in the lower reaches, like Graham Taylor, Harry

Redknapp or Martin O'Neill, are still with us. But we live in the era of the young superstar boss, and very few of that breed are given the time or the space to successfully make the immediate transition from player to manager. Mark Hughes, David Moyes, Steve Bruce and Gareth Southgate deserve tremendous credit for what they've achieved in the top tier, under those circumstances.

Arguably Keane's achievement so far is as good as any of them.

His four peers all inherited Premier League clubs. In the space of two years, Keane had taken his club from the foot of the Championship, into the Premier League and kept it there, breaking the yo-yo sequence. Ultimately, Keane did his job in his first Premier League season – keeping Sunderland up. That was critical because for Sunderland to progress, it had to continue drinking from the riches flowing from the top table.

Keane was right when he said just because Sunderland had stayed up was not a time for laurel resting. Sunderland would need to improve further.

He had said promotion and survival were achievements not worth over-celebrating for a club like Sunderland. Now he was looking towards achievements which were worth Sunderland celebrating. Keane was adamant he did not want to endure another season of scrapping around the lower reaches, of hoping to avoid the bottom three come its close. How much he would succeed in that ambition would be dictated largely by the budget he was given and the willingness of the club to break, not only transfer records, but its wage structure.

But all the signs were that he would find what he was given in the transfer market more than acceptable.

In return though, the board would expect Keane, too, to step up his game. 'I made hundreds of mistakes in the season,' he said, with refreshing frankness. And his ultimate, if harsh, verdict on himself after considering how many defeats the club had had was, 'I'm lucky to be in a job.'

But there was no getting away from the fact that Keane's iron resolve and determination from the touchlines had dragged Sunderland through trying times, just as much as it had when those qualities were being put to use in his playing days.

As the season reached its end he wasted no time in putting into practice things he had learned. Five out-of-contract players were moved on before May was out. A sixth, Yorke, was offered a coaching rather than a playing contract. Already a changing of the guard. When the season came to a close Keane flew off to spend some down time in Dubai. Then it was off to New Zealand to complete his UEFA Pro Licence, by studying the All Blacks approach to fitness and training. A big fan of the legendary rugby team, Keane remained eager to glean, from any source, something he could use to further the professional ethos at Sunderland Football Club. A busman's holiday to be sure, but still a break from football he had denied himself a year previously. He did not spend the early weeks of preseason, as he had done last time around, on an endless series of fruitless phone calls at a time when football was having its annual break.

But, where it was most vital he showed he had learned lessons was the area where there has never been any guarantees in football – the transfer market. In his first season in charge of Sunderland, Keane had possessed the Midas touch. Almost every single one of his transfers came off and had played a major part in the club's promotion. In his second season, not so much.

Veterans Cole and Harte cost the club little to recruit but were never able to nail down a first-team place. Anderson got injured and was loaned out. Prica scored on his debut but then disappeared off the map. Halford ended up on loan to Championship Charlton from January onwards. Some others could only be called qualified successes. Then there was the thought that if Keane had been successful in his pursuit of his strikers the previous summer he might have ended up with Mido and Nugent as his first-choice partnership – a pairing that would have yielded just two Premier League goals between them all season.

Keane himself admitted: 'I bought one or two last summer, and I look now and we should have stepped back from the deals. That's part of the learning curve and I will be in a stronger position this summer.'

He had though, got it spectacularly right in the January transfer window. In the signings of Jonny Evans, Phil Bardsley and Andy Reid lay the saving of Sunderland's season.

No one doubts that he learns from his mistakes and, having made so many in his first season in the top flight, he will be twice the manager on his return. Keane will probably never have a harder transfer window than the one he had in Sunderland's first season, when the highest quality players could not be attracted and he had to gamble on players he believed would be able to step up. As someone who was one himself, he's an impeccable judge of the richer talents. With Sunderland staying in the top flight, he now had a chance to go shopping for them. It was an exciting time for Sunderland, and a long way removed from what fans have come to expect over the vast majority of the last five decades.

Certainly the likes of Gordon and Jones had proven their worth. As Sunderland went into the close season, Keane described them as his 'untouchables' – players he would not look to sell at any cost; players he wanted to build a team around. Jones in particular had shown enough to suggest that Keane had got an absolute bargain for the £6 million paid.

Although the big man suffered ligament damage in an international friendly against England at the end of May, which would sideline him for months, there was no doubting his long-term value, or the fact that Keane was determined Sunderland would be far more than a one-man band. When the new fixture list came out in mid-June the club's tough task could hardly have been made clearer – Liverpool in the first game of the season, Chelsea in the last. Champions League opposition lying in wait at its beginning and end.

Keane was insistent those were the sort of fixtures Sunderland should look forward to rather than dread. With Quinn, Keane would spend the summer looking to get in the players who would help bridge the gap between the strugglers and the established. Keane had asked Quinn and his consortium to rise to the challenge in four transfer windows now and open their purse strings. They had not let him down and were determined they would find the funds to keep their demanding manager happy.

Sunderland got its hooks into Quinn, still so adored by its fans, and he forsook an easy life to come to its rescue. I think it has its hooks in Keane now, because managing Sunderland Football Club has become so much more to him than either a job or a stepping stone. He says himself he realised the potential of the club from the start, but I think that's even more the case now. And his special privilege is to be able to mould the club in his own image.

The underachievement of the second half of Sunderland's history stands in stark contrast to the first. But that's in

Quinn's and Keane's favour. They're painting on a blank canvas. Keane isn't burdened down, as he might have been at other clubs, by either the weight of expectation or the success of preceding managers and their teams.

What lies ahead, no one knows.

There is a chance now that with the board's backing, coupled with Sunderland's revival as a club of significance and the possibility that Keane might go on to justify Sir Alex Ferguson's billing of him as a genius. The sky could be the limit. A sustained stay in the top half of the top tier might beckon; Europe maybe, successful cup runs, fans can even dream one day of the Champions League without which, Keane said, he felt his managerial CV would be incomplete. Certainly there's every chance that Quinn's and Keane's Sunderland will come to stand for something; something worthwhile in football. A club where football is about character, conviction and commitment rather than WAGS, bling and baby Bentleys.

It was widely believed when Quinn's ambitious consortium took over the club that a five-year plan was drawn up: two years to win promotion, two years to establish it in the top flight and a final year to push on to Europe and beyond. Promotion and survival in Keane's first two seasons has put the club ahead of that schedule and Keane, by his own admission, is eager to progress at an ever faster pace.

'I know these things take time, but I'm impatient,' he said.

Whatever is achieved in the seasons to come, the roots of any success will trace back to this campaign. A campaign of struggle and survival when players and manager were stretched to the limit and came through.

Everyone learns from their mistakes. With Keane's estimate of his running into the hundreds, that's a lot of learning to benefit from. The members of the squad who survive into next season, along with their boss, will be all the better for the experience. For Keane it was where he learnt so much more about himself as a manager. It was where he made mistakes and got away with them, made mistakes and paid for them, where he learned about his own and his team's limitations, as well as the pitfalls and potential which lie in front of him.

All these things, he and the club experienced over a tumultuous ten months.

The nothing season.

That's how it will appear in the history books.

But in reality it was far from it. Anything but. A crippling injury list, learning curve mistakes and perverse refereeing decisions had all been overcome on the way to the club staying up.

For Quinn and his board the future now looks bright, the chairman's magic carpet still on the rise. There remains the question of Keane's contract, which has only one year to run on it. But Quinn is hopeful that will soon be resolved, and supporters hope the same.

For the fans want only one man at the helm leading the club forward for years to come. That man will be Keane, they trust.

SUNDERLAND'S 2007-08 GAMES

denotes booking + denotes sending off.

Aug 11: Sunderland 1 Tottenham Hotspur 0

Scorer: Chopra (Sunderland) 93.

Sunderland: Gordon, Whitehead*, Nosworthy, McShane, Wallace, Edwards, Etuhu, Yorke, Richardson, Stokes, Murphy.
Subs used: Collins, Chopra.

Referee: Alan Wiley.

Attendance: 43,967

Position: 8th.

Aug 14: Birmingham City 2 Sunderland 2

Scorers: Kelly (Birmingham City) 28, Chopra (Sunderland) 75, O'Connor (Birmingham City) 81, John (Sunderland) 90.

Sunderland: Gordon, Halford, Nosworthy, McShane, Collins, Edwards, Etuhu*, Whitehead, Wallace, Chopra, Connolly.
Subs used: O'Donovan, Miller, John.

Referee: Keith Stroud.

Attendance: 24,898

Position: 4th.

Aug 18: Wigan Athletic 3 Sunderland 0

Scorers: Heskey (Wigan) 18, Landzaat (Wigan) 61(p), Sibierski (Wigan) 67 (p)

Sunderland: Gordon, Halford, Nosworthy, McShane, Wallace, Stokes, Etuhu*, Yorke, Richardson, Chopra, Murphy.
Subs used: Anderson, Collins, Miller.

Referee: Mike Riley.

Attendance: 18,639.

Position: 7th.

Aug 25: Sunderland 0 Liverpool 2

Scorers: Sissoko (Liverpool) 37, Voronin (Liverpool) 87.
Sunderland: Gordon, Halford, Nosworthy, McShane, Wallace, Miller, Etuhu*, Yorke, Richardson, Chopra, Murphy.
Subs used: Stokes, Leadbitter, Connolly.
Referee: Mark Halsey.
Attendance: 45,645.
Position: 14th.

Aug 28: (CC2) Luton Town 3 Sunderland 0

Scorers: Bell (Luton Town)16, Furlong (Luton Town) 42, 75.
Sunderland: Ward, Halford+, Nosworthy, Anderson, Wallace*, Leadbitter, Etuhu*, Miller, Stokes, Chopra, Murphy.
Subs used: Connolly*, O'Donovan, Yorke.
Referee: Trevor Kettle.
Attendance: 4,401.

Sept 1: Manchester Utd 1 Sunderland 0

Scorer: Saha (Manchester United) 71.
Sunderland: Gordon, McShane, Nosworthy, Higginbotham, Collins, Leadbitter, Etuhu, Yorke, Wallace, Chopra, Jones, Murphy.
Subs used: Stokes, Miller.
Referee: Martin Atkinson.
Attendance: 75,648.
Position: 17th.

Sept 15: Sunderland 2 Reading 1

Scorers: Jones (Sunderland) 28, Wallace (Sunderland) 47, Kitson (Reading) 85.
Sunderland: Gordon, McShane, Nosworthy, Higginbotham, Collins, Leadbitter, Etuhu, Yorke, Wallace, Chopra, Jones.
Subs used: Stokes, Miller, Murphy.
Referee: Steve Tanner.
Attendance: 39,272.
Position: 14th.

Sept 22:   Middlesbrough 2 Sunderland 2

Scorers: Leadbitter (Sunderland) 2, Arca (Middlesbrough) 13, Downing (Middlesbrough) 68, Miller (Sunderland) 89.

Sunderland: Gordon, Halford, McShane, Higginbotham, Collins, Leadbitter*, Etuhu*, Yorke, Wallace, Chopra*, Jones.
Subs used: Miller*, Stokes, O'Donovan.

Referee: Howard Webb.

Attendance: 30,675.

Position: 13th.

Sept 29:   Sunderland 1 Blackburn Rovers 2

Scorers: Bentley (Blackburn Rovers) 54, Santa Cruz (Blackburn Rovers) 56, Leadbitter (Sunderland) 89

Sunderland: Gordon, McShane, Nosworthy, Higginbotham, Collins, Leadbitter, Miller, Yorke, Wallace, Chopra, Jones.
Subs used: Connolly, Murphy, O'Donovan.

Referee: Peter Walton.

Attendance: 41,252.

Position: 15th.

Oct 7:   Arsenal 3 Sunderland 2

Scorers: Van Persie (Arsenal) 7, 79, Senderos (Arsenal) 13, Wallace (Sunderland) 25, Jones (Sunderland) 48.

Sunderland: Gordon, McShane+, Nosworthy, Higginbotham, Collins, Leadbitter, Miller, Yorke, Wallace, Chopra*, Jones*.
Subs used: Stokes, Etuhu, Harte.

Referee: Rob Styles.

Attendance: 60,098.

Position: 16th.

Oct 21: West Ham Utd 3 Sunderland 1

Scorers: Cole (West Ham) 9, Jones (Sunderland) 51, Gordon (Sunderland) OG 77, Bellamy (West Ham) 91.

Sunderland: Gordon, Halford*, Nosworthy, Higginbotham, Collins, Leadbitter*, Miller, Etuhu, Wallace, O'Donovan, Jones.
Subs used: Chopra, Stokes, Harte.

Referee: Chris Foy.
Attendance: 34,913.
Position: 16th.

Oct 27: Sunderland 1 Fulham 1

Scorers: Davies (Fulham) 32, Jones (Sunderland) 85.

Sunderland: Gordon, Halford+, Nosworthy, Higginbotham, Collins, Leadbitter, Miller, Etuhu, Wallace, Chopra, Jones.
Subs used: Murphy, Stokes, Harte.

Referee: Andre Marriner.
Attendance: 39,392.
Position: 15th.

Nov 5: Manchester City 1 Sunderland 0

Scorer: Ireland (Manchester City) 66.

Sunderland: Gordon, Nosworthy*, Collins, Higginbotham, Harte, Leadbitter, Miller, Etuhu, Murphy, Stokes, Jones.
Subs used: Wallace, Chopra.

Referee: Alan Wiley.
Attendance: 40,038.
Position: 15th.

Nov 10: Sunderland 1 Newcastle United 1

Scorers: Higginbotham (Sunderland) 52, Milner (Newcastle United) 65

Sunderland: Gordon, Nosworthy, McShane, Higginbotham, Harte, Edwards, Leadbitter, Etuhu, Wallace, Chopra*, Jones.
Subs used: Collins, Stokes.

Referee: Martin Atkinson.
Attendance: 47,701.
Position: 16th.

Nov 24: Everton 7 Sunderland 1

Scorers: Yakubu (Everton) 12, 72, Cahill (Everton) 17, 61, Pienaar (Everton) 43, Yorke (Sunderland) 45, Johnson (Everton) 79, Osman (Everton) 84.

Sunderland: Gordon, Whitehead, McShane*, Higginbotham, Harte, Edwards, Yorke, Etuhu, Leadbitter, Chopra, Jones.
Subs used: Wallace, Collins, Cole.

Referee: Phil Dowd.
Attendance: 38,594.
Position: 18th.

Dec 1: Sunderland 1 Derby County 0

Scorer: Stokes (Sunderland) 92.

Sunderland: Ward, Halford, McShane, Higginbotham, Collins, Edwards, Whitehead, Leadbitter, Wallace, Cole, Jones.
Subs used: Chopra, Stokes*, Miller.

Referee: Mark Halsey.
Attendance: 42,380.
Position: 14th.

Dec 8: Chelsea 2 Sunderland 0

Scorers: Shevchenko (Chelsea) 23, Lampard (Chelsea) (p) 75.

Sunderland: Ward, Halford, McShane, Higginbotham, Collins, Miller+, Whitehead, Etuhu, Wallace, Leadbitter, Jones.
Subs used: Murphy, Stokes.

Referee: Peter Walton.
Attendance: 41,707.
Position: 15th.

Dec 15:   Sunderland 1 Aston Villa 1

Scorers: Higginbotham (Sunderland) 10,
Maloney (Aston Villa) 74.

Sunderland: Ward, Whitehead*, McShane, Higginbotham,
Collins, Wallace, Yorke* , Etuhu, Murphy, Stokes,
Jones, Leadbitter.
Subs used: Chopra, Cole.

Referee: Steve Bennett.

Attendance: 43,248.

Position: 17th.

Dec 22:   Reading 2 Sunderland 1

Scorers: Ingimarrson (Reading) 69,
Chopra (Sunderland) 81 (p), Hunt (Reading) 91.

Sunderland: Gordon, Whitehead, McShane, Higginbotham, Collins,
Chopra, Yorke*, Leadbitter*, Murphy*, Cole, Jones*.
Subs used: Etuhu, Wallace, Stokes.

Referee: Steve Tanner.

Attendance: 24,082.

Position: 18th.

Dec 26:   Sunderland 0 Manchester United 4

Scorers: Rooney (Manchester United) 20, Saha (Manchester
United) 29, 84 (p), Ronaldo (Manchester United) 45.

Sunderland: Gordon, Whitehead*, McShane*, Higginbotham,
Collins, Chopra, Yorke, Etuhu, Wallace,
Waghorn, Jones.
Subs used: Leadbitter, Richardson, O'Donovan.

Referee: Uriah Rennie.

Attendance: 47,360.

Position: 19th.

Dec 29:   Sunderland 3   Bolton Wanderers 1

Scorer: Richardson (Sunderland) 13, Jones (Sunderland) 32, Diouf (Bolton) 41, Murphy (Sunderland) 91.

Sunderland: Gordon, Whitehead, McShane, Higginbotham, Collins, Chopra, Miller, Etuhu, Richardson*, Cole, Jones.
Subs used: Leadbitter, Murphy, O'Donovan.

Referee: Phil Dowd.

Attendance: 42,058.

Position: 17th.

Jan 2:   Blackburn Rovers 1   Sunderland 0

Scorer: McCarthy (Blackburn) 56 (p)

Sunderland: Gordon, Whitehead, McShane, Higginbotham*, Collins*, Wallace, Miller, Yorke+, Richardson, Murphy, Jones.
Subs used: Leadbitter, Waghorn, Cole.

Referee: Rob Styles.

Attendance: 23,212.

Position: 18th

Jan 5:   (FA3) Sunderland 0   Wigan Athletic 3.

Scorers: Scharner (Blackburn) 19, McShane (Sunderland) OG 56, Cotterill (Blackburn) 76.

Sunderland: Gordon, Nosworthy, McShane, Evans, Collins, O'Donovan, Whitehead, Kavanagh, Richardson, Waghorn, Murphy.
Subs used: Leadbitter, Cole, Connolly.

Referee: Mike Riley.

Attendance: 20,821

Jan 13:   Sunderland 2   Portsmouth 0

Scorers: Richardson (Sunderland) 33, 43.

Sunderland: Gordon, Whitehead, Nosworthy, Evans, Collins*, Stokes, Miller, Yorke*, Richardson* , Murphy, Jones.
Subs used: Leadbitter, McShane, O'Donovan.

Referee: Chris Foy.

Attendance: 37,369.

Position: 18th.

Jan 19:   Tottenham 2 Sunderland 0

Scorers: Lennon (Spurs) 2, Keane (Spurs) 92.
Sunderland: Gordon, McShane*, Nosworthy, Evans, Collins, Stokes, Miller, Yorke, Whitehead, Murphy, Jones.
Subs used: Chopra, Cole.
Referee: Lee Mason.
Attendance: 36,070.
Position: 18th.

Jan 29:   Sunderland 2 Birmingham City 0

Scorers: Murphy (Sunderland) 15, Prica (Sunderland) 65.
Sunderland: Gordon, Bardsley, Nosworthy, Evans, Collins, Stokes, Miller, Yorke, Whitehead, Murphy, Jones.
Subs used: Prica*, O'Donovan.
Referee: Mark Halsey.
Attendance: 37,674.
Position: 14th.

Feb 2:   Liverpool 3 Sunderland 0

Scorers: Crouch (Liverpool) 56, Torres (Liverpool) 69, Gerrard (Liverpool) 88 (p).
Sunderland: Gordon*, Bardsley, Nosworthy, Evans, Collins, Chopra, Miller*, Whitehead, Richardson, Murphy, Jones.
Subs used: Prica, O'Donovan, Waghorn.
Referee: Rob Styles.
Attendance: 43,244.
Position: 16th.

Feb 9:   Sunderland 2 Wigan Athletic 0

Scorers: Etuhu (Sunderland), Murphy (Sunderland) 75.
Sunderland: Gordon, Bardsley, Nosworthy, Evans, Collins, O'Donovan, Etuhu, Whitehead, Murphy, Chopra, Jones.
Subs used: Prica, Reid, Leadbitter.
Referee: Mike Dean.
Attendance: 43,600.
Position: 14th.

Feb 23: Portsmouth 1 Sunderland 0

Scorer: Defoe (Portsmouth) 70 (p)

Sunderland: Gordon, Bardsley, Nosworthy, Evans, Collins*, Leadbitter, Etuhu, Whitehead, Reid, Murphy, Jones.
Subs used: Yorke*, Prica, Chopra.

Referee: Phil Dowd.

Attendance: 20,139.

Position: 15th.

Mar 1: Derby County 0 Sunderland 0

Scorers: None.

Sunderland: Gordon, Bardsley, Nosworthy, Evans, Higginbotham, Chopra*, Whitehead, Reid, Richardson, Murphy, Jones.
Subs used: Leadbitter, Stokes.

Referee: Mike Riley.

Attendance: 33,057.

Position: 15th.

Mar 9: Sunderland 0 Everton 1

Scorer: Johnson (Everton) 55.

Sunderland: Gordon, Bardsley*, Nosworthy, Evans, Collins, Stokes, Whitehead*, Leadbitter, Richardson, Murphy, Jones.
Subs used: Chopra, Reid, Prica.

Referee: Alan Wiley.

Attendance: 42,595.

Position: 16th.

Mar 15: Sunderland 0 Chelsea 1

Scorer: Terry (Chelsea) 9.

Sunderland: Gordon, Bardsley, Nosworthy, Evans, Collins, Edwards, Whitehead*, Leadbitter*, Reid, O'Donovan, Jones.
Subs used: Prica, Yorke, Harte.

Referee: Mike Dean.

Attendance: 44,679.

Position: 16th.

Mar 22: Aston Villa 0 Sunderland 1

Scorer: Chopra (Sunderland) 84.

Sunderland: Gordon, Bardsley*, Nosworthy, Evans, Collins, Edwards, Whitehead, Reid, Richardson, O'Donovan*, Murphy.
Subs used: Chopra, Leadbitter, Yorke.

Referee: Howard Webb.

Attendance: 42,640.

Position: 16th.

Mar 29: Sunderland 2 West Ham United 1

Scorers: Ljungberg (West Ham) 17, Jones (Sunderland) 28, Reid (Sunderland) 96.

Sunderland: Gordon, Bardsley, Nosworthy, Evans, Collins, Chopra, Whitehead, Reid*, Richardson, Murphy, Jones.
Subs used: Edwards, Leadbitter, O'Donovan*.

Referee: Andre Marriner.

Attendance: 45,690.

Position: 13th.

April 5: Fulham 3 Sunderland 1

Scorers: Collins (Sunderland) 44, Chopra (Sunderland) 67, Healy (Fulham) 73, Jones (Sunderland) 75.

Sunderland: Gordon, Bardsley, Nosworthy, Evans, Collins, Edwards, Whitehead, Reid, Richardson, Murphy, Jones.
Subs used: Chopra, Leadbitter, O'Donovan.

Referee: Mark Halsey.

Attendance: 25,053.

Position: 13th.

April 12: Sunderland 1 Manchester City 2

Scorers: Elano (Manchester City) 77 (p) Whitehead (Sunderland) 81, Vassell (Manchester City) 87.

Sunderland: Gordon, Bardsley*, Nosworthy*, Evans, Collins, Chopra, Whitehead*, Reid, Richardson, Murphy, Jones.
Subs used: Leadbitter, Edwards, O'Donovan.

Referee: Mike Riley.

Attendance: 46,797.

Position: 14th.

April 20: Newcastle 2 Sunderland 0

Scorers: Owen (Newcastle) 4, 44.

Sunderland: Gordon, McShane, Nosworthy*, Higginbotham, Collins, Edwards, Whitehead*, Miller*, Reid*, Murphy*, Jones.
Subs used: Richardson, Chopra, Harte.

Referee: Mike Dean.

Attendance: 52,305.

Position: 15th

April 26: Sunderland 3 Middlesbrough 2

Scorers: Tuncay (Boro) 4, Higginbotham (Sunderland) 6, Chopra (Sunderland) 45, Alves (Boro) 73, Murphy (Sunderland) 92.

Sunderland: Gordon, Whitehead*, Nosworthy, Higginbotham, Collins, Edwards, Miller, Reid, Richardson*, Chopra*, Jones.
Subs used: Leadbitter, Murphy.

Referee: Steve Bennett.

Attendance: 45,069.

Position: 13th.

May 3: Bolton Wanderers 2 Sunderland 0

Scorers: Diouf (Bolton) 41, Murphy (Sunderland) OG 82.

Sunderland: Gordon, Nosworthy, Higginbotham, Evans, Collins, Miller, Whitehead, Richardson, Reid, Chopra, Jones.
Subs used: Leadbitter, Murphy, O'Donovan.

Referee: Martin Atkinson.

Attendance: 25,053.

Position: 15th.

May 11: Sunderland 0 Arsenal 1

Scorer: Walcott (Arsenal) 26.

Sunderland: Fulop, Whitehead, Nosworthy, Evans, Collins*, Edwards, Leadbitter, Yorke, Reid, Wallace, Jones.
Subs used: O'Donovan, Miller, Chopra.

Referee: Keith Stroud.

Attendance: 47,802.

Final position, season end: 15th.

GOALSCORERS

	Lge	CC	FA	Total
Jones	7	0	0	7
Chopra	6	0	0	6
Murphy	4	0	0	4
Higginbotham	3	0	0	3
Richardson	3	0	0	3
Leadbitter	2	0	0	2
Wallace	2	0	0	2
Collins	1	0	0	1
Etuhu	1	0	0	1
John	1	0	0	1
Miller	1	0	0	1
Prica	1	0	0	1
Reid	1	0	0	1
Stokes	1	0	0	1
Whitehead	1	0	0	1
Yorke	1	0	0	1

APPEARANCES:

SAFC APPEARANCES AND GOALS CURRENT SEASON 2007-08

	LGE APPS	LGE GLS	LC APPS	LC GLS	FAC APPS	FAC GLS	TOTAL APPS	TOTAL GLS
Anderson	0+1	0	1	0	0	0	1+1	0
Bardsley	11	0	0	0	0	0	11	0
Chopra	20+11	6	1	0	0	0	21+11	6
Cole	3+4	0	0	0	0+1	0	3+5	0
Collins	32+5	1	0	0	1	0	33+5	1
Connolly	1+2	0	0+1	0	0+1	0	1+4	0
Edwards	11+2	0	0	0	0	0	11+2	0
Etuhu	18+2	1	1	0	0	0	19+2	1
Evans	15	0	0	0	1	0	16	0
Fulop	1	0	0	0	0	0	1	0
Gordon	34	0	0	0	1	0	35	0
Halford	8	0	1	0	0	0	9	0
Harte	3+5	0	0	0	0	0	3+5	0
Hartley	0	0	0	0	0	0	0	0
Higginbotham	21	3	0	0	0	0	21	3
Jones	33	7	0	0	0	0	33	7
John	0+1	1	0	0	0	0	0+1	1
Kavanagh	0	0	0	0	1	0	1	0
Leadbitter	17+14	2	1	0	0+1	0	18+15	2
McShane	20+1	0	0	0	1	0	21+1	0
Miller	16+8	1	1	0	0	0	17+8	1
Murphy	20+8	4	1	0	1	0	22+8	4
O'Donovan	4+13	0	0+1	0	1	0	5+14	0
Prica	0+6	1	0	0	0	0	0+6	1
Nosworthy	29	0	1	0	1	0	31	0
Reid	11+2	1	0	0	0	0	11+2	1
Richardson	13+2	3	0	0	1	0	14+2	3
Stokes	'8+12	1	1	0	0	0	9+12	1
Varga	0	0	0	0	0	0	0	0
Waghorn	1+2	0	0	0	1	0	2+2	0
Wallace	17+3	2	1	0	0	0	17+3	2
Ward	3	0	1	0	0	0	4	0
Whitehead	27	1	0	0	1	0	28	1
Wright	0	0	0	0	0	0	0	0
Yorke	17+3	1	0+1	0	0	0	17+4	1

BIBLIOGRAPHY

Reference books:

Rothmans Football Yearbooks

SkySports Football Yearbooks

Sunderland The Complete Record, by Rob Mason *(Breedon Books 2005)*

The History of Sunderland AFC, by Bob Graham *(Wearside Publications 1995)*

Sunderland Football Club An A-Z, by Dean Hayes *(Aureus Publishing 1999)*

Into The Light, by Roger Hutchinson *(Mainstream Publishing 1999)*

Sunderland A Club Transformed, by Jonathan Wilson *(Orion Books 2007)*

Keane: The Autobiography, by Roy Keane *(Penquin 2003)*

Niall Quinn: The Autobiography *(Headline 2002)*

Alice in Sunderland: An Entertainment, by Bryan Talbot *(Jonathan Cape 2007)*

Provided You Don't Kiss Me, by Duncan Hamilton *(Harper Collins 2007)*

This Is The One, by Daniel Taylor *(Aurum Press 2007)*

Staying Up, by Rick Gekoski *(Little Brown Company 1998)*

Meet Me In The Roker End, by Martin Howey and David Bond *(Vertical Editions 2004)*

Newspapers and magazines:

The Sunderland Echo

The Football Echo

The Newcastle Journal

The Northern Echo

The Independent on Sunday

Cork Examiner

Ireland on Sunday

The Irish Times

The Irish Examiner

The News of the World

The Sunday Mirror

The People

The Sunday Sun

The Daily Telegraph

The Daily Mail

The Sun

The Mirror

The Daily Star

The Roscommon Herald

A Love Supreme

OK Magazine